THE
UNITED
STATES
AND
ASIA

Toward a New U.S. Strategy and Force Posture

Zalmay Khalilzad ~ David T. Orletsky ~ Jonathan D. Pollack

Kevin Pollpeter ~ Angel M. Rabasa ~ David A. Shlapak

Abram N. Shulsky ~ Ashley J. Tellis

Project AIR FORCE
RAND

Prepared for the United States Air Force · Approved for public release, distribution unlimited

The research reported here was sponsored by the United States Air Force under Contract F49642-01-C-0003. Further information may be obtained from the Strategic Planning Division, Directorate of Plans, Hq USAF.

Library of Congress Cataloging-in-Publication Data

The United States and Asia : towards a new U.S. strategy and force structure / Zalmay Khalilzad ... [et al.].
    p. cm.
    "MR-1315."
    Includes bibliographical references.
    ISBN 0-8330-2955-X
    1. United States—Military policy. 2. Asia—Strategic aspects. 3. United States. Air Force. I. Khalilzad, Zalmay.

UA23. .U68 2001
327.7305—dc21

2001019597

Published 2001 by RAND
1700 Main Street, P.O. Box 2138, Santa Monica, CA 90407-2138
1200 South Hayes Street, Arlington, VA 22202-5050
201 North Craig Street, Suite 102, Pittsburgh, PA 15213-1516
RAND URL: http://www.rand.org/
To order RAND documents or to obtain additional information, contact Distribution Services: Telephone: (310) 451-7002; Fax: (310) 451-6915; Internet: order@rand.org

This report focuses on the question of how the United States should deal with the changing security environment in Asia—a vital and dynamic region of the world that may be entering a period of increased instability. It then addresses the implications for the U.S. Air Force in shaping the environment, responding to potential crises, and preparing for the long term.

This project was conducted in the Strategy and Doctrine Program of Project AIR FORCE under the sponsorship of the Deputy Chief of Staff for Air and Space Operations, U.S. Air Force (AF/XO), and the Commander, Pacific Air Forces (PACAF/CC). The report should be of interest to the national security community and to segments of the general public. Comments are welcome and may be addressed to the project leader, Dr. Zalmay Khalilzad.

Research was completed in fall 2000.

PROJECT AIR FORCE

Project AIR FORCE, a division of RAND, is the Air Force federally funded research and development center (FFRDC) for studies and analyses. It provides the Air Force with independent analyses of policy alternatives affecting the development, employment, combat readiness, and support of current and future aerospace forces. Research is performed in four programs: Aerospace Force Development; Manpower, Personnel, and Training; Resource Management; and Strategy and Doctrine.

CONTENTS

FIGURES

TABLES

Over the past 20 years, Asia has undergone a remarkable transformation. Under an umbrella provided by U.S. security guarantees and American military presence, the region has witnessed tremendous economic growth, an expansion of its democratic institutions, and relative peace. Although several countries suffered serious economic setbacks in 1997–1998, most, with the notable exception of Indonesia, have recovered.

The United States has a profound interest in seeing that events in Asia continue down the path of economic development, democratization, and regional peace. However, Asia faces potentially serious problems that could unravel the fabric of peace and prosperity. India and, especially, China are rising powers that seek their place in the world and, in the process, could potentially disrupt the regional order. At the same time, India is involved in an ongoing confrontation with Pakistan that now extends to nuclear weapon capabilities on both sides. Pakistan also confronts a deep crisis of governance. Beijing glares covetously at Taiwan, maintaining a threatening posture toward it in both word and deed. Indonesia, the most populous country in Southeast Asia, is rent by ethnic and religious tensions, which could bring about its fragmentation. Malaysia and the Philippines suffer their own internal unrest. And overshadowing all else, from the U.S. perspective, the military confrontation on the Korean peninsula has now entered its sixth decade, notwithstanding favorable political trends.

To help shape events in Asia in the interests of ensuring peace and stability, the United States must successfully manage a number of critical challenges. Among these—the one that must occupy the immediate attention of the United States—is Korea. The U.S. military posture in Northeast Asia must continue to deter and defend against North Korea. Over the longer term, however, it is possible that the North Korean threat will disappear as a result of the political unification of the Korean peninsula, an accommodation between North and South, or a collapse of the North Korean regime. The June 2000 summit meeting between South Korean president Kim Dae Jung and North Korean leader Kim Jong Il offers evidence that the political-military situation in Asia may change much more quickly than had once been thought.

Even if the Korean threat persists, the rest of Asia is changing in ways that seem likely to require major adjustments in U.S. strategy and military posture. One of the most important changes is the emergence of China as a rising power, its military modernization program, and its enhanced role in the East Asian region.[1] For the U.S. military, this highlights the *near-term* question of how to respond to a possible Chinese use of force against Taiwan. In the *long term,* China's increased power will entail substantial implications for the region and for U.S. strategy and its military—particularly if China pursues a policy of regional primacy.

But Korea and China are not the only parts of this dynamic region where important changes are occurring. India too has begun to assume a larger role in regional political-military affairs, and it also faces Pakistan-supported insurrection in Kashmir, a situation made more dangerous by the nuclear tests conducted in 1998 by both countries. In Southeast Asia, the turmoil surrounding the fall of the Suharto regime, together with Indonesia's separatist movements and civil strife, highlights growing uncertainty about the country's territorial integrity and stability. As the largest country in Southeast Asia, Indonesia will have a significant impact on the region as a whole. In addition, Japan and Russia aspire to enhanced political and military status. A unified Korea could similarly play a major political-military

---

[1]See Zalmay M. Khalilzad, Abram N. Shulsky, Daniel L. Byman, Roger Cliff, David T. Orletsky, David Shlapak, and Ashley J. Tellis, *The United States and a Rising China: Strategic and Military Implications,* Santa Monica: RAND, MR-1082-AF, 1999, for a discussion of the political-military implications of China's emergence for the United States.

role in the region. Even without unification, South Korea appears to be developing the economic, technological, and military resources to pursue a more active regional policy.

U.S. OBJECTIVES

In order to meet all these potential challenges, the United States must begin to formulate an integrated regional strategy. The overall long-term U.S. objective for the region should be to preclude in Asia the growth of rivalries, suspicions, and insecurities that could lead to war. This overall objective necessitates, in turn, three subordinate goals:

- **Prevent the rise of a regional hegemon.** Any potential Asian hegemon would seek to undermine the U.S. role in Asia and would be more likely to use force to assert its claims. Given Asia's human, technological, and economic resources, the domination of the region by a hostile power would pose a global challenge and threaten the current international order.

- **Maintain stability.** Stability has been the foundation of Asia's prosperity. If Asia is to become more prosperous and more integrated, each country must be free to develop peacefully.

- **Manage Asia's transformation.** The United States may not be able to be actively engaged in all disputes in Asia, but it can try to influence events so that they do not spiral out of control.

In addition, the United States wishes to maintain and increase economic access to the region as a whole. This implies a continuation of policies favoring free trade that have underpinned the region's prosperity in recent decades.

U.S. STRATEGY: TOWARD A NEW EQUILIBRIUM

To achieve these goals, an integrated political-military-economic strategy is required. A necessary precondition for this strategy is continued American global leadership. This assumes, in turn, that the United States will continue to make the necessary political, technological, and military investments to ensure its global preeminence. Economically, the United States should further Asia's development by continuing to support the expansion of free-trade policies—e.g., by the expansion of the World Trade Organization (WTO) to include China as well as other countries.

In political-military terms, a four-part strategy is required.

First, the United States should both deepen and widen its bilateral security alliances to allow for the creation of a comprehensive partnership. This multilateralization—which would serve as a complement to rather than a substitute for existing bilateral alliances—could ultimately include the United States, Japan, South Korea, Australia, and perhaps Singapore, the Philippines, and Thailand. Initially, however, the United States will need to promote trust among its allies and encourage them to create militaries that can respond to regional crises as coalitions. Improved relations between Japan and South Korea, for example, would facilitate the future cooperation of these countries on security issues. As part of this effort, the United States should also encourage information sharing among these nations. Moreover, the United States should support Japan's efforts to revise its constitution to allow it to expand its security horizons beyond its territorial defense and acquire appropriate capabilities for supporting coalition operations.

Second, the United States should pursue a balance-of-power strategy among the major rising powers and key regional states in Asia—including China, India, and a currently weakened Russia—that are not now part of the U.S. alliance structure. The objective of this strategy must be to deter any of these states from threatening regional security or dominating each other, while simultaneously preventing any combination of these states from "bandwagoning" to undercut critical U.S. strategic interests in Asia. Developing a stable balance of power among major powers in Asia will require great political and strategic agility. Washington should seek strengthened political, economic, and military-to-military relations with all, but especially those least likely to challenge U.S. strategic interests.

Third, the United States should address those situations that could tempt others to use force. The United States should clearly state, for example, that it opposes the use of force by China against Taiwan (as well as a declaration of independence by Taiwan).[2] At the same time, it should work to resolve territorial disputes in the South China Sea and oppose the use of force there, while emphasizing its commitment to freedom of navigation and to adherence to an agreed code of conduct in the area. The United States should also promote the cohesion, stability, and territorial integrity of Indonesia and other Southeast Asian states and foster security cooperation and interoperability, and it should similarly use its influence to encourage the resolution of the Kashmir dispute through peaceful means and prevent an outbreak of a regional nuclear war. The United States should, moreover, encourage Russia to resolve its territorial dispute with Japan over the Northern Territories.

Finally, the United States should promote an inclusive security dialogue among *all* the Asian states.[3] This dialogue would not only provide for a discussion of regional conflicts and promote confidence building but also encourage states to enter into a multilateral framework at some point in the future. The United States should also maintain flexibility of relations with as many countries as possible for ad hoc coalitions to deal with specific future challenges—challenges that might concern not only the United States and its allies but many others in the region as well.

TOWARD A NEW MILITARY POSTURE

Implementing such a wide-ranging and flexible strategy in Asia will require major adjustments to the current U.S. military posture. Since the 1950s, the focus of U.S. attention in Asia has been in the northeast, oriented toward the Soviet Union (until the end of the Cold War) and North Korea. This posture will need to shift broadly

---

[2]Should the United States and China come into conflict over Taiwan or some other issue, the American military would confront an adversary having capabilities—an arsenal of theater ballistic missiles, evolving capabilities for information and counterspace operations, and, of course, the means to strike U.S. targets with nuclear weapons—well beyond those fielded by other potential adversaries. While a critical U.S. objective must be to avoid making an enemy of China, the U.S. Air Force and its sister services should think through how best to counter these capabilities if American military power must at some future time be projected into East Asia in the face of active Chinese opposition.

[3]This is important in order to address the reluctance of many Asian states to engage in cooperative efforts that might offend the People's Republic of China (PRC).

southward. To be sure, this does not mean that the United States should abandon its existing security arrangements in Northeast Asia; even if the confrontation on the Korean peninsula should end, the United States would benefit from maintaining basing and access in both South Korea and Japan. In fact, modifying access in Japan by establishing possible forward operating locations (FOLs) for U.S. Air Force (USAF) fighters in the southern Ryukyu Islands would be of great help were the U.S. military called on to support Taiwan in a conflict with mainland China. However, this may be politically problematic in Japan.

Elsewhere in Asia, the United States should seek to solidify existing access arrangements and create new ones. For example, Manila appears interested in improving relations with the United States, and the Philippines' location makes it an attractive potential partner. In the longer term, Vietnam could provide additional access in Southeast Asia beyond that which Singapore and Thailand offer.

South Asia presents many distinct challenges. Critical in and of itself—it is probably the world's most likely nuclear battleground—the region is also an important link between Asia proper and the Middle East and Central Asia. Yet the United States currently lacks reliable access to the subcontinent. Pakistan—currently under military rule and at risk of implosion—is hardly a reliable partner and current domestic trends promise to make it even less so. Relations between the United States and India are still in an early stage of post–Cold War thawing and have yet to overcome the differences and hesitancy bequeathed by the past. Of the basing possibilities in the region, Oman is one of the closest to the Indian-Pakistani border—about 500 nautical miles. Relations between the government of Oman and the United States are good, and Oman has shown itself to be a reasonably steadfast ally. In addition, the basing infrastructure in Oman is well developed.

Knitting together a coherent web of security arrangements among the United States and its core partners in Asia—Japan, Australia, and South Korea—that might expand to Southeast Asia will demand military as well as political steps. Training exercises will need to be expanded to include all the parties; planning forums will need to be established; and some degree of hardware standardization will be necessary to foster human and technical interoperability.[4] Particularly useful in this regard could be the deployment of procedures and mechanisms for greater information sharing between the United States and its core regional partners at the strategic, operational, and tactical levels.

The overall U.S. posture in the Western Pacific would benefit from three additional steps. First, Guam—a sovereign U.S. territory—should be built up as a major hub for power projection throughout Asia. Sufficient stockpiles of munitions, spare parts, and other equipment should be established to support the rapid deployment and employment of a sizable tranche of USAF assets—say, 100 to 150 fighters and up to 50 bombers—anywhere in the region. Within C-130 range of the Philippines, northwest Australia, Malaysia, Indonesia, Singapore, Vietnam, and Thailand, assets could be quickly moved from Guam to FOLs across much of the region.

Second, the USAF and the U.S. Navy should work to develop new concepts of operations that maximize the leverage their combined forces could offer to a joint commander in a future Pacific crisis. With basing for land-based fighters at a premium in much of the region, the USAF and the U.S. Navy should, for example, plan and practice tactics and procedures to enable carrier-based fighters to provide air-to-air and defense-suppression support for Air Force bombers and in turn to be supported by USAF tankers and command, control, communications, computers, intelligence, surveillance, and reconnaissance (C^4ISR) platforms.

Third, the USAF should review its future force structure and consider whether it might not benefit from a mix that places greater emphasis on longer-range combat platforms. In this context, acquiring additional heavy bombers might be one option. Another option that is often discussed is the arsenal plane, an aircraft capable of delivering a large number of smart munitions from a stand-off range beyond the enemy's defensive envelope. A third option would be to develop

---

[4]These steps could provide the political benefit of helping dispel the lingering distrust and animosity between South Korea and Japan.

and deploy a small fleet of high-speed, long-range strike aircraft.[5] Asia is vast, and options for basing large numbers of land-based combat aircraft are few and far between; long range and high speeds have payoffs that might not be evident when looking at contingencies in more-compact theaters, such as Korea, Europe, or even the Persian Gulf.

---

[5]By "high speed" we mean roughly a Mach-2 supercruise and by "long range" a minimum 2500-nm unrefueled range. If fitted with a dozen or so 250-pound small smart bombs (SSBs), such an aircraft could conduct missions currently executable only by B-1 or B-2 bombers at a sortie rate more comparable to that achieved by current fighter-bombers such as the F-15E or F-117. Preliminary calculations suggest that such a platform would be about the size of an F-4. See John Stillion and David T. Orletsky, *Airbase Vulnerability to Conventional Cruise-Missile and Ballistic-Missile Attacks: Technology, Scenarios, and U.S. Air Force Responses*, Santa Monica: RAND, MR-1028-AF, 1999; and D. A. Shlapak, J. Stillion, O. Oliker, and T. Charlick-Paley, *A Global Access Strategy for the U.S. Air Force*, Santa Monica: RAND, MR-1216-AF, forthcoming.

ACKNOWLEDGMENTS

Project AIR FORCE's work on "Future Asian Security," whose results are summarized in this report, could not have been conducted without the strong support of its sponsors, General Patrick Gamble, Commander, Pacific Air Forces; Lieutenant General Robert H. Foglesong, Deputy Chief of Staff, Air and Space Operations; and Lieutenant General (Retired) Marvin Esmond. We are grateful to them for their continuing faith and interest in our work.

Our action officers, Lieutenant Colonel Max Hanessian, Major Milton Johnson, and James Hertsch, have been very helpful in opening doors for us and helping ensure our work's relevance to the concerns of the senior USAF leadership.

The appendices on the changing political-military environment in Northeast Asia, Southeast Asia, and South Asia were prepared by Jonathan D. Pollack, Angel Rabasa, and Ashley J. Tellis.

We have benefited from conversations with our RAND colleagues Robert Mullins, Roger Cliff, Michael Swaine, Tanya Charlick-Paley, Rachel Swanger, and James Mulvenon and from the assistance of Tatsuro Yoda. Of course, they bear no responsibility for the final product. Kurt Campbell and Douglas Paal reviewed an earlier draft of the report and made many helpful suggestions, but they too are innocent of the final result. We express our gratitude to our editor, Andrea Fellows.

Last but certainly not least, we wish to thank our secretaries, Luetta Pope, Joanna Alberdeston, and Karen Echeverri, for their steadfast and good-natured support in preparing this report.

ACRONYMS

ABM — Antiballistic missile

AoR — Area of Responsibility (of a U.S. Joint Command)

APEC — Asia-Pacific Economic Cooperation

APOD — Aerial port debarkation

ARF — ASEAN Regional Forum

ASEAN — Association of Southeast Asian Nations

AWACS — Airborne warning and control system

BARCAP — Barrier CAP

BJP — Bharatiya Janata Party (Indian political party, literally "People's Party of India")

C^2 — Command and control

C^3 — Command, control, and communications

C^4ISR — Command, control, communications, computers, intelligence, surveillance, and reconnaissance

CAP — Combat air patrol

CENTO — Central Treaty Organization

CNP — Comprehensive national power

COB — Collocated operating base

COMINT   Communications intelligence

CPP   Communist Party of the Philippines

CSCAP   Council for Security Cooperation in the Asia Pacific

CSIS   Center for Strategic and International Studies

CTBT   Comprehensive Test Ban Treaty

DCINC   Deputy commander-in-chief

DMZ   Demilitarized zone (between North and South Korea)

DPP   Democratic Progressive Party (ROC political party)

EEZ   Exclusive Economic Zone (200-mile zone extending outward from a country's coast)

ELINT   Electronic intelligence

EU   European Union

FFB   Federal Financing Bank

FMCT   Fissile Material Cutoff Treaty

FMS   Foreign Military Sales (U.S. program)

FOL   Forward Operating Location (USAF)

FSL   Forward support location

GAM   Gerakan Aceh Merdeka (Acehnese separatist movement, Indonesia)

GCC   Ground Component Command

GDP   Gross domestic product

GNP   Gross national product

HNS   Host-nation support

ICBM	Intercontinental ballistic missile
IMET	International military education and training (U.S. program)
ISR	Intelligence, surveillance, and reconnaissance
JDA	Japan (Self-)Defense Agency
JSF	Joint Strike Force
KMT	Kuomintang
LAC	Line of Actual Control (de facto border between India and China)
LOA	Letter of offer and acceptance
MASINT	Measurement and signature intelligence
MFA	Ministry of Foreign Affairs (PRC)
MILF	Moro Islamic Liberation Front (Philippines)
MND	Ministry of National Defense (ROK)
MNLF	Moro National Liberation Front (Philippines)
MOB	Main operating base
MOOTW	Military operations other than war
MOU	Memorandum of understanding
MRC	Major regional contingency
MTCR	Missile Technology Control Regime
MTW	Major theater war (U.S. defense-planning scenario)
NEFA	Northeast Frontier Agency
NEO	Noncombatant evacuation operation
NMD	National missile defense

NPT	[Nuclear] Non-Proliferation Treaty
NTW	[U.S.] Navy Theater Wide (ballistic missile defense program)
OPCON	Operational control
PACOM	U.S. Pacific Command
PAS	Islamic Party of Malaysia
PfP	Partnership for Peace
PKO	Peacekeeping operations
PLA	People's Liberation Army (PRC)
PRC	People's Republic of China
PULO	Pattani United Liberation Organization (Thailand)
RMB	Renminbi (PRC currency)
ROC	Republic of China (Taiwan)
ROCAF	Republic of China Air Force
ROK	Republic of Korea (South Korea)
RTC	Resolution Trust Corporation (U.S.)
SIGINT	Signals intelligence
SLOC	Sea line of communication
SOE	State-owned enterprise (PRC)
SOF	Special operations forces
SRBM	Short-range ballistic missile
SSB	Small smart bomb
SSM	Surface-to-surface missile
TMD	Theater missile defense

UAV	Unmanned aerial vehicle
UCP	Unified Command Plan
UMNO	United Malays National Organization
USAF	U.S. Air Force
USCENTCOM	U.S. Central Command
USFK	U.S. Forces Korea
USPACOM	U.S. Pacific Command
VFA	Visiting forces agreement (between the United States and a nation hosting U.S. military forces)
WMD	Weapons of mass destruction (nuclear, chemical, or biological weapons)
WTO	World Trade Organization

Chapter One

INTRODUCTION: THE USAF AND ASIA[1]

The past 20 years in Asia have been a time of relative peace that has seen Asian governments set aside their differences in order to concentrate on economic growth. At the same time, however, Asia's economic success—notwithstanding the financial crisis of 1997–1998—is providing many states with the means to act on latent rivalries and ambitions that had previously been subordinated to economic growth. Nationalism, territorial disputes, nuclear rivalry, and the potential rise of a hegemon may all disrupt the present political-military balance in Asia. In short, serious problems confront Asia that, if not well managed, could spell an end to the relative peace the continent has enjoyed for the past two decades.

Asia is, moreover, a region fraught with rivalry, suspicion, and insecurity.[2] As China becomes more powerful, it may well become more assertive. India also has ambitions of becoming a major continental actor and, as evidenced by its 1998 nuclear tests, regards China as its

---

[1]For the purposes of the report, Asia is considered to include Northeast, Southeast, and South Asia as well as China, Australia, and New Zealand. It is roughly equivalent to the U.S. Pacific Command (PACOM) area of responsibility (AoR), minus the small island-states and territories of the south and southwest Pacific, but including Pakistan. The inclusion of Pakistan is necessary to discuss questions concerning the future of South Asia and U.S.-Indian relations.

[2]Aaron Friedberg ("Will Europe's Past Be Asia's Future?" *Survival*, Vol. 42, No. 3, Autumn 2000, pp. 147–160) raises the question of whether the current international political situation in Asia possesses disquieting similarities to that of late 19th- and early 20th-century Europe, suggesting that an awareness of these similarities may be an important prerequisite to avoiding the fate of Europe in 1914. In reviewing an earlier draft of this report, Douglas Paal suggested that the appropriate comparison might be to the Asia of a century ago.

primary long-term rival. Similarly, Japan may ultimately move toward a more independent foreign policy. More immediately, Korean unification or reconciliation could change the balance of power in Northeast Asia.

The principal challenge for U.S. regional strategy is to prevent 21st-century Asia from becoming unstable and producing massive conflagrations. Toward this goal, the United States must begin to formulate policies that will enable Asia to develop peacefully and in ways compatible with U.S. national interests. The United States cannot hope to resolve every regional security issue in Asia, but together with its allies it can strive to focus on the larger issues while shaping the smaller ones so that they remain manageable. At the same time, the United States must build a framework for greater regional cooperation in Asia. Enhanced communication and more fully integrated economies will reduce misunderstanding and increase interdependence, thereby diminishing the likelihood of major-power rivalry and armed conflict. Expanded security alliances will further aid in deterring aggression.

To understand the region's future prospects and potential challenges to U.S. strategy, Chapter Two first examines the changing political-military environment in Asia and discusses possible outcomes. Chapter Three then deals with U.S. strategy for the region. It examines several alternatives for shaping and responding to the future Asian political-military environment and finally recommends a strategy of creating a "dynamic peace."

Chapter Four examines the military implications of the proposed strategy. It also focuses on possible military missions that the U.S. armed forces might be called on to perform in furtherance of that strategy and the implications for the U.S. Air Force (USAF).

Four appendices examine in greater detail the changing political-military environments in Northeast Asia, China, Southeast Asia, and South Asia.

Chapter Two

THE CHANGING ASIAN POLITICAL-MILITARY ENVIRONMENT[1]

IS ASIA HEADING TOWARD RIVALRY?

A Period of Relative Peace: 1980–2000

Compared to its experience since the 1930s, Asia has enjoyed relative peace during the past two decades. There have been no major wars comparable to World War II, the Korean War, the French and American wars in Vietnam, or the Indo-Pakistani wars of 1965 and 1971. Nor has China engaged in combat as it did during the offshore-islands crises of 1954–1955 and 1958, the Sino-Indian border war of 1962, its border skirmishes with the Soviet Union in 1969, and its "defensive counterattack" against Vietnam in 1979. Similarly, China no longer supports communist insurgencies in the region.

Of course, the past 20 years have hardly been free of tension and rivalry. First, Asia contains the one ongoing Cold War conflict in the world—the tense, militarized standoff between North and South Korea. It is also home to the seemingly intractable rift between China and Taiwan. In 1996, the United States responded militarily to Chinese missile tests directed at waters adjacent to Taiwan's two main ports—tests that were apparently intended to intimidate the Taiwanese electorate on the eve of the March 1996 presidential

---

[1]This chapter draws heavily on the four appendices, which discuss the changing political-military environment in Northeast Asia, China, Southeast Asia, and South Asia.

election. The presidential election of 2000 was also the occasion for Chinese fulminations.

The past 20 years have also seen violence in Cambodia; the secession struggle in East Timor and the Indonesian army's brutal response to that struggle; insurgency and terrorism in Kashmir and the southern Philippines; and minor naval clashes in the South China Sea. Nevertheless, compared to the major military conflicts of the previous half-century, the Asian region has remained relatively tranquil.

Will It Continue?

Asia's relative tranquillity over the past 20 years is attributable primarily to the fact that most Asian nations have concentrated on economic development. Indeed, it is this emphasis on development that underlies whatever unity the region may have, given its vast differences in culture, religion, and historical experiences.[2] The key question is whether we can expect this trend to continue.

On the positive side, most countries in the region have adapted to the U.S.-led liberal trading order as the best means of achieving their top priority: national economic and technological development. Indeed, the Asian financial crisis of 1997 has weakened the appeal of the "Asian model" of development, which has come to be referred to disparagingly as "crony capitalism." In South Korea and Taiwan, free-market authoritarianism has been replaced by democracy, thus belying the argument that the latter is a Western import unsuited to Confucian societies. Indonesia—the country with the largest Islamic population in Asia—has also moved away from free-market authori-

---

[2]The importance of this emphasis on development is neither a new phenomenon nor a new observation. Writing in the mid-1980s, Lucian Pye (*Asian Power and Politics: The Cultural Dimensions of Authority*, Cambridge, MA: Harvard University Press, 1985) noted this trend and viewed it as the grounds for talking about Asia as a single entity:

> The common element in Asia is that it is a continent in pursuit of economic growth, national power, and all that can be lumped together under the general label of modernization. The unity of Europe lies in its history; the unity of Asia is in the more subtle, but no less real, shared consciousness of the desirability of change and of making a future different from the past.

What is different now is that the formula for achieving this progress is more evident than ever before, and the international environment is more supportive.

tarianism, although its democracy is much less entrenched than that of South Korea or Taiwan. Conversely, India, which has continued to maintain a democratic government despite its substantial poverty, is moving—albeit in fits and starts—away from its traditional Fabian socialism toward a free-market economy.

On the negative side, a variety of factors may hinder this positive trend. Of the world's remaining communist regimes, for example, all but one remain in Asia. Democracy and support for human rights are not as universally accepted as is the case in Europe, and some Asian countries continue to view authoritarianism as necessary for political stability and economic success.[3] Similarly, the international institutional framework of the region remains relatively undeveloped, and there is less cultural commonality and interchange than in Europe. Nationalist sentiments, often fueled by resentment over past injustices suffered at the hands of colonial powers, remain strong in most Asian countries and were not mitigated by the experience of World War II as they were in Europe. Perhaps most significant, however, is the fact that Japan—the region's strongest and most successful democracy—seems highly unlikely to serve as a model given its cultural singularity and its tardiness in coming to terms with its record of colonialism in the 20th century.

Asia's economic growth also carries with it the possibility of increasing military power. Over the past several decades, most of the nations of the region have not spent high percentages of their GDP on defense and have not increased their defense expenditures at a rate commensurate with their economic growth. This may, however, be changing. Over the past several years, both China and India have—in contrast to past behavior—increased defense spending at rates exceeding their GDP growth. In 2000, for example, China's defense budget increased 12.7 percent compared to a 1999 GDP growth of 7.2

---

[3]The relevance of these facts for Asia's peaceableness depends, of course, on the much-debated theory of "democratic peace." Critics of that theory could argue that, whatever its merits elsewhere, it is likely to be inapplicable to Asia given that nationalist sentiment remains strong among many populations. It remains, however, a fundamental component of U.S. policy toward the region and will therefore be discussed in this context.

percent, while India's defense budget increased 28.2 percent compared with a 1999 GDP growth of 5.8 percent.[4]

Asia further lacks common institutions analogous to NATO and the European Union (EU), which buttressed security and promoted regional cooperation during Europe's transition from the Cold War. Institutions such as the Association of Southeast Asian Nations (ASEAN) and its security counterpart, the ASEAN Regional Forum (ARF), have remained weak given their member states' reluctance to criticize each other. Although the Philippines and Thailand have at times been openly critical of their neighbors, the majority of Asian governments prefer inclusion and consensus building rather than confrontation.

At the same time, Asia is host to a variety of unresolved border disputes that serve to perpetuate mistrust in the region. For example, the South China Sea and its islands and reefs have been claimed in whole or in part by Brunei, China, Taiwan, Malaysia, the Philippines, and Vietnam. In addition, disputes have arisen among China, Taiwan, and Japan over the Senkaku/Diaoyu Islands; China has had land or maritime border disputes with India, Russia, and Vietnam; South Korea and Japan have laid claim to the Tokto/Takeshima Islands; and Russia and Japan continue to vie for the Northern Territories. Yet while all of these disputes have the potential to escalate into violence, none is so volatile as that between India and Pakistan over Kashmir, where border incursions, insurgency, terrorism, and nuclear weapons make for a dangerous mix that continues to have a destabilizing effect on the region.

Finally, Asia is home to two aspiring great powers—India and China. China's rapid economic growth and its steadily growing military strength may ultimately prompt it to become more forceful in pressing its territorial and sovereignty claims. Both China and India may also want more of a say in shaping regional and continental in-

---

[4]China's defense-budget data are derived from "China Military Budget Up 12.7% for 2000," *China Online,* March 8, 2000, available at http://www.chinaonline.com; China's GDP data are from *Country Report: China and Mongolia,* London: Economist Intelligence Unit, 2000, p. 6; India's defense-budget data are from "Defense Spending Could Spiral Out of Control," *Asia Times,* March 4, 2000, available at http://www. asiatimes.com/indpak/BCO4Df02.html; and India's GDP data are from "Economic Indicators," *Far Eastern Economic Review,* April 13, 2000, p. 75.

stitutions and events. Whether India and China will be able to assume the role of dominant regional or continental powers remains uncertain, but the fact that both countries aspire to great-power status may in itself prove to be a source of conflict in the years to come.

Asia's political-military situation is thus becoming increasingly fluid. Many countries have more resources—both economic and technological—and may also have greater incentive to transform those resources into military power. Indeed, one analyst has termed the region "ripe for rivalry."[5] Below the surface, various countries are building up their potential strength. If or when they enter the geopolitical arena as confident "actors," they may find themselves engaged in heightened political-military competition or even conflict with their neighbors. Nevertheless, there are some positive indications as well. Most governments in the region seem to understand that peace and stability are highly preferable as conditions for promoting their economic and technological development.

WHITHER A UNIFIED KOREA?

Among the geopolitical changes taking place in Asia, those on the Korean peninsula loom large. The June 2000 Pyongyang summit between the leaders of South and North Korea raised the possibility that the two parts of the Korean peninsula could ultimately reach a fundamental reconciliation or even formally unite. As part of this process, North Korea has somewhat relaxed its hostile public posture toward the South. At Pyongyang, the two leaders agreed on a series of steps—including "visits by separated family members" and "economic cooperation and exchange in all fields"[6]—that, while bolstering North Korea economically, would open it up to outside influence to an unprecedented extent. This would appear to pose a serious risk to the stability of the North Korean regime.

---

[5]The term is taken from Aaron Friedberg, "Ripe for Rivalry: Prospects for Peace in a Multipolar Asia," *International Security*, Vol. 18, No. 3, Winter 1993/1994, pp. 5–33.

[6]Citations are from the joint declaration issued by the two leaders. See *ROK News Agency Carries "Unofficial Translation" of South-North Joint Declaration*, FBIS-EAS-2000-0614, reprinted from Yonhap, June 14, 2000.

The predominant motivation of the North Korean leadership is the continued receipt of economic assistance necessary to prevent catastrophe. However, since North Korea's extraction of aid has to date depended largely on its perceived willingness to undertake dangerous military adventures, it is unclear whether North Korea could afford to adopt a policy of straightforward accommodation toward the South.[7] Despite the positive atmospherics surrounding the November 2000 visit to Pyongyang by then–U.S. Secretary of State Madeleine Albright, it thus seems more likely that any process of reconciliation will at a minimum be punctuated by periods of North Korean–provoked crisis and tension, if only to keep international economic aid flowing. It is also possible, although not likely, that a unified Korea would come about as a result of the collapse of the North Korean regime.[8]

A unified Korea would in any event face a completely changed security environment and would have to make several fundamental decisions. Among these would be whether to continue to host U.S. military forces on its territory; whether to maintain the relatively large military establishments of North and South Korea, particularly the North's ballistic missile forces and nuclear weapon program;[9] and what posture to adopt toward China and Japan. A unified Korea could seek an autonomous role in the region but would be relatively weak compared with its closest neighbors, China, Japan, and (to a lesser extent) Russia.

Some of these issues are likely to arise even in the absence of unification. For example, North and South Korea might become recon-

---

[7]One could argue that the military threat could be replaced as a motivation for aid and investment by (1) the South's desire that the North not collapse (in order to avoid the costs of reunification) and (2) the benefit accruing to the South's corporations from the exploitation of the North's large pool of relatively cheap, Korean-speaking labor. One wonders, however, whether these factors would be sufficient to motivate the large financial transfers that the North will require.

[8]Although economic difficulties alone rarely cause a regime to collapse, they can lead to intra-élite conflicts that get out of hand.

[9]It is not known whether North Korea now possesses a nuclear weapon or sufficient fissile material to manufacture one; in any case, a unified Korea would inherit whatever nuclear facilities had not yet been dismantled in accordance with the U.S.–North Korean Agreed Framework of 1994. Combined with South Korea's generally higher technological capabilities, these facilities would be a major step toward a nuclear capability if such a capability did not already exist.

ciled to such an extent that they would no longer regard each other as their main security threat, or the economic collapse of North Korea could sharply limit the threat to the South.

A major potential effect of unification or reconciliation would be pressure on the United States to abandon its military bases in South Korea. The primary justification for these bases has heretofore been the defense of South Korea from another North Korean invasion. Without the threat of military invasion, many parties could question the continued stationing of U.S. troops in a postunification or reconciliation environment.[10]

Unification or reconciliation could also provoke nationalist sentiment in Korea, which would in turn intensify opposition to a continued U.S. presence. In response, the United States would have to make the case to the Korean government and public that the presence of its forces served the overall goals of regional stability and hence was advantageous to Korea even in the absence of an immediate threat. It might also be necessary to investigate what steps could be taken to reduce the impact and visibility of U.S. forces so as to help placate any nationalist sentiments that might be unleashed by the unification of the peninsula.

Some support for a continued U.S. presence has unexpectedly emanated from the North. Until the June 2000 summit, North Korea had always been a vociferous opponent of U.S. bases in the South. At that summit, however, Kim Jong Il purportedly expressed the view that it would be beneficial for a unified Korea to retain a U.S. military presence in order to fend off pressures from Korea's larger neighbors, China, Russia, and Japan. Although this makes sense from a realist perspective (as a strong but distant power, the United States would be an ideal ally for a unified Korea), it also represents an extraordinary statement on the part of the world's last Stalinist regime—one

---

[10]According to the South Korean Institute of Foreign Affairs and National Security, a research arm of the Ministry of Foreign Affairs and Trade, a poll conducted in late 1998 indicated that "70% of South Koreans would be opposed to the continued presence of American troops in a unified Korea." See *South Korea: IFANS Report on Presence of U.S. Forces After Unification,* FBIS-EAS-99-020, reprinted from Yonhap, January 21, 1999.

that has previously been vituperative in its stance toward the U.S. military presence in South Korea.[11]

Whatever the North Korean view may be, the United States may in any case have to deal with Chinese opposition to its troops in South Korea. To be sure, China has not officially demanded that the United States withdraw its forces from South Korea after a Korean unification or reconciliation. It has, however, demanded that remaining U.S. forces be used only for bilateral contingencies and not for operations that could support other regional contingencies—e.g., a crisis over Taiwan. Even if its security concerns might be addressed, China would likely prefer not to have U.S. forces stationed in Korea. As a result, depending on how unification or reconciliation was accomplished, China might attempt to make the withdrawal of the U.S. military a quid pro quo for its acquiescence to unification.

Indeed, China's current helpfulness on behalf of Korean reconciliation[12] may well be motivated by a desire to force an abandonment of the U.S. military presence in South Korea. Beijing may even hope that such a result would place U.S. access to Japanese bases in doubt as well,[13] thereby greatly complicating any possible U.S. response to a Chinese use of force against Taiwan.

China may also play a critical role in determining the manner in which unification or reconciliation is achieved. At least two factors

---

[11]Doug Struck, "South Korea Says North Wants U.S. Troops to Stay," *Washington Post*, August 30, 2000, p. A1.

[12]For example, the arrangements for the June 2000 Pyongyang summit were negotiated in Beijing. In addition, China's encouragement of economic reform in North Korea has probably contributed to the current North Korean policy of seeking southern investment.

[13]For example, a *People's Daily* "news analysis" (Ma Shikun and Zhang Yong, "The United States Makes Quicker Adjustment to DPRK Policy," *Renmin Ribao [People's Daily]*, June 24, 2000, p. 3, reprinted as *Analysis of U.S. Adjustment to DPRK Policy*, FBIS-CHI-2000-0624) suggests that Korean reconciliation could undermine "U.S. strategic interests in Asia":

> The U.S. government and military have said that they will not hastily withdraw the ROK [Republic of Korea]-based U.S. troops and shut down the military bases, but *the development of the situation is something independent of the United States' will.* Besides, once reconciliation has been achieved on the Korean peninsula, *the ROK-U.S. and Japan-U.S. military alliances will lose their archrival and the grounds of existence, and U.S. strategic interests in Asia will be challenged* [italics added].

could be important in this regard. First, if unification involved some military action, obtaining China's acquiescence to forestall any Chinese interference would presumably be an important policy objective. Achieving this objective might require some understanding with the Chinese concerning the role of U.S. forward-based forces in a unified Korea. For example, it might be advisable to agree that no U.S. forces would be permanently based in the former North Korea.

Any decision on the continued stationing of U.S. forces would also be greatly affected by the status of relations between Korea and China. If those relations were good, Korea would seek some way to reassure China concerning any continued U.S. presence, perhaps by limiting such presence to the southern part of the peninsula. Conversely, if relations with China were bad, Korea would have a greater stake in retaining U.S. forces on its territory, if only as an indicator of U.S. commitment to its defense. How vigorously China would oppose continued U.S. basing would then depend on the future status of Sino-U.S. relations.

At the same time, however, a unified Korea is more likely to view Japan as its main regional rival—and perhaps even as a security threat. Again, much will depend on the circumstances of Korea's unification and on whether Japan is seen as hostile to it. In addition, Japan's reaction to South Korea's inheritance of the North's missile and nuclear programs could play a pivotal role. A unified Korea with nuclear and missile programs, backed by South Korea's economic strength, would form the basis of a significant military force and would thus raise concerns in Japan. This, together with historical antagonisms that have not been fully resolved, could lead to worsening relations between Korea and Japan and to a concomitant tendency on Korea's part to seek improved relations with China.

If the postunification relationship between Japan and Korea turns out to be a troubled one, the United States, as the closest ally of both countries, would find itself in a challenging situation. From a *realpolitik* perspective, one might argue that this could have some advantages in that it could provoke each country to "bid" for U.S. support against the other. Handled deftly, the situation could thus prove advantageous to U.S. interests, as both countries could be more willing to provide access to U.S. forces and to respond favorably to U.S. requests in order to ensure that the United States did not "tilt" toward its rival. On the other hand, the result could just as easily be disappointment and resentment on the part of each country at U.S. unwillingness to take its side of the quarrel.

As a practical matter, however, this situation would be difficult to manage, since popular resentment in each country would probably be high whenever the United States took an action that could be construed as favoring the other side. Thus, a more favorable outcome for the United States would be a Korean-Japanese rapprochement that ensured that the United States would not be caught between the two entities. Some progress has already been made along these lines. In October 1998, for example, the Japanese delivered their most complete apology to date for their colonial activities in Korea. Similarly, in 1999, Japan and Korea conducted their first joint naval exercise involving "a maritime search aid rescue drill for peaceful purposes."[14]

Finally, given its overall weakness, Russia is not likely to be a major factor in any calculation of Korea's security threats and interests. That could change, however, if the Russian economy were to recover and were Russia to rebuild its military might, especially in the Far East. This would give Korea more flexibility in balancing among the "whales" in whose midst it must continue to live.

Of the four major powers with which Korea must concern itself— China, Russia, Japan, and the United States—the United States stands out as being the most powerful and the farthest away. Thus, the United States is Korea's most desirable ally *if* the Koreans have confidence in its staying power. As an ally of the Republic of Korea (ROK) against North Korea, the United States has proved its reliability over time. In the more fluid environment that might follow Korean reunification or reconciliation, however, the United States might appear to have a lesser stake in the future of the Korean peninsula and hence be less likely to remain a reliable ally.

---

[14]*ROK, Japanese Navy Officials Agree to Hold Joint Exercise,* FBIS-EAS-1999-0213, reprinted from *Korea Times* (Internet version), February 13, 1999.

THE U.S.-JAPAN ALLIANCE

North Korea's nuclear and missile programs, as well as China's military modernization, confront Japan with a host of new security challenges. The most fundamental question, however, is whether Japan will continue to rely on U.S. protection against these new threats as it did with respect to the Soviet threat during the Cold War. In addition, the mere passage of time and generational change may weaken the antimilitarism that has characterized Japanese public opinion during the post–World War II period. Occasionally politicians or others give voice to the sentiment that Japan's reliance on the United States should come to an end. Japan may thus be facing some major strategic decisions in the next decade.

To be sure, Japan has already begun to build up its military strength in response to the challenges noted above and has been willing to become more active militarily. It has participated in U.N. peacekeeping operations (PKO) and has been more forceful in its attitude toward North Korean intrusions into its territorial waters. The key question in this regard, however, is whether Japan's military buildup and increased willingness to contemplate the use of military force are occurring within the context of the U.S.-Japan alliance[15] or as a step toward breaking free of that alliance. Thus far, it would appear that the former is the case, with the United States tending to encourage these Japanese activities.

At the same time, the Japanese may well be concerned either that the United States may wish to reduce its commitment to the region or that Japan might face a threat against which the United States would not prove a reliable ally. The belief that U.S. intelligence failed to alert the Japanese about the 1998 North Korean missile launch, for example, raised doubts in Japan about U.S. reliability and provided an impetus for the authorization of funds to procure four reconnaissance satellites. Further incidents of this kind could encourage Japan to take on a greater burden for its own defense. In addition, the Japanese may believe that a unified Korea could not only pose a security challenge but could provoke conflicts in which the United

---

[15]Even within the context of the alliance, Japan could come to play a more active role in international affairs; in particular, the alliance itself could evolve in a way that gives Japan more influence in terms of decisionmaking.

States might be reluctant to take sides. For this reason, it is worth considering the choices Japan would face were it to decide to adopt a more independent national security posture, however remote such a possibility may be.

Given its economic strength, Japan could elect to become a major military power capable of defending itself and its sea lines of communication (SLOCs). This course of action would, however, have serious drawbacks—for not only would the attendant economic sacrifice be great, but the increased military expenditures it would involve would come on top of the large financial demands Japan currently faces in dealing with its aging population and shrinking labor force. Assuming that it would be unable to cope with the cultural shock involved in accepting large numbers of immigrants, Japan would thus face the necessity to conserve on manpower in both the economy and its military—a goal that, although attainable, would require widespread economic reform and large investments in labor-saving technology for both the economy and the military.

In addition, the pursuit of an independent national security policy would probably require the acquisition of nuclear weapons—if not openly, at least on the Israeli model. Although one could argue that the nuclear option could save Japan money (as compared to trying to achieve a comparable capability by conventional means), it would be very costly from a political standpoint both domestically and in terms of Japan's relations with other East Asian and Southeast Asian states.

Even if Japan were willing to expend the necessary economic and political resources on the development of its military forces, it would have to make still other changes to bring its military strength in line with its economic prowess. Aside from the constitutional issue, for example, its Self-Defense Agency would have to be given the status of a full-fledged ministry, toward which goal either a draft would have to be introduced or steps would have to be taken to raise the prestige of military service so as to attract large numbers of high-quality personnel.

An alternative strategy for Japan would be to seek a *modus vivendi* with China as the region's rising power. This would not be inconsistent with modern Japanese history, which has twice seen Japan make an alliance with the predominant power—Britain in the pre–World War I period and the United States in the post–World War II period—the bulwark of its security policy.[16] Given China's residual ill will toward Japan, however, the latter might find it difficult to reach a satisfactory *modus vivendi* with China;[17] presumably, such an understanding could come about only as a result of a traumatic event that led the Japanese to lose all faith in U.S. support. On the other hand, China would have a great deal to gain from such an arrangement (e.g., relatively unfettered access to Japan's world-class technological capability), and thus a pragmatic Chinese leadership might well prove willing to suppress its—and its population's—anti-Japanese sentiments in order to facilitate an understanding with Japan.

The formation of such a relationship would, however, deal a fatal blow to U.S. political and military influence in East Asia. Presumably, for example, such a relationship would lead to the expulsion of U.S. forces from Japan and would place potentially insurmountable pressure on U.S. bases in Korea—assuming that such bases had not already been eliminated. As part of the deal, Japan would probably be required to go beyond its current "One China" policy and put additional pressure on Taiwan to accede to reunification. The result could be a loss of confidence on Taiwan, which would result in its acceptance of reunification on the best terms it could get.

Finally, Japan could attempt to balance Chinese power by seeking out other allies in the region, the most obvious of which would be India, Vietnam, and, depending on circumstances, perhaps a unified Korea (although Korea might prefer to remain equidistant from both China and Japan or even to "tilt" toward China). India might be tempted to seek closer relationships, if not alliances, with other Asian powers were it to see the need to balance Chinese power. In the absence of a strong tie to the United States, the Indian navy would appear to Japan as an important factor in securing (or threatening) its vital SLOCs to the Persian Gulf.

---

[16]Perhaps the same idea lay behind the Tokyo-Berlin-Rome axis of the 1930s, but in this case Japan miscalculated.

[17]In addition, it should be noted that Britain and the United States are distant liberal states, whereas China is a neighboring authoritarian one; reliance would thus be a more risky proposition in any case.

However, even assuming—as seems likely—that Japan does not make any major change in its national security strategy, the United States must consider the effects that Korean reconciliation, and concomitant pressure on U.S. military bases in South Korea, could have on U.S. military access to Japan. There could be some difficulties concerning U.S. bases in the aftermath of Korean unification, not least if the United States had to remove its forces from Korea. Japan might not wish to be the sole host of U.S. military forces in the region, and the disappearance of the North Korean threat might lead popular opinion to suppose that U.S. forces no longer had a role to play in Northeast Asian security.

ADJUSTING TO THE EMERGENCE OF CHINA[18]

Assuming that China's economic, technological, and military development proceeds on its current course, its potential threat to the United States and its interests will rest on two major factors: first, the evolution of the Taiwan issue, and second, whether a more powerful China will seek to reduce U.S. influence and presence in East Asia.

The Taiwan issue seems capable of becoming more contentious and dangerous over time in that Taiwanese society is evolving in a direction unfavorable to unification while Chinese nationalist sentiments appear to be growing stronger. Beijing insists that Taiwan adopt China's definition of the One China formula and also regards the issue of reunification as potentially vital to the continuation of communist rule. Taiwan, for its part, exists in an uneasy in-between world: A vibrant new democracy with a booming economy, it treads a fine and dangerous line while sustaining its separation from China. The mainland, meanwhile, has made it quite clear that it retains the option of employing military force to effect reunification. Even if violence is averted, the issue will thus remain a volatile one.

Of course, even a "straight line" projection might yield unanticipated results. Economic factors, for example, could work to bring the two societies closer together by leading the benefits of economic cooperation to outweigh political differences. Even more optimistically,

---

[18]The question of whether China will in fact emerge as a great power is discussed in detail in Appendix B.

favorable changes in China in the direction of greater openness, democracy, and respect for human rights could weaken Taiwanese distrust and pave the way for a peaceful settlement.

Quite apart from this issue, China's declared preference in the international arena is that the world move toward multipolarity—i.e., that U.S. power and influence, viewed in China as excessive, be "cut down to size." Thus, although the Chinese probably recognize that the United States will remain the world's dominant power for the foreseeable future, their hope will continue to be to constrain the exercise of U.S. power in Asia. As a result, China will presumably work to limit U.S. military basing and access in East and Southeast Asia while seeking to dilute U.S. ties to alliance partners such as Japan and South Korea as well as to a unified Korea.

At the same time, it is not clear whether these policies would in the long run be in China's interests. Weakening the U.S.-Japan alliance, for example, could easily lead Japan to pursue a more independent geopolitical course. If deprived of U.S. support, Korea too could increase its military power, perhaps to include the acquisition of nuclear weapons. More generally, multipolarity would imply that both India and, if it recovers, Russia would become potential rivals of China. India has, in fact, already embarked on a course of pursuing great-power status—and although Chinese observers do not list India among the "poles" of a future multipolar system, it is hard to see how China could prevent that from occurring. In a similar manner, the current era of good Sino-Russian relations rests both on Russian weakness and on Russia's and China's common opposition to U.S. "hegemony." Yet in a multipolar setting, a revived Russia and China could easily become competitive. The possible risks of a multipolar world thus suggest that the alternative option of a "strategic partnership" with the United States might have its attractions for China.[19] At

---

[19]A real strategic partnership would imply a willingness on the part of both countries to cooperate closely in dealing with major world issues. Aside from the joint statement issued by the two countries following the South Asia nuclear tests ("Joint Statement by Chinese and U.S. Heads of State on the South Asian Issue, 27 June 1998, Beijing," Xinhua, June 27, 1998, reprinted in FBIS-CHI-98-178), it is difficult to find publicly known instances of even ostensible cooperation on a major international issue, although it is often claimed that China has, at various times, placed helpful (from a U.S. standpoint) pressure on North Korea with regard to nuclear weapons and ballistic missile issues.

the moment, however, China's preference for multipolarity and hence for bringing the United States down in power terms from superpower to great-power status appears to remain firm.

How the rest of Asia will adjust to increased Chinese power is perhaps the single most critical question weighing on the future regional security environment. From a theoretical perspective, the fundamental choice for China's neighbors would appear to be between "balancing" and "bandwagoning"—that is, between seeking allies[20] to help resist any pressure China might apply, on the one hand, and on the other aligning with China in the hope that the required accommodation to Chinese interests will not be too costly and that Chinese friendship will benefit other national security interests.

The perceived reliability of the United States as a potential ally and "balancer" will have a pivotal effect on the strategic choices of China's neighbors. As a potential ally and balancer, the United States has two crucial advantages: It is powerful, and it is far away and hence less likely to be seen as a direct threat. On the other hand, regional states may believe that the United States is unlikely to remain militarily engaged in Asia over the long term and may thus fear that too heavy a reliance on the United States will make them vulnerable to potential U.S. pressures in other areas such as human rights and trade policies.

Most regional states, however, do not see the situation in such stark terms. At least in the short run, for example, they do not see China as an imminent threat and may well believe that China will be unwilling or unable to throw its weight around in the region at any time soon. Indeed, during the 1990s China's behavior was generally conciliatory, with the major exceptions of (1) its 1995 occupation of Mischief Reef, and (2) the military exercises and diplomatic efforts it has undertaken to pressure Taiwan.

To be sure, the first event did produce a major reaction in the region, when the Philippines raised the issue with its ASEAN allies. Up to that point, China's claims to the South China Sea had been forcefully

----

[20]China's neighbors may also seek to increase their own military power; however, except for Russia, India, and Japan, China's neighbors cannot hope to be able to stand up to a powerful China on their own.

vindicated only against Vietnam, and the other claimants may have felt that they were immune to Chinese pressure. The Mischief Reef incident thus served as something of a "wake-up" call for Asia even though its long-term effects remain uncertain. On May 16, 2000, the Chinese foreign minister agreed with his Philippine counterpart that the two sides "will contribute positively toward the formulation and adoption of the regional Code of Conduct in the South China Sea."[21] This appeared to augur well in that China's usual stance has been that disputes over the South China Sea should be settled bilaterally rather than in multilateral forums (where the Chinese power advantage over any one other claimant would be diluted). It is unclear, however, whether this agreement represented a change in Chinese policy or merely a tactic to defuse tensions in the South China Sea in the wake of further Chinese construction on Mischief Reef in 1998.

Chinese military pressure against Taiwan in 1996 prompted the United States to send two aircraft carriers to the region but elicited little public support from Asian countries. Since then, the Chinese white paper of February 21, 2000 (entitled "The One China Principle and the Taiwan Issue"[22]), which restated China's claim that it is entitled to use force against Taiwan and officially[23] extended the circumstances that might trigger the use of force to include Taiwanese refusal "*sine die*" of "the peaceful settlement of cross-Straits reunification through negotiations," has put this issue back on the front burner.

---

[21]"Joint Statement of the Chinese Foreign Minister and Philippine Secretary of Foreign Affairs," Xinhua, May 16, 2000, reprinted as *China, Philippines Sign Joint Statement*, FBIS-CHI-2000-0516.

[22]Taiwan Affairs Office and Information Office of the State Council of the People's Republic of China, "The One China Principle and the Taiwan Issue," February 21, 2000, available at http://www.fmprc.gov.cn/english/dhtml/readsubject.asp?pkey=20000222170511.

[23]China had previously implied (and perhaps stated unofficially) that it would use force against Taiwan if Taiwan sought to perpetuate its current status of de facto independence by refusing "over a long period of time" to negotiate on reunification. See Roger Cliff, "China's Peaceful Reunification Strategy," *American Asian Review*, Vol. 14, No. 4, Winter 1996, p. 100. It appears, however, that China had not previously stated this condition in such an authoritative manner.

The publication of the white paper has led to some speculation[24] that Beijing may set an internal deadline for the recovery of Taiwan, perhaps before 2010. If there is any truth to this speculation, the next decade may see forceful Chinese actions with respect to Taiwan that could have a major effect on the policies of regional states.

Despite the escalation of this war of words, it remains unclear how regional states might react to a Chinese use of force against Taiwan. It is possible that, as noted, such states might regard Taiwan as a special case and hence might not view the use of force against it as a sign of more general aggressive tendencies on China's part—i.e., as tendencies that could hurt them in the future. Even if this were the case, however, the regional states would carefully monitor U.S. reaction. Failure on the part of the United States to react, for example, might be attributed to an unwillingness to risk a military conflict with China.[25] If this were so, then America's failure to react could have devastating effects on U.S. credibility in the region and might lead regional states to believe that they had no choice but to seek accommodation with a rising China. The United States could then find itself in a dilemma in which regional states were unwilling to support U.S. action to defend Taiwan but would react adversely to U.S. failure to support Taiwan.

Beyond the immediate sovereignty issues with respect to the South China Sea and Taiwan, many regional states wonder whether a strong China might not have additional ambitions. Over its history, the People's Republic of China (PRC) has made territorial claims on many of its neighbors.[26] In the case of India, no territorial settlement has been reached, although the land border has been quiet and the

---

[24]See, for example, Willy Wo-Lap Lam, "Deadline Debated as Taiwan Stakes Raised," *South China Morning Post,* February 22, 2000.

[25]Rather than to a principled adherence to a One China policy. In particular, it might make a significant difference how China itself interpreted the U.S. failure to react. To the extent that, as seems likely, China attributed U.S. restraint to a weakness of will, fear of confronting China militarily, concern about damaging economic interests relative to China, and the like, other regional states would be likely to do so as well. In any case, they would have to be concerned that China would be less likely to be deterred from any action in the region by fear of U.S. resistance.

[26]China's attitude toward territorial claims is assessed in Michael D. Swaine and Ashley J. Tellis, *Interpreting China's Grand Strategy,* Santa Monica: RAND, MR-1121-AF, 2000, pp. 129–133.

two sides have agreed to abide by the current de facto border. In addition to the conflicting claims in the South China Sea, maritime territorial disputes still exist with Vietnam and Japan. In the cases of Vietnam, Burma (Myanmar), and the states of the former Soviet Union, formal agreements settling the various disputes over land borders have been reached or appear to be close at hand. In the long run, regional states may fear that a strong China might revive and prosecute some of these claims. In addition, a strong China might wish to acquire a "sphere of influence" in East Asia—i.e., a position of influence such that neighboring states felt obliged to take its interests into account in making any major national security decisions.

Be this as it may, most of the states in the region appear to regard any such Chinese threat as a matter for the longer term—i.e., as something that need have only a minor influence on their policies for the present. India and Japan may constitute partial exceptions to this generally relaxed posture concerning China's status as a potentially rising power. The Indian nuclear tests of 1998 were explicitly linked by senior Indian officials to Chinese military power. Indian ballistic missile developments also seem to be explicable only in this context. The ranges of the new Indian ballistic missile are greater than those required for targeting Pakistan. The Agni series of missiles, for example, will eventually be able to reach Beijing with a nuclear warhead. On the other hand, such posturing may reflect India's sense of its own future as a great power with an autonomous foreign policy rather than any settled suspicion of or hostility toward China. Yet potential difficulties remain in the Sino-Indian relationship, as discussed at greater length later in this chapter.

In the case of Japan, there seems to be a heightened sense of a potential challenge from China as well, perhaps reflected most clearly in the revised U.S.-Japan Defense Guidelines that followed in the wake of Chinese military pressure against Taiwan. Indeed, Japan has perhaps two related worries on this score: increasing Chinese power and the fear that, under some circumstances, China could achieve a status such that U.S. relations with China might compromise Japanese interests. To some extent, the revision of the defense guidelines addressed both concerns by emphasizing the importance of the Japanese relationship to the United States.[27]

On the other side of the equation, some regional states may be more tempted to "bandwagon" with China. Aside from Pakistan, which relies on China for support against India, the main states that might fall into this category are Thailand, Russia, and perhaps South Korea. Historically, the Thais have not seen China as a threat. Thailand has no claims in the South China Sea, and in contrast to other Southeast Asian states, the ethnic Chinese community in Thailand is well integrated into Thai society. In addition, the Thai-Chinese relationship has a strategic component: After Vietnam's invasion of Cambodia, Thailand cooperated with China in opposing Vietnamese regional hegemony and, in doing so, became a conduit for logistical support of the anti-Vietnamese forces in Cambodia. On the other hand, Vietnam's withdrawal from Cambodia and its entry into ASEAN diminished the strategic rationale for Thai Chinese security cooperation. At the same time, China's expanding military ties with Burma and possible Chinese use of Burmese facilities on the Indian Ocean have created some concern in Thailand.

Thus far, Russia has for its part seen China more as a potential ally and business partner than as a threat. In the global context, both countries have focused on U.S. preeminence as their key concern and hence have seen each other as strategic partners—at least at the rhetorical level—against U.S. "hegemony." In addition, China has the hard currency with which to purchase weaponry from Russia, thus helping keep Russian arms producers afloat. Finally, the two countries share similar concerns over the threat of Islamic fundamentalism both with respect to separatist movements on their own territory in Chechnya and Xinjiang and with respect to the Central Asian nations.[28] Thus, in the near term at least, Russia probably does not have any reason to be concerned about increasing Chinese power. In the long run, however, it would have to wonder whether

---

[27]See Appendix A for a more detailed discussion of this point.

[28]See Mark Burles, *Chinese Policy Toward Russia and the Central Asian Republics*, Santa Monica: RAND, MR-1045-AF, 1999, Chapter 3, for a discussion of Sino-Russian relations with respect to Central Asian issues.

the demographic pressures created by the difference in population density on the two sides of the border might not cause difficulties.[29]

The most interesting case is that of South Korea. South Korea's establishment of diplomatic relations with China in 1992 put pressure on the North Korean regime and suggested that China could provide a useful avenue of approach toward reconciliation or even unification (although one could easily argue that Korean unification is not in China's interests). For example, the initial secret negotiations that led to the June 2000 summit took place in Beijing and Shanghai. In addition, Kim Jong Il's surprise secret visit to Beijing was closely followed by the summit itself. As the country with the greatest influence on North Korea, China is obviously important for the South, and its goodwill is worth cultivating. As long as South Korea follows a policy of seeking better relations with the North, it would seem to have a strong incentive to maintain good relations with Beijing as well.

Another interesting case is that of Vietnam. Historically, Vietnam has seen China as the major threat to its security—and with the expulsion of the United States from Vietnam in 1975, this historic pattern recurred with a vengeance, culminating in China's 1979 invasion. At the moment, both sides are working to improve relations and have resolved their dispute concerning the land border. The maritime disputes, which concern both the division of the Gulf of Tonkin and conflicting claims in the South China Sea,[30] have been put on the back burner as well. In the long run, however, it is hard to believe that Sino-Vietnamese relations will remain untroubled. Vietnam's interest in rapprochement with the United States, despite its leadership's concerns that any type of opening or reform will endanger its domestic political control, seems to attest to an abiding suspicion of China.

Most of the remaining states of the region tend to be wary of China but are far from having decided to adopt an anti-Chinese posture.

---

[29]Burles (1999), p. 45, summarizes this issue.

[30]These led China to use force in 1974 and 1988 over the Paracel Islands and the Spratlys, respectively. The forces the Chinese ousted from the Paracel Islands in 1974 were South Vietnamese; presumably the Chinese wished to secure those islands before they were inherited by North Vietnam.

China's action in building permanent structures on Mischief Reef has led the Philippines to reverse course with respect to military ties with the United States, resulting in the signing of a visiting forces agreement (VFA) on February 10, 1998.

Thus, while the emergence of China probably represents one of the most important trends affecting Asia's future security environment, we are still in the very early stages of this development, and it is too soon to tell what its major implications will be. Nevertheless, under the surface, regional states will be at least quietly assessing Chinese political-military developments and considering their options.

INDIA'S FUTURE ROLE

One of the largest uncertainties in the region is whether India will be able to emulate China's sustained economic dynamism, thereby laying the foundation for an expanded political-military role. Compared to China, India has many advantages that could well enable it to become the region's next economic success story. It has a vigorous high-tech sector supported by high-quality academic institutions; it enjoys a functioning legal system that can protect property rights; it will not face an aging-population problem in the next two decades or a gender imbalance over the longer term; and, most important, it has a political system that is not threatened by opening up to the world. Although India faces a large task in privatizing various state-owned industries, it does have the legal infrastructure in place for doing so. Moreover, unlike China, India need not be concerned that increasing links to the rest of the world and growing prosperity will place potentially fatal stresses on its political system; if anything, such forces could be expected to strengthen India's democracy.

Still other recent developments bode well for India's continued growth. In the early 1990s, for example—in the face of a foreign exchange crisis—the Indian government began an economic reform process that has led to increased rates of growth (about 5.5 percent annual GNP growth over the period 1988–1998).[31] By the end of the 1990s, India had made its mark in the global software market, with

---

[31]"India at a Glance," World Bank fact sheet, March 28, 2000, available at http://www.worldbank.org/data/countrydata/aag/ind_aag.pdf.

several of its new software companies having become highfliers on Wall Street.[32] Lured by the opportunities created by this economic reform, entrepreneurial members of the Indian diaspora, including the hugely successful Indian population of Silicon Valley, have been investing their effort and money in developing India's high-technology sector.

On the other hand, India faces a number of disadvantages that could prevent it from attaining China's level of economic success. Its basic educational system is not well funded, and literacy rates are lower; it has not overcome the effects of the caste system; it is subject to internal strains and secessionist tendencies that have the potential to cause more disruption than similar problems in China (e.g., Tibet and Xinjiang); and, most important, its leadership has followed a less pragmatic economic policy. Although India has embarked on a path of economic reform, it has not done so as decisively as has China over the past two decades, in part because of the populist pressures surfacing in its democratic system. It is hard, for example, to imagine an Indian leader echoing Deng Xiaoping's sentiment that "it doesn't matter whether the cat is black or white as long as it catches mice." As a result, foreign direct investment in India totaled $2.2 billion in 1998,[33] well below Chinese levels. In a similar manner, India's democratic system—while an advantage in the long run—stands in the way of many reforms that make economic sense. Thus, it remains to be seen whether the Indian reform process will culminate in a dynamic economy that enjoys East Asian–style rates of growth.

In any case, if India's economic and technological development can be sustained and accelerated, India should be in a position to claim a larger role for itself in world affairs. One possible way in which this claim might find expression would be in a campaign to obtain permanent membership (with veto power) on the U.N. Security Council. It is unclear whether the question of India's status with respect to the Nuclear Non-Proliferation Treaty (NPT) will become a major obstacle to achieving this goal (as well as to improving U.S.-Indian rela-

---

[32]Sadanand Dhume, "No Holds Barred," *Far Eastern Economic Review*, February 24, 2000, pp. 40–41, discusses the competition between the New York Stock Exchange and the Nasdaq to attract new stock listings by Indian companies.

[33]"India's Economy," *The Economist*, March 4–10, 2000, p. 72.

tions). Presumably, India would like to see its status as a nuclear weapon state accepted in the eyes of the international community (although if its economy "takes off," this may prove to be irrelevant for most practical purposes)—and this would seem to imply some modification of the NPT to include India as a nuclear weapon state. It is not clear, however, that this is possible, as it would require Chinese agreement, or even that the United States would favor it. In the absence of such a step, however, India's possession of nuclear weapons could be a continuing irritant and thus serve as an impediment to India's emergence on the world stage as a recognized and accepted great power.

During the Cold War, India's orientation toward the Soviet Union defined its relationship with the United States. Since the end of the Cold War, India has to some extent been left out in the cold and, as the rhetoric surrounding its nuclear tests indicated, has been concerned about its potential military imbalance in relation to China. Thus, the incentive exists for a closer relationship with the United States.

As the Indian nuclear tests of 1998 suggest, it would seem likely that India will maintain a wary posture toward China. Whether this posture will degenerate into outright political-military competition, however, is less clear. India will most likely continue to develop its nuclear deterrent capability vis-à-vis China[34]—and while the Chinese will not like this (they reacted vociferously to India's 1998 nuclear tests), their options for dealing with it would appear to be limited. In any case, India's goal will probably be merely to establish a credible deterrent against any Chinese attempt to use nuclear blackmail against India—a goal that may not in itself threaten any vital Chinese interests. Overall, China's reaction to India's ongoing nuclear and ballistic missile development programs may thus be muted.

Aside from India's development of a nuclear deterrent posture targeted primarily against China, there are several other possible areas of contention between the two powers. These include:

---

[34]See Ashley J. Tellis, *India's Emerging Nuclear Posture: Between Recessed Deterrent and Ready Arsenal,* Santa Monica: RAND, MR-1127-AF, 2001, for a discussion of India's nuclear posture.

- the ongoing border issue, which was put on the back burner in 1993;

- political-military rivalry in Southeast Asia (especially Burma) and the adjacent maritime areas;

- Chinese attitudes toward Indian "regional hegemony" in South Asia; and

- evolution of the situation in Tibet and in the Indian northeast.

The border issue has been quiescent since the "peace and tranquillity" agreement was signed in September 1993, according to which both India and China agreed to respect the "Line of Actual Control" (LAC) pending a final settlement.[35] This implies a recognition of Chinese claims in the west (Ladakh area) and Indian claims in the east (Northeast Frontier Agency). Although no final settlement of these conflicting claims has yet been reached, it seems unlikely that this issue will flare up again unless one of the countries decided to raise it for other reasons. Thus, any future border conflict is likely to be a symptom rather than a cause of strained Sino-Indian relations.

One of the more likely possible causes of political-military rivalry between China and India would be continued Chinese pursuit of a significant presence in Burma. Burma's pariah status, which is due to the oppressive rule of its military junta, has rendered that country vulnerable to Beijing's blandishments. According to one observer, it

> has given obeisance to China in exchange for its independence and minimal intervention in its internal affairs. However, arms transfers and economic ties have dramatically increased China's influence within Burma. In fact, a few years of trade and military aid have turned the non-aligned state of Burma into China's client state—an objective which the three decades of Beijing-supported insurgency and Burmese Communist Party's armed struggle failed to achieve.[36]

Neighboring states have reacted to this development in several ways. In 1997, for example, Burma—despite the unsavory character of its

---

[35]J. Mohan Malik, "China-India Relations in the Post-Soviet Era: The Continuing Rivalry," *China Quarterly*, No. 142, June 1995, p. 317.

[36]Malik (1995), pp. 340–341.

regime—was tentatively approved for membership in ASEAN. In India, the "Look East" policy was adopted, partially as a response to China's interest in Burma, as a means by which India could seek to enhance its ties with the Southeast Asian nations.[37] One should probably expect to see an ongoing Sino-Indian rivalry for influence in Southeast Asia, with Vietnam leaning toward India, Thailand toward China, and Burma caught in the middle. The fact that several members of ASEAN have claims in the South China Sea that conflict with China's could give India an advantage in this competition, but the predominant goal of the Southeast Asian states (with the possible exception of Malaysia) will probably be to balance China and India against each other to prevent either from obtaining too much influence.

In the wake of the Indian nuclear tests in 1998, the official Chinese press carried several blasts against India's supposed policy of becoming the "regional hegemon" in South Asia.[38] Indeed, over the years China has often sought to help South Asian states resist Indian influence and power, most notably in the case of Pakistan. In particular, the Chinese facilitated the Pakistani nuclear program with transfers of key equipment.

---

[37]This is discussed in greater detail in Appendix D. Sino-Indian rivalry in Southeast Asia is not a new phenomenon. In particular, India's friendship with Vietnam has been of significance in this regard. Interestingly, India's foreign minister (now prime minister), Atal Behari Vajpayee, was visiting Beijing when the Chinese attacked Vietnam on February 17, 1979; this visit marked a thaw in the two countries' relations, which had been strained since their 1962 border war. China's ability to achieve tactical surprise (despite the fact that it had been broadcasting its intention to "punish" Vietnam) may have depended in part on the fact that Vietnam did not "[expect] China to spoil this new thaw by mounting an attack on India's friend Vietnam while Vajpayee was still in China. In fact, Hanoi was so confident that on February 16 Premier Pham Van Dong, along with Chief of Staff Van Tien Dung and other senior leaders, had left for Phnom Penh on a four-day visit. See Nayan Chanda, *Brother Enemy: The War After the War,* San Diego CA: Harcourt Brace Jovanovich, 1986, p. 356.

[38]For example, an article in the People's Liberation Army (PLA) newspaper claimed that the objectives of India's strategy were "to seek hegemony in South Asia, contain China, control the Indian Ocean and strive to become a military power in the contemporary world." See Liu Yang and Guo Feng, "What Is the Intention of Wantonly Engaging in Military Ventures—India's Military Development Should Be Watched Out For," *Jiefangjun Bao (Liberation Army Daily),* May 19, 1998, p. 5, reprinted in FBIS-CHI-98-141, May 21, 1998.

In yet another case, China tried unsuccessfully to help one of the states on the Himalayan border, Nepal, gain more international autonomy from India. After Nepal turned to China to buy arms that India had refused to sell it, India imposed a partial trade blockade on land-locked Nepal and eventually forced it to reaffirm its subordinate status.[39] Similarly, China has not recognized the 1975 incorporation of Sikkim into the Indian Union, a failure that occasions complaints in the Indian media.[40]

In general, however, China has been careful not to push too far in its South Asian activities and has not been willing to actively encourage India's neighbors to resist its influence.

Finally, there is the question of Tibet. Upon obtaining independence from Great Britain, India at first appeared to wish to inherit Britain's position of influence in Tibet. Prime Minister Nehru, however, acquiesced in the Chinese invasion of Tibet in 1950 and recognized Tibet as an integral part of China. Following the Tibetan revolt of 1959 and the flight of the Dalai Lama, India provided a refuge for the Tibetan religious leader in Dharmsala but has prevented him from engaging in high-profile political activities in India. India has also decided to grant refuge to the 17th Karmapa—a 14-year-old who, prior to his escape to India in February 2000, had been the highest-ranking Buddhist religious figure residing in Tibet to be recognized both by the Dalai Lama and by the PRC—despite Chinese warnings against doing so.[41] China is thus likely to regard India's attitude toward Tibet as potentially troubling—and while India has not taken any action to destabilize Chinese rule in Tibet, the mere presence of major Tibetan religious figures on Indian territory provides some support for the forces of Tibetan resistance to Chinese rule. If the Tibetan resistance

---

[39]John W. Garver, "China-India Rivalry in Nepal: The Clash over Chinese Arms Sales," *Asian Survey*, Vol. 31, No. 10, October 1991, pp. 956–975.

[40]See, for example, Mira Sinha Bhattacharjea and C. V. Ranganathan, "India and China—I," *The Hindu*, May 8, 2000, reprinted as *Daily Analyzes India-China Relations*, FBIS-CHI-2000-0508.

[41]In March 2000, Chinese Foreign Ministry spokesman Zhu Bangzao said at a press briefing that "the Indian government should tread carefully on granting asylum. India should 'proceed from the overall interest of bilateral relations and handle this issue prudently and properly.'" See "China Says Dalai Lama Using Escaped Karmapa for Own Purpose," Beijing, Agence France-Presse, March 9, 2000.

should become stronger and more active in the future, it could lead to a worsening of relations between China and India.

Underlying all these issues is the question of how the two countries will see their future relationship. India believes that the relationship should be one of equals. China, on the other hand, tends to regard India as distinctly inferior. At present, the "world community" implicitly sides with China in this dispute: China is a permanent member of the U.N. Security Council and a recognized nuclear power under the terms of the NPT, whereas India is not. A recent review of Chinese scholarship on the question of India's future suggests that there is a wide variety of opinion concerning India's future importance. In general, however,

> India's economic reforms are judged insufficient to catch up with China and enter the multipolar world as a sixth pole. India's CNP [comprehensive national power] scores for 2010 place it no higher than number nine [Academy of Military Sciences] or thirteen [Chinese Academy of Social Sciences], only about half of China's CNP score in 2010.[42]

Regardless of how the Sino-Indian relationship develops, India appears likely to pursue a more active political-military role in the world, of which its nuclear tests in 1998 and its expressed interest in becoming a permanent member of the U.N. Security Council may serve as indicators. Another manifestation of this desire may be more diplomacy with other countries in Asia and the Middle East. India's Look East policy of closer relations with the nations of Southeast Asia has already been noted. More speculatively, one might envisage that India will look farther afield as well. For example, India and Japan could see a common interest in balancing Chinese influence in the region and in protecting SLOCs from the Middle East.[43] While at present India probably sees Japan's close ties to the United States as an obstacle to cooperation, that could change either if

---

[42]Michael Pillsbury, *China Debates the Future Security Environment*, Washington, D.C.: National Defense University Press, 2000, p. 153.

[43]Nayan Chanda ("After the Bomb," *Far Eastern Economic Review*, April 13, 2000, p. 20) claims that "there are signs that an informal security-cooperation chain is forming between India, Japan, and Vietnam." One focus of Japanese-Indian cooperation has been antipiracy training for the Japanese coast guard and the Indian navy.

Japan becomes a more independent actor or if U.S.-Indian relations improve. Similarly, India, Iran, Russia, and even the United States share a common concern with respect to Pakistan's influence in Afghanistan and its support for the Taliban. In general, except for its Cold War friendship with the Soviet Union, India has tended to pursue an independent path and eschew close alliances; this could change in the future if India decides to play a larger role in international politics.

PAKISTAN AS A FAILED STATE?

Although the shape of Sino-Indian relations may be the most significant issue influencing the future Asian political-military environment, the current concern in South Asia centers on relations between Pakistan and India, especially as it is manifested in Pakistani support for the Islamic insurgency in Kashmir. The nuclear tests of 1998 appear to have convinced Pakistan that a nuclear standoff exists between India and Pakistan, thus making the situation safer for lower-level conflict. An example of such lower-level conflict was the invasion, in the spring of 1999, of the mountainous Kargil region of the Indian-Pakistani border by Pakistani-supported forces; ultimately the forces were driven out by a large Indian military effort.

For Pakistan, this type of low-level harassment of India represents its best chance—albeit not a very good one—of gaining control of Kashmir. As long as the indigenous insurgency is not fully suppressed, Pakistan can support it at a low cost to itself while imposing a larger cost on India. While it may seem remote, Pakistan may hope that the victory over the Soviets in Afghanistan can be duplicated in Kashmir. In any case, the struggle in Kashmir provides a rare point of unity for Pakistan, and it employs Islam-inspired guerrilla warriors who might otherwise cause trouble in Pakistan itself—a nation in which Islamic fundamentalism is gaining in political influence.

In the past, India has adopted a defensive stance toward this sort of Pakistani harassment. A repetition of the Kargil incident could, however, lead India to consider whether a more forceful response might not be advisable to solve the problem once and for all. Some observers have argued that we may be seeing the beginning of a major change in opinion in New Delhi, from a relatively relaxed posture toward Pakistan to one that actively questions whether the stability of Pakistan is in India's interests.

This view could be bolstered by a sense that Pakistan may in any case be on its last legs. The current military government may be Pakistan's last chance to get its economic house in order; while some positive steps were initially taken,[44] the pace of reform seems to have slowed. If the military government fails, separatist and Islamic forces are in the wings. A failing Pakistan might both invite and compel India to react more forcefully to the next Kargil episode.[45]

In contrast to the situation in Kashmir, Pakistan has been more successful in Afghanistan, where its backing of the Taliban has enabled it to take control of almost the entire country. However, most of Afghanistan's other neighbors remain suspicious of the Taliban and fearful that its religious extremism will harm their stability; indeed, even Iran is hostile. Thus, Pakistan's success in Afghanistan has had the effect of furthering its isolation and providing Russia, China, Iran, and the Central Asian states with a motive for uniting in opposition to it.

THE FUTURE OF RUSSIA

The Asian region could also be significantly affected by developments in Russia, which tended to disappear during the 1990s as a factor in the Asian security environment. The reappearance of the Russian factor could come about either because of Russian weakness or by virtue of a revival of Russia's strength. Continued Russian weakness could create a vacuum in the Russian Far East, leading either to encroachments by surrounding countries (such as China) or to secessionist tendencies by local leaders, who would then have to contend with their neighbors on their own. Conversely, renewed Russian strength might lead to a revival of tensions with China and Japan over immigration and border issues.

---

[44]These steps include cracking down on the looting of the nation's bank by well-connected members of the elite, suppressing sectarian violence, and attempting to reform the economic system.

[45]These are discussed in detail in Appendix D.

In any case, now that it no longer represents an ideologically based threat, Russia is capable of acting more flexibly in the region than was the case during the final decades of the Soviet era. An agreement with Japan concerning the disputed Northern Territories (although not reached during Russian President Vladimir Putin's visit to Tokyo in September 2000)[46] could allow for increased economic interaction involving Japanese investment and exploitation of the natural resources of the Russian Far East. With respect to China, Russia shares some common concerns, including fears regarding Islamic political movements and terrorism as well as displeasure with the predominant global role the United States currently enjoys.

If Russia remains weak, it will probably continue to seek close relations with China, both as a counterweight to the United States and because China could be an important source of funds to keep its military-industrial complex in operation. In the case of a recovering Russia, on the other hand, the economic motive for good relations with China would be smaller.

With respect to the United States, Russia and China share several major concerns. First, U.S. and NATO action in Kosovo seemed to set a precedent that both countries, plagued as they are by unrest in regions populated by ethnic minorities, found troubling. At their summit meeting in July 2000, the presidents of Russia and China emphasized both countries' opposition to "any attempts to split the country from within or outside the country."[47]

Second, both Russia and China oppose any U.S. plan to build ballistic missile defenses, fearing that they would be unable to compete in this new arena and that the value of their offensive strategic nuclear force would be reduced.[48] Finally, in rhetorical terms at least, both

---

[46]Doug Struck, "Russia, Japan Oceans Apart on Islands," *Washington Post*, September 5, 2000, p. 16.

[47]"Beijing Declaration by the People's Republic of China and the Russian Federation," PRC Ministry of Foreign Affairs, July 20, 2000, point V, available at http: //www. fmprc.gov.cn/english/dhtml/readhomepage.asp?pkey=2000071819160807/20/ 2000.

[48]At the July 2000 summit, the two presidents issued a joint statement condemning U.S. missile defense efforts.

countries are committed to the "multipolarization of the world"[49]—i.e., to the elimination of the preeminent international position now enjoyed by the United States.

In any case, over the longer term Russia must be concerned that the military and demographic imbalance in the Far East could lead to some sort of Chinese pressure against Russian territory there. Demographically, the Russian population of its far eastern territories is relatively small and declining; not only is the total population of Russia decreasing, but with the collapse of the subsidies provided by Moscow, many economically unviable towns and projects in Siberia and the Far East are being abandoned. Across the border is the vastly larger and economically more dynamic Chinese population of Manchuria and the northeast.

In 1993, Russian authorities in the Far East cracked down on illegal Chinese immigration in the region. Since that time, the situation has been quiet, but the raw demographic facts suggest that problems could arise at any time.[50] Over the years, one would expect that inexpensive Chinese consumer goods would make major inroads into the market in the Russian Far East and that Chinese merchants and traders would come to play a significant if not dominant role in the region's economic life.

Similarly, in Central Asia, Russian and Chinese interests are largely congruent at the present time. Both countries are concerned with Islamic fundamentalism as a threat to their own territorial integrity in Chechnya and Xinjiang, and both see a threat from growing Turkish influence. The rulers of the Central Asian states themselves are concerned about fundamentalist influences in their own countries and have generally been cooperative with China in fighting Uighur separatism in Xinjiang. In particular, the Central Asian states of Kyrgyzstan, Tajikistan, and Kazakhstan have joined with China and Russia in an informal grouping called the Shanghai Five. In addition,

---

[49]PRC Ministry of Foreign Affairs (2000), point III. In this declaration, the push for "multipolarization" was linked to China's and Russia's status as permanent members of the U.N. Security Council; this may be a way of dealing with the awkward (for China) fact that Japan would in all likelihood become one of the "poles" in a future multipolar world.

[50]Burles (1999), p. 45.

both China and Russia have reasons to oppose U.S.-led plans to build a pipeline that could transport Central Asian as well as Azerbaijani oil and gas to the West without transiting either Iran or Russia.[51] Over the longer run, however, Russian and Chinese interests could come into conflict if both sought to increase their influence in Central Asia.

Although these regional issues will no doubt play an important role in Sino-Russian relations, they do not appear—with the possible exception of the question of Chinese demographic pressure on the Russian Far East—to be as important as both sides' assessment of the overall global balance of power. For the moment, it would thus appear that the desire to create a counterweight to the United States will provide an incentive to both China and Russia for closer ties.

SOUTH CHINA SEA

Southeast Asia lies at the intersection of two of the world's most heavily traveled SLOCs. The East-West route connects the Indian and Pacific Oceans, while the North-South route links Australia and New Zealand to Northeast Asia. Nearly half of the world's merchant fleet capacity sails through the SLOCs of the South China Sea and the waters surrounding Indonesia. These SLOCs serve as the economic lifelines by which the economies of Northeast Asia receive oil and other critical inputs and export finished goods to the rest of the world. Moreover, much intraregional trade depends on these waterways. A closure or prolonged blockade of any of the Southeast Asian SLOCs would seriously disrupt shipping markets and international trade.

From a military perspective, these sea lanes are critical to the movement of U.S. forces from the Western Pacific to the Indian Ocean and the Persian Gulf. During the Cold War, maintaining freedom of navigation for U.S. military vessels while denying that same freedom to the Soviet Union in the event of a conflict was the top American strategic objective with respect to these waterways, while facilitating seaborne commerce was a secondary goal. With the demise of a

---

[51]China's interest in this question is clearly less than Russia's. Nevertheless, China has no interest in increasing the access of the rest of the world to Central Asian oil.

clear and immediate global military threat, economic considerations have become more salient. Nonetheless, the United States and its regional friends must still pay attention to a range of potential threats, both conventional and nonconventional, to freedom of navigation and SLOCs and must retain the capability to deny freedom of operation to potential adversaries.

The territorial disputes concerning the South China Sea and its islands have been a continuing source of tension in Asia. China and Taiwan claim all the South China Sea, while Brunei, Malaysia, the Philippines, and Vietnam have overlapping claims to some of the islands. The area has seen disputes flare into violence. Confrontations have occurred between China and Vietnam and China and the Philippines on several occasions, between the Philippines and Vietnam, between the Philippines and Malaysia, and between Taiwan and Vietnam.[52]

Disputes continue over the islands in the South China Sea because of commercial fishing rights and the possibility of major deposits of oil and natural gas, since those possessing the islands have the right to fish and explore for oil and natural gas in the surrounding waters. Such disputes are also caused by nationalist sentiment and heightened concerns over territorial sovereignty. Although the ASEAN claimants and China have been discussing these issues in the Indonesian-sponsored dialogue, the potential for armed conflict persists. Five events that may trigger violence are:

- A Chinese attempt to interfere with maritime traffic on the South China Sea SLOCs, perhaps in an effort to coerce the United States, Japan, or ASEAN into accepting Chinese political demands.

- A Chinese effort to forcibly establish and maintain control over all or most of the Spratly Islands. Such an operation could feature the threat or use of force against an ASEAN state, either to compel acceptance of Chinese demands or to defeat opposing military forces.

---

[52]U.S. Energy Information Administration, "South China Sea Region," January 2000, available at http://www.eia.doe.gov/emeu/cabs/schinatab.html#TAB2.

- Continuation or expansion of China's "salami tactics" to gradually assert control of more territory in the disputed areas—for instance, the occupation of other reefs or the construction of new structures in already claimed reefs.

- Conflict triggered by energy exploration or exploitation activity, fishery disputes, accidents or miscalculations, regional tensions, or provocative actions by one or more parties to the dispute.

- More ambiguous uses of force by China, including selective harassment and intimidation of regional states in the guise of enforcement of Chinese maritime claims, protection of fishermen, antipiracy or antismuggling operations, or peacekeeping or order-keeping operations in the event of a breakdown of domestic or international order in the region.[53]

To address these disputes, ASEAN issued the 1992 ASEAN Declaration on the South China Sea, which "urge[d] all parties concerned to exercise restraint with view to creating a positive climate for the eventual resolution of all disputes." Despite having pledged to honor the declaration, however, China occupied Mischief Reef, also claimed by the Philippines, in 1995 and subsequently built structures on it.

Despite the 1992 ASEAN Declaration on the South China Sea and the signing of codes of conduct between China and the Philippines as well as between the Philippines and Vietnam, little has been done to resolve the underlying issue: sovereignty. Although some countries would be supportive of multilateral discussions to resolve the issues, China has refused to engage in such discussions, since doing so would improve the relative bargaining position of the ASEAN claimants vis-à-vis China. Instead, China has proposed that bilateral discussions be held with each of the countries with which it has a dispute. China has, moreover, expressed a willingness to discuss joint development of the disputed areas but not to negotiate questions of sovereignty. Yet if discussions are not held to resolve the

---

[53]All five bullets are taken from Richard Sokolsky, Angel Rabasa, and C. R. Neu, *The Role of Southeast Asia in U.S. Strategy Toward China*, Santa Monica: RAND, MR-1170-AF, 2000.

sovereignty of the islands, territorial disputes are likely to continue indefinitely and may well lead to armed conflict.

The range of opportunities for China to engage in these activities in Southeast Asia would expand in an environment of economic hardship and political and social disorder. Weakened ASEAN governments unable to control piracy or prevent attacks on ethnic Chinese communities may present Beijing with targets of opportunity for intervention. One factor that is likely to influence Chinese calculations regarding the use of force is whether ASEAN countries, either individually or collectively—or with the assistance of outside powers— have the military capabilities and political will to mount an effective defense against Chinese threats to regional security.

INDONESIA AS A DISINTEGRATING STATE?

The most important question about Indonesia's future pivots on whether the country will survive in its present configuration or whether, like Yugoslavia or the Soviet Union, it will simply disintegrate. Other second-order but nonetheless critical issues are the fate of Indonesia's democratic transformation and the future role of its armed forces.

The current disarray in Jakarta and the separation of East Timor have encouraged secessionist movements in the economically strategic provinces of Aceh, Riau—which produces half of Indonesia's oil— and Irian Jaya (Papua), the location of the world's largest gold mine and third-largest copper mine as well as the source of an estimated 15 percent of Indonesia's foreign exchange earnings. In tandem with secessionist threats, religious and ethnic violence has been escalating in eastern Indonesia. The growing sectarian violence and the demands of the outlying islands for independence or greater autonomy are generating stresses that the Indonesian political system may not be able to withstand.

Most Indonesians view the insurgency in Aceh as the most serious challenge to Indonesia's territorial integrity. Acehnese resistance to Jakarta has strong roots: strong ethnic identity, lack of trust in Jakarta, the legacy of human rights violations by the security forces, and the possession of natural resources, which in the view of the Acehnese give their province economic viability.

The Indonesian government and the Acehnese separatist movement, Gerakan Aceh Merdeka (GAM), agreed on a temporary cease-fire in May 2000. The Jakarta government has turned over internal security functions to the newly separated national police and has tried to negotiate a political settlement. The question that remains, however, is whether the government's concessions will be sufficient to satisfy Acehnese demands. At present, neither the government nor the insurgents are strong enough to defeat the other, so an accommodation that permits significant autonomy for Aceh within Indonesia may be accepted as the best possible outcome by both sides. On the other hand, a perceived weakening of Jakarta's authority or political will might stimulate demands for full independence.

At the same time, the insurgency in Irian Jaya, which did not become part of Indonesia until 1963 and which shares few cultural or social characteristics with the rest of Indonesia, is, according to one view, potentially even more dangerous than the Aceh rebellion. According to this view, the rebels are Christian and therefore more likely to receive Western support than the Muslim rebels in Aceh, and the border with Papua New Guinea affords the possibility of cross-border sanctuaries for the insurgents.

Aside from separatist insurgencies, there has been large-scale violence between Muslims and Christians in the eastern islands of Indonesia, with the epicenter on the island of Ambon in the Moluccas, and in Sulawesi. There are different theories in Indonesia on who is behind the sectarian violence; some blame Muslim radicals and others Indonesian army factions seeking to destabilize the Jakarta government. The possibility of political manipulation cannot be discarded, but probably the most likely trigger was the collapse of authority following the fall of Suharto, which unleashed pent-up tensions between the original Christian inhabitants and Muslim immigrants from Java who had moved in under the Suharto government's resettlement program. These tensions in turn developed into an economic and religious civil war.

Given the immediacy and seriousness of these internal threats to stability, external threats have taken a back seat in Indonesian defense thinking. President Wahid's government has embarked on a policy of rapprochement with China that represents a departure from the Suharto government's more suspicious attitude. Senior Indonesian military officers do not believe that China poses a direct military threat to Indonesia in the near to intermediate term. This is because of the distance from Chinese operating bases to Indonesian waters and because the Indonesians expect that the Philippines and Vietnam would block China's southern expansion. Nevertheless, they do see China as a long-term threat. In this context, they are particularly concerned about China's potential ability to intervene in and manipulate domestic Indonesian politics.

VIETNAM AS A SIGNIFICANT ACTOR?

Vietnam's leadership has been hesitant to adopt a vigorous reform program for fear that it would weaken its control over the country.[54] As a result, the country has missed out on the Asian economic boom and has been an unattractive location for direct foreign investment. At the same time, relations between Vietnam and China have generally improved: The two countries settled their land-border disputes at the end of 1999 and in December 2000 reached agreement on their maritime boundary in the Gulf of Tonkin. With respect to the South China Sea, China has turned its attention to the Philippine-claimed Mischief Reef and the Scarborough Shoal area, also located in the eastern part of the sea. In Cambodia, Hun Sen, who was originally installed in office by Vietnamese troops, has outmaneuvered and outmuscled his opponents and seems firmly in command.

Thus, Vietnam has not been a significant actor in the international politics of the region. However, this could change in the future. The most likely catalyst for such a change would be the reinvigoration of the historic hostility between Vietnam and China. In the meantime, Vietnam has been hedging its bets by improving its relations with the United States[55] and India.[56]

---

[54]For example, Vietnam has been hesitant about joining the World Trade Organization.

[55]In spring 2000, Vietnam hosted a visit by U.S. Secretary of Defense William Cohen, the first visit by a U.S. secretary of defense since the end of the Vietnam War.

[56]See the discussion above concerning joint Indian-Vietnamese naval exercises.

CONCLUSION

As this short summary indicates, a host of trends and possible events in Asia have the potential to change the overall character of the region's geopolitical environment for the third time since the end of World War II. Roughly speaking, an initial postwar period of more than three decades was characterized by anticolonial and ideological conflicts. A succeeding period of more than two decades was characterized by an intensive concentration on economic development; this period saw the success of export-led, free-market economies, although often with strong governmental intervention and direction.

We are now at the beginning of a third period. As a result of the successful developmental efforts of the second period, many of the nations of the region possess more resources and more confidence in their ability to play a role in the world. The effects of this may vary; in some cases, there is an increase in nationalist sentiment, perhaps leading to a greater willingness to pursue geopolitical ambitions. At the same time, in some societies the result has been a greater pressure for democratization, as the educated middle class that was spawned by the decades of economic development demands the right to participate in the political life of its nation.

Geographically, this third period appears to be characterized by a shift in focus from Northeast Asia, where the remaining ideological conflict of the preceding periods may be winding down, to other subregions of Asia. Greater attention will have to be paid to Taiwan, where the conflict between the mainland's desire for unification and the development in Taiwan of a separate identity, bolstered by the island's economic and domestic political success, may be coming to a head; to Southeast Asia, which is undergoing a period of instability; and to South Asia, where the ongoing conflict between India and Pakistan has been made potentially more dangerous by both sides' acquisition of nuclear weapons in the face of a regional power transition and by Pakistan's increasing internal instability.

Chapter Three

U.S. STRATEGY FOR A CHANGING ASIA

U.S. OBJECTIVES IN THE REGION

As Chapter Two attests, the changing character of the Asian political and military environment presents the United States with a host of critical challenges. If it is to meet these challenges, the United States must begin to formulate a strategy aimed at a pivotal long-term objective: preventing a worsening of the security situation in Asia. Central to this objective is the need to preclude the rise of a regional or continental hegemon. This is important for two main reasons:

- To prevent the United States from being denied economic, political, and military access to an important part of the globe; and

- To prevent a concentration of resources that could support a global challenge to the United States on the order of that posed by the former Soviet Union.

At the moment, no nation in Asia is close to becoming a regional or continental hegemon, but this is not to say that such a threat could not arise. In fact, one major power in Asia or a coalition thereof could readily choose to devote maximum effort to building up armed might in efforts to challenge the United States in the region. Although currently only a remote possibility, the outcome of such a buildup would be sufficiently adverse to U.S. interests to warrant priority.

The United States must also seek to maintain stability in the region through "shaping" activities aimed at providing positive incentives for cooperative behavior and disincentives against the use of force to achieve geopolitical goals. These shaping activities must seek to convince the nations of the region that their security will be attained more easily if the United States maintains an active military role in the region than would be the case if it did not. The acceptance of this role should in turn strengthen the ability of the United States to bolster international norms and influence regional developments in a positive manner. If Asian states are to develop their economies and evolve as free societies, they must be free from the threat of armed attack or coercion. Stability will reduce the need for states to devote resources to the military beyond what is needed for their own defense.

Finally, the United States, in cooperation with its allies, must be able to help manage Asia's ongoing transformation. To be sure, the wide variety of challenges Asia faces suggests that the United States is unlikely to prevent every problem or significantly influence every scenario, but it should be able to shape most scenarios so that they do not spiral out of control. Ultimately, the United States should seek to influence the region in a manner that fosters the development of democratic, market-oriented societies that are willing and able to abide by current international norms of behavior and, eventually, to cooperate in the manner of the democratic European nations so that major armed conflicts among them become unthinkable.

These objectives imply a large number of subsidiary goals that the United States should pursue as well. In dealing with current "hot spots" such as Taiwan and Korea, the United States seeks to deter the use of force or defend allies and states to whose defense it is committed. Aside from strengthening the barriers against the use of force, such actions protect U.S. credibility in the region. The general belief that the United States will remain engaged and that nations that depend on it will not be left in the lurch provides the strongest basis for the region's continuing stability.

In addition, the United States wishes to maintain undiminished economic access to this dynamic region. This implies a continuation of policies toward free trade that have underpinned the region's prosperity so far.

STRATEGIC OPTIONS

Given these objectives, the United States could pursue any of several alternative strategies.

At one end of the spectrum would be a strategy built on ensuring and strengthening U.S. hegemony in Asia. The key to this strategy would lie in maintaining and increasing the U.S. position of preeminent power in the region—if necessary by taking steps to constrain the economic and military growth of any other country that could threaten that preeminence. Such a strategy would require maximum vigilance as well as the expenditure of money and effort and, as such, would probably prove incompatible with U.S. domestic political requirements. It may also make demands on regional friends and allies that might undercut the very stability Washington seeks to reinforce.

A less ambitious strategy would lie in forming a "condominium" with one of Asia's major powers—e.g., India, Japan, or China. In this scenario, the United States would share the military and political burden with its partner at the cost of reducing its ability to act independently, since the interests and wishes of that partner would have to be taken into account and accorded equal weight. However, none of the possible candidates for the role of partner seems suitable owing to the disproportion in power between the United States and each of its potential partners; the reaction of neighboring states to the enhanced political role of that partner; specific bilateral differences between the United States and its potential partner; and, more generally, the incompatibility of such a *Realpolitik* approach with U.S. domestic political realities.

An even less ambitious strategy would call for the United States to adopt the role of "balancer" among the major regional powers. This strategy envisages the transformation of Asia into a multipolar system in which several major powers of significant strength—e.g., China, Japan, India, and Russia, with perhaps Vietnam, a unified Korea, and Indonesia present as important but middle-rank powers—contend for influence and advantage in the region. The United States would have certain structural advantages in such a multipolar system: As a major power involved in the Asian balance but situated far away (and hence less likely to be seen by any country as a direct threat), it would enjoy maximum flexibility to make and shift alliances. This strategy would mean, however, that the United States could not effectively pursue any objective that was not already the objective of one or more of the region's major powers. It would also mean that the United States would in general have to subordinate its ideological interests to the demands of its role as balancer.

An alternative strategy, and one that reflects a non-*Realpolitik* approach, would involve the creation of a collective security system embracing all the states in the region. Such an arrangement would reinforce stability by guaranteeing each state against aggression. By requiring a mechanism for either solving or shelving the various disputes over sovereignty that currently afflict the region, this approach would have to confront the weaknesses that have bedeviled previous attempts at collective security since the days of the League of Nations.

A final possible strategy would hinge on a U.S. disengagement from Asia, trusting to the mutual rivalries and suspicions of the regional powers—along with whatever diplomatic or political influence the United States could exert—to prevent any single power from becoming predominant. In the short run, such a strategy would be the cheapest and easiest to pursue. In the long run, however, it would run two major risks. First, a U.S. withdrawal could undermine the peaceful stability that has been the foundation on which Asia's decades-long economic growth and political transformation have been built. The resulting loss of stability would cause severe and pervasive harm to both the United States and its regional friends. Second, U.S. withdrawal would raise the specter—at present remote but nonetheless worrisome—that a single power would achieve regional hegemony in Asia, bringing the economic and technological resources of Asia under its influence and control and potentially posing a security threat to the United States.

A PROPOSED U.S. STRATEGY FOR ASIA

The optimal U.S. strategy would involve elements of most of these options and would seek both to preserve U.S. influence in the region and to bolster Asian stability. While preserving a leading role for the United States, this strategy would seek to share responsibility with U.S. allies to the extent possible. At the same time, it would rely on a balance among regional powers where appropriate and useful.

This strategy would be integrated across political, military, and economic dimensions, and a necessary precondition would be continued American global leadership. It assumes that the United States will continue to make the necessary political, technological, and military investments in cementing its global preeminence. Economically, the United States should further the development of Asia by continuing to support the expansion of free-trade policies—e.g., by expanding the World Trade Organization (WTO) to include not only China but Taiwan and Vietnam as well. In political-military terms, a four-part strategy is required.

First, the United States should deepen as well as widen its bilateral security alliances to create a larger partnership. This multilateralization—which would be a complement to and not a substitute for existing bilateral alliances—should include the United States, Japan, South Korea, Australia, and perhaps Singapore, the Philippines, and Thailand. Initially, however, the United States will need to promote trust among its allies as well as encourage them to build military capabilities that can respond to regional crises as part of potential coalitions. For example, improved relations between Japan and South Korea should be encouraged in order to facilitate their cooperation on security issues. The United States should support Japanese efforts to gradually become a normal state, which would allow for national participation in collective self-defense, expand its security horizon beyond its territorial defense, and permit Japan to acquire appropriate capabilities for supporting coalition operations.

Second, the United States should pursue a balance-of-power strategy among those major rising powers and key regional states in Asia which are not part of the existing U.S. alliance structure—including China, India, and a currently weakened Russia. The objective of this balance-of-power component is twofold: It seeks to prevent any one of these states from effectively threatening the security of another while simultaneously preventing any combination of these states from "bandwagoning" to undercut critical U.S. strategic interests in Asia. Developing a stable balance of power among these major powers will require great political and strategic agility on the part of the United States. Washington should thus seek strengthened political, economic, and military-to-military relations with all, but especially those least likely to challenge U.S. strategic interests.

Third, the United States should address those situations which, because of a power vacuum or for some other reason, tempt others to use force. The United States should, for example, clearly state that it opposes the use of force by China against Taiwan and likewise any declaration of independence by Taiwan. The United States should also work to resolve the territorial disputes in the South China Sea while emphasizing its commitment to freedom of navigation and the adherence to an agreed code of conduct in the area. It should, moreover, promote the cohesion, stability, and territorial integrity of Indonesia and other Southeast Asian states and foster security cooperation and interoperability among them as well as with the United States and its allies. In addition, the United States should use its influence to encourage the resolution of the Kashmir dispute through peaceful means and prevent an outbreak of a regional nuclear war in South Asia. It should also encourage Japan and Russia to resolve their territorial dispute over the Northern Territories.

Finally, the United States should promote an inclusive security dialogue among *all* the states of Asia. This dialogue would not only provide for a discussion of regional conflicts and promote confidence building but also encourage states to enter into the U.S.-led multilateral framework at some time in the future. At the same time, the United States should maintain flexibility of relations with as many countries as possible to support the formation of ad hoc coalitions to deal with challenges that might concern not only the United States and its allies but many others in the region as well.

Adapting the U.S. Position in Northeast Asia

Maintaining access to facilities in Northeast Asia is an important prerequisite to implementing such a strategy.

Looking Toward a United Korea. The United States must look forward to the possibility that Korea will be reunified or that North and South Korea will reconcile to such an extent that the possibility of military conflict between the two can be disregarded as a military planning contingency. In such a circumstance, the issue of the continued basing of U.S. forces on the Korean peninsula would come to the fore.

There are important political reasons for the United States to try to maintain at least some presence in Korea even when the prospect of war is removed from the peninsula. If all U.S. forces were to leave Korea, Japan would be left as the sole host of permanent U.S. military installations in East Asia, and it is questionable how satisfied Tokyo would be with such an arrangement given its history of uneven popular support for foreign bases. This would particularly be the case if China and Russia applied heavy pressure on Japan to expel American forces. The historic animosity between Korea and Japan has also been somewhat mitigated by the ongoing U.S. presence in both countries and by their mutual participation in security arrangements with Washington. Keeping even a small presence in a unified or reconciled Korea could thus help the United States continue to play a catalytic role in smoothing relations between its two key Asian allies.

If the process of unification involves a conflict or serious military confrontation, however, obtaining Chinese acquiescence in order to forestall any interference from Beijing could be an important policy objective. Achieving this might require some understanding with the Chinese concerning the role of U.S. forward-based forces in a unified Korea.

Korean-Japanese Relations. As already noted, a unified Korea might come to see Japan as its main security threat. The United States, however, can play an important role in strengthening trust between a unified Korea and Japan. By maintaining bases on their respective territories, the United States can reassure Korea and influence Japan toward peaceful behavior. In addition, as part of a nascent multilateral relationship, military-to-military exchanges and military exercises should be encouraged between the United States, Japan, and Korea.

The Role of Russia in Northeast Asia. Russian power in its Far East has been declining, and Moscow is unable at present to play a major role in the politics of Northeast Asia. Whether this will change depends heavily on developments in European Russia. Until Russia is able to complete its transition to a market economy and establish the legal institutions to support such a transition, it seems unlikely that the Russian Federation will even be able to support its current posture in the Far East, much less reinvigorate it.

Russia and Japan have both voiced the intention to solve the long-standing problem of the Northern Territories—the four disputed islands and island groups stretching north from Hokkaido. Although the two sides failed to reach an agreement on the issue during Russian President Vladimir Putin's September 2000 visit to Japan, such an agreement should be encouraged both for economic reasons (to facilitate Japanese investment in the Russian Far East) and to give both parties more diplomatic flexibility vis-à-vis China should that be required in the future.

One area in which Russia has been active is in arms sales to China. Unable to find reliable suppliers in the West, China has turned to Moscow for advanced weapon systems. Chinese purchases of Russian equipment include Su-27 fighters, Kilo-class submarines, SA-10 surface-to-air-missile systems, Sovremenny destroyers, SS-N-22 "Sunburn" missiles, and, reportedly, airborne warning and control system (AWACS) aircraft. This relationship has proved beneficial to both sides, with China acquiring advanced military hardware and the Russian arms industry remaining afloat by virtue of Beijing's purchases. However, the relationship poses problems for the United States in that Russian weapons at least modestly strengthen China's military power, which could in turn be used to create mischief in Asia to the detriment of American interests.

At the same time, Russian arms sales to China are probably motivated more by economic concerns than by a "strategic partnership" designed to bolster the two countries' leverage vis-à-vis the United States. Some Russian military leaders have in fact expressed concern that these weapons could one day be used against Russia. Hence, U.S. policy toward Russia should pivot on encouraging Russia not to sell certain types of weapons to China.[1] Russia's further economic development and integration with Western economies could be used as a leverage on this issue.

Future of Japanese Security Policy. The United States should support Japanese efforts to play a greater role in its own defense (e.g., through the revision of its constitution). Such measures could start

---

[1]See Zalmay M. Khalilzad, Abram N. Shulsky, Daniel L. Byman, Roger Cliff, David T. Orletsky, David Shlapak, and Ashley J. Tellis, *The United States and a Rising China: Strategic and Military Implications*, Santa Monica: RAND, MR-1082-AF, 1999.

out small; for example, air refueling equipment could be installed on Japanese military aircraft and air refueling planes purchased. The United States should also support Japanese efforts to play a more active role in U.N. peacekeeping missions as well as to engage in more frequent military exercises with the United States. Ultimately, the United States would like to see Japan evolve into a country with a more normal geopolitical status—one that is respected but not feared. By slowly introducing its military to Asia through multilateral alliances, Japan can redefine its historical role in Asia as well as permit other nations to become comfortable with its more active posture. Unified Germany's cautious and gradual emergence on the European stage over the past decade could serve as something of a model for this transition.

Taiwan. The United States should continue to assert its interest in the peaceful resolution of the Taiwan situation. The question that remains, however, is whether the current posture of "strategic ambiguity" about U.S. intentions in the event of a Chinese attack on the island is adequate for what seems to be the more threatening future we face with respect to this issue. One alternative would be a more explicit approach in which the United States makes clearer its intention to defend Taiwan against an unprovoked Chinese attack while also clarifying to Taiwan exactly what it would regard as a provocation.

Such a policy would require securing the confidence of both sides. Taiwan would have to believe that the United States would not be tempted to sell it out for the sake of better Sino-U.S. relations, while China would have to believe that the United States would maintain its commitment to a One China policy. If this confidence were not secured, Taiwan might be tempted, when it thought circumstances were favorable, to force the hand of the United States by deliberately taking more provocative stances than the United States had "allowed," believing that the United States, both for the sake of its credibility in the region and by virtue of U.S. domestic political factors, would have to come to its defense in any case. China, on the other hand, might treat the U.S. commitment to defend Taiwan against an unprovoked attack as tantamount to an abandonment of "One China" and to the adoption of a containment policy.

Maintaining the status quo, however, does have its own dangers for China. By freezing the de jure situation, the policy would allow social and political forces on Taiwan to continue to evolve in the direction of normalization of Taiwan's status as a de facto independent country and toward solidification of a Taiwanese identity. The last generation of mainlanders with personal ties to their native regions and to family members who did not flee to Taiwan would pass away while intermarriage and the passage of time would erase the distinction between mainlanders and indigenous Taiwanese in favor of a "new Taiwan identity."

Economic forces, on the other hand, might have the opposite effect: Increased Taiwanese investment in China, more direct trade, travel and communication between Taiwan and China, and greater integration of the economies might increase the leverage China might be able to exercise. China could attempt to cultivate parts of the Taiwanese business community and influence them to lobby for pro-Chinese policies.[2] In addition, the military balance could shift in China's favor as the nation develops both technologically and economically.

Thus, to acquiesce in this U.S. policy, China would have to be willing to gamble either that the economic forces of integration would overpower the social and political forces of normalization or that China's military strength would increase in relation to that of the United States. In the latter case, China would be convinced not only that it could mount a successful invasion and occupation of Taiwan but also that it could either deter the U.S. against intervening or succeed against U.S. resistance.

Finally, there is the question of how China will evolve in political and social terms. If China's political system evolved in such a way as to make it more attractive to the Taiwanese population, then the salience of the reunification issue would probably diminish. A more democratic China might be less willing to risk its economic prospects

---

[2]Although these economic ties might give Taiwan some long-term leverage as well, it is likely, especially in the short term, that an authoritarian China could exploit its economic leverage more effectively than could a democratic Taiwan. In any case, China will be in a position to hold "hostage" Taiwanese-owned assets on the mainland; as cross-straits economic ties develop, these could become considerable in magnitude.

by engaging in military action with respect to Taiwan, although democratization—especially in its early stages—might provide an opportunity for demagogues to play on nationalist sentiment in a way that would enhance the risk of conflict.

Thus, Taiwan would have to believe either that China would evolve in a favorable direction that would make reunification unimportant to China or palatable to Taiwan, or that China's military strength would never be sufficient to deter the United States from living up to its commitment to defend Taiwan against unprovoked attack.

South China Sea

The United States has not taken any position with respect to the conflicting claims to the islands of the South China Sea, but a defense official has stated that if military action in the Spratlys interfered "with freedom of the seas, then we would be prepared to escort and make sure that free navigation continues."[3] In addition, the United States has a defense treaty with the Philippines—and although the U.S.-Philippines Mutual Defense Treaty deals only with attacks on the metropolitan territory of the Philippines or the Philippine armed forces, former Defense Secretary William Cohen made a statement in August 1998 that was interpreted in the Philippine press as implying U.S. support for Philippine forces that were attacked while defending such claims.[4]

The United States should continue its policy of demanding freedom of the seas and, while avoiding a direct endorsement of any of the

---

[3]Statement of Assistant Secretary of Defense for International Security Affairs Joseph Nye, as quoted in Nigel Holloway, "Jolt from the Blue," *Far Eastern Economic Review*, August 3, 1995, p. 22.

[4]It is unclear whether Secretary Cohen meant to change U.S. policy in any respect; it is significant that his remarks do not appear to have been reported in the U.S. media. The Philippine press report (Christina V. Deocadiz, *Business World* [Internet version], August 6, 1998, reprinted as *Philippines: Siazon: U.S. to "Aid" Manila in Event of Spratlys Attack*, FBIS-EAS-98-218) claimed that "the United States gave its assurance that it will come to the aid of the Philippines in case its forces are attacked in disputed territories in the South China Sea." Although the United States holds that the Mutual Defense Treaty applies only to Philippine territory as it existed in 1951 (and does not cover Philippines-claimed regions of the South China Sea), the treaty calls for bilateral consultations in case Philippine armed forces come under attack, whether or not they were inside the boundaries of the Philippines, as defined for purposes of the treaty.

claims in the South China Sea, should work to resolve the territorial disputes to the extent possible. One risk inherent in establishing a regional security institution involving the Philippines, however, is that it could prompt the Philippines to ask for U.S. assistance in protecting its claims to the South China Sea. The United States should thus emphasize the importance of a multilateral solution to the overlapping claims while offering increased training and equipment transfers that would not only strengthen the Philippines role in the multilateral institution but also enable it to unilaterally defend itself.

South Asia

A New Relationship with India. As previously discussed, India may be in the early stages of a process of economic development and modernization similar to that which China began in 1978. Indeed, India is already ahead of China in some important areas—e.g., certain high-technology fields such as software development as well as in many military dimensions, with the important exceptions of ballistic missiles and nuclear weapons.

Better relations between India and the United States make sense from a variety of perspectives. The two nations are the world's largest and second-largest democracies. The development of the Indian software industry implies a close connection between the two countries' economies, while both countries share common interests in reducing instability in Central Asia and preventing Islamic terrorism. The ultimate common interest, however, is probably the desire to hedge against the future emergence of a more powerful and assertive China. Since this is a long-term concern for both sides, however, there is no need to accelerate the process of U.S.-Indian rapprochement; indeed, Indian domestic politics limits the speed with which this process can develop.

There are, however, several steps the United States can take that could gradually improve U.S.-Indian relations by making such relations more politically palatable to Indian leaders. One such step would be to restore the regular high-level dialogue initiated in 1985; another would be to increase the number of military-to-military contacts similar to those now conducted with the Chinese. Other helpful initiatives would involve dropping the last remnants of the sanctions imposed in the aftermath of the 1998 nuclear tests by revitalizing trade and joint development in civilian high technology, information technology, and services. Yet another area of increased cooperation and informational exchange should center on training and planning for peacekeeping missions. In addition, the United States should seek opportunities to help resolve the Kashmir issue through peaceful means.

Avoiding the Isolation of Pakistan. In the process of improving relations with India, however, it is important that the United States not unnecessarily isolate Pakistan. Although the center of gravity of U.S. policy toward South Asia has shifted from Pakistan toward India, the United States should do whatever it can—consistent with its other policy interests—to prevent Pakistan from drifting into an embittered fundamentalism. In the wake of the military coup of 1999, Pakistan's prospects are not very good: It does not have promising options for carrying on its efforts to wrest Kashmir from India; its economic situation is poor; its military government seems unable or unwilling to embark on a thoroughgoing reform program; and it remains beset with internal violence, fundamentalism, and separatist tendencies.

U.S. policy toward Pakistan should thus seek to address numerous problems. First, Pakistan should be assisted in developing its economy as well as encouraged to reform the economy structurally. Second, Pakistan should be encouraged to cease its support of terrorists operating in South Asia and beyond. Specifically, the country should be urged to peacefully resolve its differences with India over Kashmir, to stop supporting Islamist militants operating there, and to cease its politico-military support of the Taliban in Afghanistan. Third, Pakistan should be encouraged to safeguard its nuclear stockpile and limit its aggressive nuclear and missile acquisition program. As with India, Pakistan should be encouraged to sign the Comprehensive Test Ban Treaty (CTBT), support a Fissile Material Cutoff Treaty (FMCT), and avoid the deployment of ready nuclear forces. It should also establish a comprehensive command-and-control (C^2) system to reduce the chances of accidental nuclear release; cease continued missile testing, production, and deployment; and institute export controls on weapons of mass destruction (WMD), their technologies, and their components.

Chapter Four

IMPLICATIONS FOR THE MILITARY AND USAF: THE CHALLENGES OF CHANGE

The USAF's ability to support U.S. national interests in a rapidly changing Asia will demand great flexibility. The existing Air Force posture in the region may, however, be inadequate or poorly configured to carry out the full range of tasks it might face. This chapter will therefore discuss steps the USAF might take to prepare for the Asian environment it could confront over the next two decades. We will focus on three broad topics: shaping the regional environment, responding to crises, and thinking about the long term.

SHAPING THE ASIAN SECURITY ENVIRONMENT

For the past 50 years, the focus of U.S. attention has been in Northeast Asia, where the Cold War confrontation between North and South Korea continues. Today and in the future, however, U.S. interests—which include coping with an uncertain China, supporting stability in the volatile countries of Southeast Asia, and reducing the risks of the Indo-Pakistani nuclear rivalry—are and will continue to be spread throughout this vast region. The U.S. military posture in the Western Pacific must therefore adapt over time to support the region's new needs.

If and when the two Koreas reach some form of stable accommodation, changes in the numbers and kinds of U.S. forces stationed in Asia will likely be forthcoming. However, any alterations in U.S. posture should be made only after considering the full range of American interests and objectives in the region. If changes are made prudently, the United States could be better prepared to protect and advance its goals in East Asia as a whole even if it is moved to reduce the absolute size of its military forces permanently stationed in the region.

The large U.S. Marine Corps force on Okinawa, for example, is a source of ongoing friction between Washington and many Okinawans. Positioned to respond quickly to a crisis on the Korean peninsula, this force may decline substantially in strategic and military value if the prospects for a second Korean War are finally reduced. Reducing and/or relocating this force—to Guam, perhaps, or to Hawaii—would remove a perennially contentious issue from the agenda of U.S.-Japanese relations while not significantly diminishing U.S. capabilities for rapidly responding to events in East Asia.[1]

The size of U.S. Army and USAF forces stationed in Korea would almost certainly be reconsidered as well should the threat of war between Pyongyang and Seoul recede. Under such circumstances, support for continued American deployments on the peninsula will likely waver in both Korea and the United States. In addition, the Korean government could resist continued payment of host-nation support (HNS) to the United States, particularly if Seoul is, as seems likely, incurring large costs as a result of reconciliation or reunification with the North. Moreover, North Korea has in the past insisted that a U.S. troop withdrawal be a precondition for reunification with the South, although this stance may be changing.[2] Finally, Korea could find itself under pressure from its regional neighbors—China and Russia in particular—to evict or at least reduce the number of U.S. forces on its territory.

As on Okinawa, it would seem that large ground-force units would be the most obvious targets for selective drawdowns. The U.S. Second Infantry Division in Korea has a unique structure and is specifically configured to fight on the peninsula. Unlike lighter formations such

---

[1]At least at first glance, the most likely conflicts in a post-Korea Asia—China-Taiwan, India-Pakistan, or an Indonesian implosion—do not seem to be the kinds of scenarios that call for the commitment of a large combined-arms Marine force. While smaller Marine units and specialized Marine capabilities may be valuable in many future Asian contingencies, the maintenance of a large U.S. Marine Corps presence on Okinawa may not be an effective use of limited U.S. political capital in the region.

[2]See Struck, "South Korean Says North Wants U.S. Troops to Stay" (2000), p. A1.

as the 82nd Airborne or 10th Mountain divisions, it is not designed to be strategically mobile and hence would not necessarily be appropriate for a post-Korean unification role as a rapid-reaction force for contingencies across Asia at large. Therefore, some reduction in the number of Army troops deployed in Korea might be an initial option if some U.S. withdrawals become necessary.

The USAF currently deploys four fighter squadrons at two main operating bases (MOBs) in South Korea. The strategic reach of airpower may make it desirable to try to keep these forces in place even after Korean reconciliation, but pressures to reduce may eventually prove irresistible. At the least, the Air Force should be prepared to consider the implications of eliminating one MOB and moving one or two squadrons elsewhere in the region, perhaps to Guam.

There are important political reasons to try to maintain at least some presence in Korea even after the threat of a North Korean invasion has disappeared. As discussed in Chapter Three, for example, the departure of all U.S. forces from Korea would leave Japan the sole host of permanent U.S. military installations in East Asia, and how satisfied Tokyo would be with such an arrangement given its history of uneven popular support for foreign bases—particularly if China and Russia applied heavy pressure on Japan to expel the Americans— is unclear. In addition, the lingering animosity between Korea and Japan has been mitigated by the ongoing U.S. presence in both countries, arguing for the retention of a U.S. presence in a unified or reconciled Korea.

RESPONDING TO CRISES

It is easy to forget just how large and diverse Asia is. The tyranny of this vast geography (Figure 4.1 identifies, on maps drawn to scale, USAF bases in Asia and those used during the 1990–1991 Gulf War) has much to say about how the USAF should position itself to enable quick and effective reaction to emerging crises. To better reflect this geographic diversity, we have divided the discussion into four sections, each dealing with one area: Northeast Asia, Taiwan, Southeast Asia, and South Asia.

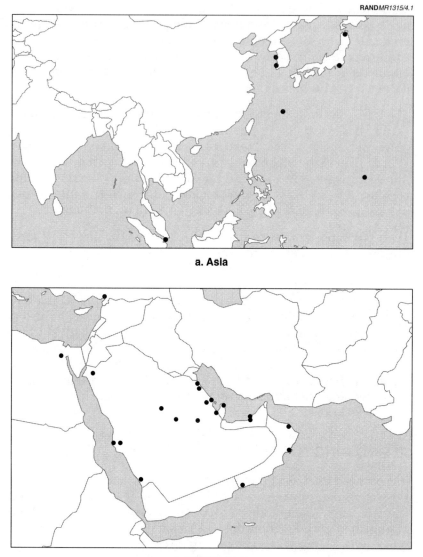

RAND*MR1315/4.1*

a. Asia

b. Persian Gulf

Figure 4.1—Comparative Sizes of Asia and the Gulf War Theater

As Figure 4.1 illustrates, the availability of adequate basing is a critical component that will help shape the USAF response to any crisis in Asia. We have examined a number of bases across Asia and have evaluated the capacity to support USAF flight operations. This assessment focused on the five key attributes shown in Table 4.1: the length of the runway(s) at the facility, runway width, the amount of ramp space, the number of fighter-sized parking spaces available, and whether or not weapon storage was available. We also looked at pavement-loading characteristics (which are critical to operating large, heavy aircraft such as airlifters), the availability of fuel, and other factors.

Although the suitability of a base is specific to mission and aircraft type, the number of bases and facilities at each of those bases can be used as a measure of a region's capability to support USAF operations. For analytical purposes, we divided the bases we examined into four broad categories: minimal, small, large, and support.[3] A "minimal" airfield is the smallest base from which any sort of fighter operations could be conducted. Such an installation has short runways that are near the bare minimum of many fighters and C-130 aircraft along with limited parking areas that could support a squadron or two of fighter aircraft at most. A minimal base is not suitable for sustained fighter operations but could be used if better alternatives were not immediately available.

Table 4.1

Airfield "Class" Minimum Requirements

Airfield Attributes	Minimal	Small	Large	Support
Runway length (feet)	4000	7500	8500	11,000
Runway width (feet)	75	100	140	140
Ramp space (square feet)	100,000	200,000	200,000	1,000,000
Number of fighter parking spaces	24	48	72	0
Weapon storage	yes	yes	yes	yes

---

[3]See D. A. Shlapak, J. Stillion, O. Oliker, and T. Charlick-Paley, *A Global Access Strategy for the U.S. Air Force*, Santa Monica: RAND, MR-1216-AF, forthcoming.

A "small" base is one that is fairly well suited to fighter operations. A small base has runway dimensions significantly larger than those of a minimal base and parking space for two or three squadrons of aircraft types. The longer runways could also support the operation of some larger aircraft.

A "large" base is well suited to conducting a wide range of combat operations. Such a facility has ample parking space for at least a wing of fighter-size aircraft and runway dimensions adequate for the majority of USAF aircraft, including heavy bombers and strategic airlifters.

Finally, we define a "support" base as one that is suitable for large-scale aerial port debarkation (APOD) operations. This base is characterized by very long runways and vast amounts of ramp space.

Throughout this chapter, these classes of airfields will be used to identify current capability in each of the regions discussed. In many cases, the requirement for munitions storage inhibits a base from appearing on our list. Although munitions storage could be added as well as runways lengthened or widened or concrete strength enhanced, our purpose was to identify bases that would likely require limited USAF improvement to support military operations. Immediate ease of use is especially important to an air force based around an expeditionary mindset.

The identification of bases that are currently capable (or nearly so) of supporting USAF operations has both political and financial advantages. There appears to be little appetite, either in the United States or in the region, for the construction of additional American military installations in Asia. The bases identified in this analysis should not require significant upgrades that could be costly in terms of either USAF budget dollars or American political capital.

The United States does enjoy close relations with a number of Asian countries besides Japan and Korea and should work to further expand its network of friends in the region. In the near term, access strategy for Asia should center on increasing opportunities for deployments and exercises and on the development of contingency agreements with a number of potential security partners in the area. Depending on the closeness of the resulting relationship, this could include measures to tailor local infrastructure to USAF operations by extending runways, improving air traffic control facilities, repairing parking aprons, and the like.

Northeast Asia

Northeast Asia, which includes both Japan and Korea, has been the long-time focus of U.S. attention in the Western Pacific. As such, it is well served by the existing U.S. base structure in the region: All permanent USAF bases in Asia, with the exception of Guam and Diego Garcia, are in the northeast.

The most likely crisis to erupt in Northeast Asia remains a conflict between North and South Korea. The centerpiece of U.S. Pacific planning for nearly a half-century, war in Korea would see hundreds of combat and support aircraft poured into a small area of operations. Geography would thus seem to dictate that all short-range combat aircraft be based either in Japan or on the peninsula itself.

Current USAF bases located in South Korea and Japan are shown in Figure 4.2. The circles in this figure indicate distance from the Korean demilitarized zone (DMZ), with the inner circle being 500 nautical miles in radius and the outer circle 1000 nautical miles. Current U.S. bases have well-developed infrastructure to support combat operations. The two bases in Korea, Osan and Kunsan, are within 500 nautical miles of the DMZ, while Misawa, Yokota, and Kadena are between 500 and 1000 nautical miles away. In addition to the current USAF bases in the area, a number of other airfields exist with well-developed infrastructure. Figure 4.3 shows all bases in the region that meet the minimum requirements in Table 4.1. The USAF could not operate in the near term from all airfields presented in Figure 4.3, but this information gives an indication of the degree of development of the airfield infrastructure in this region.

Considering the current size and sophistication of North Korea's missile arsenal, Pyongyang cannot realistically hope to degrade USAF flight operations with conventionally armed Scuds, FROGs, and Nodongs.

The USAF strategy of short-range operations, however, could become increasingly dangerous if the current standoff between Seoul and Pyongyang continues long enough to permit the North to effec-

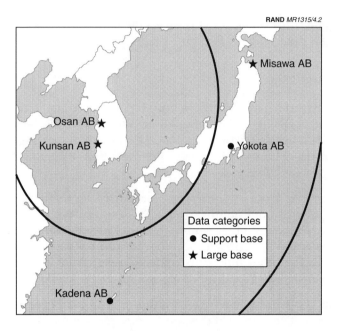

Figure 4.2—USAF Bases in South Korea and Japan

tively deploy a larger force of more modern missiles that proved capable of striking installations in South Korea and Japan. A new generation of ballistic missiles could be accurate enough to impede USAF operations using conventional warheads (especially if the North could successfully integrate submunition-dispensing warheads on the weapons).[4] Current North Korean missiles could have a major impact on USAF operations if they were fitted with chemical or nuclear warheads. Bases in South Korea would probably also come under intense attacks by North Korean special operations forces (SOF), which could cause extensive damage and disruption either independently or coupled with missile strikes.[5]

---

[4]For a thorough discussion of the possible effects of conventional missile attacks on airbases, see John Stillion and David T. Orletsky, *Airbase Vulnerability to Conventional Cruise-Missile and Ballistic-Missile Attacks: Technology, Scenarios, and U.S. Air Force Responses*, Santa Monica: RAND, MR-1028-AF, 1999.

[5]See David A. Shlapak and Alan Vick, *"Check Six Begins on the Ground": Responding to the Evolving Ground Threat to U.S. Air Force Bases*, Santa Monica: RAND, MR-606-AF, 1995, for a discussion of the potential risks posed by SOF attacks on airbases.

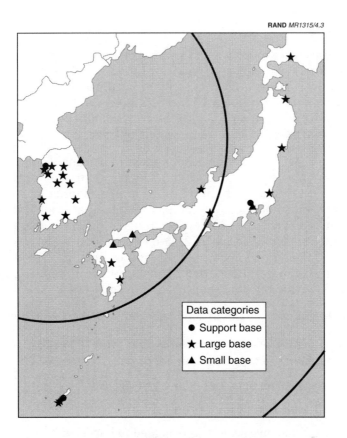

RAND *MR1315/4.3*

Figure 4.3—Northeast Asian Airfields

The USAF may therefore wish to consider what steps would be appropriate to maintain its ability to fight effectively in Korea if it appears that reunification or reconciliation there is going to be indefinitely prolonged.[6] Highly effective defenses against missile and SOF attacks may be needed as well as the reliable capability to sustain high-tempo combat operations in the face of enemy attacks.

---

[6]Despite the hopes raised by the June 2000 summit and related developments, it may nonetheless be prudent for military planners to continue contemplating how best to defend the peninsula against a future threat from North Korea lest some future White House be caught unprepared when, all forecasts of imminent collapse aside, the North chooses or feels compelled to strike.

Taiwan

In contrast to a Korean war, a Taiwan scenario could present the U.S. armed forces with a host of relatively unexamined issues that would have to be resolved quickly to facilitate a sufficiently rapid response. Thinking about this potential mission, however, is complicated not only by the political sensitivities involved but also by a lack of clarity about what the conflict scenario would look like.

In the near term, China does not appear to be capable of mounting an invasion of Taiwan.[7] If China does decide to use force against Taiwan, it is much more likely to do so in a manner calculated to achieve a quick political/psychological effect that would induce the Taiwanese to seek some sort of accommodation. Since there are several different ways in which this could be done, the U.S. armed forces, if they are assigned the mission of helping defend Taiwan against a Chinese attack, must consider how the effect could be thwarted no matter which approach China chooses.

Possible Chinese courses of action short of invasion could include:

- provocative exercises and tests (e.g., the 1996 missile tests to ocean areas near Taiwan's major ports);

- provocative air activities near or over Taiwan;

- small-scale missile attacks on Taiwan;[8]

- larger-scale missile attacks designed to harm Taiwan's economy, degrade its self-defense capabilities, and demoralize its population;

- interference with SLOCs via mining, submarine attacks on commercial shipping, and blockade;

---

[7]See the discussion of Taiwanese air base survivability in David A. Shlapak, David T. Orletsky, and Barry Wilson, *Dire Strait? Military Aspects of the China-Taiwan Confrontation and Implications for U.S. Policy*, Santa Monica: RAND, MR-1217-SRF, 2000.

[8]According to press reports, during a trip to China in late 1994, former Assistant Secretary of Defense Charles Freeman was told that "the People's Liberation Army had prepared plans for a missile attack against Taiwan consisting of one conventional missile strike a day for 30 days." See Patrick E. Tyler, "As China Threatens Taiwan, It Makes Sure U.S. Listens," *New York Times*, January 24, 1996, P. A3.

- seizing of an offshore island, one or more of the Pescadore Islands (in the Taiwan Strait), or Taiping Island (the Taiwanese-held island in the South China Sea); or

- missile and air attacks against Taiwan designed to destroy Taiwanese military capabilities.

None of these options would be sufficient to compel the Republic of China (ROC) government to surrender, nor presumably would they be intended to do that. Instead, their purpose would be to demoralize the Taiwanese population, create financial and economic havoc, and bring about a collapse of the ROC's resistance to "one country, two systems." Accordingly, the point of any U.S. military action would be primarily to counteract the psychological pressure being inflicted by the Chinese, much as the dispatch of two carrier battle groups in 1996 served as a counterweight to the Chinese missile tests directed at the waters near Taiwan's two main harbors. U.S. response to a future Chinese pressure campaign against Taiwan should similarly be designed to reassure Taiwan that China cannot successfully escalate its use of force so as to inflict a decisive military defeat; to help defend Taiwanese economic and other assets; and, more generally, to bolster Taiwanese morale and prevent panic.

U.S. military assistance must therefore be available promptly to counteract the shock of Chinese action before Taiwan's will to resist begins to fade. It must also be effective, at least in the sense of being seen to respond to the military threat.[9] While China's ability to harass Taiwan can be only partially affected by whatever military steps the United States takes in response, the psychological effect of that harassment can be negated, at least in part.

To maintain the option to assist Taiwan in case of a future conflict with China, USAF planners must come to grips with the operational requirements of projecting power into the East China Sea. Basing is

---

[9]Perhaps regardless of its actual military utility. For example, the Patriot missiles sent to Israel in response to the Iraqi Scud attacks during the Gulf War served the political purpose of reassuring the Israelis and dissuading them from retaliating against Iraq; the actual military effectiveness of the Patriots, on the other hand, is still being debated. The Scuds, whose military effectiveness, thanks to their inaccuracy, was quite small, were a psychological (or terrorist) weapon against Israel, and they were met with a primarily psychological defense.

one crucial problem confronting the USAF in any Taiwan scenario. As Figure 4.4 shows, a 500-nm-radius circle drawn from the approximate center of the Taiwan Strait encompasses vast areas of ocean but very little land (outside of mainland China).[10] In the near term, there would thus appear to be two options: basing on Taiwan itself and basing in Japan.[11]

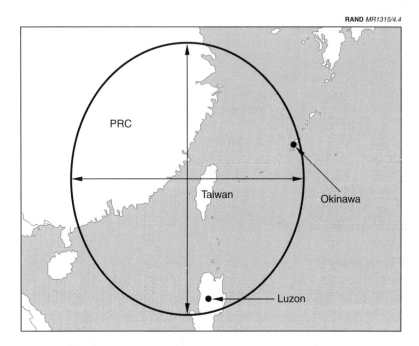

RAND *MR1315/4.4*

Circle is 500 nm in radius. It appears elliptical owing to the curvature of the earth

Figure 4.4—Bases Within 500 nm of Taiwan

---

[10]We picked 500 nm as a rough estimate of the unrefueled combat radius of current and next-generation U.S. fighter aircraft such as the F-15, F-16, F-22, and Joint Strike Force (JSF). The actual operational range of these aircraft will vary with their configuration and mission profile, but our analysis suggests that 500 nm is a fair heuristic. See Shlapak et al. (forthcoming).

[11]U.S. bases in Korea are more than 800 nm from the Strait, Misawa in northern Japan is more than 1400 nm away, and Guam is more than 1500 nm distant. Fighters can operate from these ranges, but sortie rates can suffer significant degradation unless substantial aerial refueling resources and additional crews are deployed. See Shlapak et al. (forthcoming), especially Chapter Three.

The critical question regarding basing in Taiwan is not principally whether the Taiwanese would permit the United States to use their bases, as the answer is almost certainly affirmative. Indeed, it is difficult to imagine anything that would make Taipei happier than to have USAF jets sitting on Taiwanese soil during a crisis with the mainland. However, it is also difficult to imagine anything that would anger Beijing more than seeing U.S. forces arrive in Taiwan during a period of heightened tension between the PRC and ROC. Indeed, it seems likely that any deployment of foreign forces into Taiwan would serve as a trigger to transform a simmering crisis into outright conflict.[12] Politically, then, USAF basing on Taiwan is an explosive and potentially unrealistic option.

From an operational perspective, basing on Taiwan is similarly problematic. To avert catastrophic political consequences, any deployment would probably have to be delayed until substantial hostilities were already under way, meaning that USAF forces would be landing at air bases that could be under heavy bombardment by Chinese missiles and aircraft and under assault by SOF.[13] Yet the Air Force has little if any practical experience in commencing and sustaining operations under such conditions, and even if potential USAF operating locations were not under attack when forces arrived, deploying units would essentially be moving onto the bull's-eye for virtually every offensive system in the Chinese inventory.

Taiwan's basing infrastructure is also limited, with only six to eight bases designed to support high-tempo fighter activity. ROC air force (ROCAF) units, of course, occupy and use most of these installations, but visits to two active ROCAF bases and discussions with Taiwanese officers suggest that these bases were neither built nor intended to accommodate foreign expeditionary forces. Unlike Saudi Arabia, there is not an abundance of extra infrastructure available into which USAF forces could easily flow.

Further, existing ROCAF bases would offer limited operability and sustainability in the face of large-scale attacks. The bases rely on

---

[12]The positioning of foreign forces on Taiwan is one of Beijing's often-stated conditions for initiating the use of force against the island.

[13]Taiwan's air bases would almost certainly be a focal point of any large-scale Chinese offensive against the island.

above-ground fuel storage, for example, and fuel distribution depends on tanker trucks rather than on the much more survivable system of buried pipelines and in-shelter hydrants used on many NATO bases. We observed a number of unhardened maintenance and control facilities at the bases we visited, and the Taiwanese have only limited capability to perform rapid runway repair. Absent significant improvements in various areas of survivability, the bases will grow increasingly vulnerable to attack as Chinese short-range ballistic missiles (SRBMs) grow both more numerous and more sophisticated.[14]

If basing in Taiwan appears both politically and militarily imprudent, what about Japan? It seems likely that the Japanese would grant use of their bases to the United States for certain operations in defense of Taiwan provided that China could be clearly implicated as the aggressor (i.e., provided that Taipei had not done anything unreasonably provocative, such as declare independence). Limitations on the employment of forces from Japanese bases could, however, be strict. For example, Tokyo could well decide not to permit strikes on China itself to be launched from its territory. Nonetheless, our assessment is that there is a good chance Japan would permit its facilities to be used for missions against Chinese forces in international or Taiwanese airspace.

As Figure 4.4 shows, however, the current USAF base at Kadena is nearly 500 nm away from the Strait. As a result, F-15 or F-16 fighters operating from that base would probably need to maintain combat air patrol (CAP) orbits near Taiwan, since they could not launch and transit in response to warnings of a Chinese air attack headed for Taiwan. This is in contrast to, say, a carrier stationed 50 nm off Taiwan's east coast, whose aircraft would need to fly only about 175 nm to get to the centerline and could therefore be more responsive to incoming raids.[15]

---

[14]See the discussion of Taiwanese air base survivability in Shlapak et al. (2000).

[15]We have not performed detailed analysis on the difference that the F-22 would make were it operating from Kadena. However, simple mathematical calculations suggest that employing its supersonic "supercruise" capability might enable the F-22 to cover the distance from Okinawa to the centerline quickly enough to responsively engage an attacking Chinese force that was detected early. This assumes that the F-22 can transit, fight, and disengage to a safe distance without needing to refuel; presumably

Kadena may also suffer from limitations in its ability to support high-tempo operations by a large force of combat aircraft. The base currently hosts two squadrons totaling 48 F-15C fighters, a special operations group, an air refueling squadron, a reconnaissance squadron, an AWACS squadron, and a search-and-rescue squadron.[16] In addition, it is an important transit point for airlift activity in the Western Pacific. Kadena is, in other words, a busy place even day to day, and it is not clear how many more aircraft could be operated out of the base under combat conditions.

Longer-range aircraft, such as surveillance platforms and heavy bombers, could operate out of Guam to support the defense of Taiwan. Assuming that the United States decides to intervene in a major Taiwan crisis, preliminary RAND analysis suggests that B-52s armed with Harpoon antiship missiles could play an important role in defeating Chinese maritime operations in the Taiwan Strait.[17] Currently, however, there would appear to be few alternatives available to Japan for supporting efficient fighter operations in this area (although Korea might fill that role if sufficient tanker assets could be committed and securely bedded down; like those in Japan, U.S. bases in Korea are inside the range rings for many Chinese surface-to-surface weapons[18]).

Creative USAF-U.S. Navy joint operations may provide one near-term option. For example, carrier-based fighters could be used for air superiority and defense suppression while the USAF provides intelligence, surveillance, and reconnaissance (ISR), battle management, and support functions (e.g., tankers) using longer-range aircraft based at more distant bases. Such an arrangement would exploit the carriers' freedom of operation in international waters

---

the fighters could rendezvous with tankers on their way home. The Chinese could attempt to counter these tactics by using low-level flight profiles to minimize U.S. and Taiwanese detection time and/or by stationing their own barrier caps (BARCAPs) between Okinawa and Taiwan to intercept or divert U.S. fighters attempting to intervene.

[16]Information is taken from the Kadena Air Base public Web site (http://www. kadena af.mil/).

[17]See Shlapak et al. (2000).

[18]Kunsan, for example, is about 350 nm from possible surface-to-surface missile (SSM) launch areas in the "camel's nose" part of Shandong Province. Okinawa is nearly 100 nm farther from the nearest PRC territory.

while perhaps facilitating access to foreign bases, since they would be used for support rather than combat aircraft. Heavy bombers could operate from U.S. territory on Guam.

In the longer term, the USAF should strive to develop a more robust posture to support Taiwan should the necessity arise. One step could be to expand cooperation with the Philippines. Whereas Manila is approximately 650 nm from the centerline of the Taiwan Strait, a base in northern Luzon would be about 450 nm away (i.e., a little closer to the Taiwan Strait than is Kadena). Even more proximate is Batan Island, which is on the order of 300 nm from the likely area of operations. Although it is unlikely that the United States desires or could obtain permanent basing in the Philippines, recent improvements in relations between Washington and Manila could lead to increased access. The USAF's goal might be to develop, in the mid to long term, arrangements with the Philippines not dissimilar to those enjoyed with Singapore today. Such a relationship would not involve permanent American presence but would permit frequent rotational deployments that would allow for infrastructure improvements and keep facilities "warm" to enable the rapid start of operations in a crisis.[19]

In the north, the United States may also have options to better exploit its close security relationship with Japan. Should the U.S. Marine Corps force on Okinawa be reduced or even eliminated, the United States should investigate the possibility of establishing the current Marine Corps air station at Futenma as a collocated operating base (COB) for USAF fighters. Kept in a caretaker status during peacetime, the base would be prepared to accept a rapid influx of combat and support aircraft in a crisis. An auxiliary Marine Corps airfield on Ie Jima could also be used, and the USAF may be able to deploy some assets to the Japan air self-defense force base at Naha.[20]

---

[19]This strategy would be facilitated by setting up Guam as a well-stocked forward support location (FSL) for USAF power projection throughout the Western Pacific and East Asia. The benefits of FSLs are described briefly in Shlapak et al. (2000) and are laid out more fully in R. S. Tripp, Lionel Galway, Timothy L. Ramey, Mahyar Amouzegar, and Eric Peltz, *Supporting Expeditionary Aerospace Forces: A Concept for Evolving to the Agile Combat Support/Mobility System of the Future*, Santa Monica: RAND, MR-1179-AF, 2000.

[20]Presumably the Ie Jima facility would need to be made capable of supporting the logistics demands of a combat force.

Okinawa itself lies only about halfway down the Ryukyu Island chain. Further southwest—and hence considerably closer to Taiwan—are a number of islands. Figure 4.5 shows the locations of a number of existing airfields in these islands, and Table 4.2 displays some of their more salient characteristics.[21] Shimojishima, for example, is less than 250 nm from Taipei and has a commercial airport with a 10,000-foot runway; the island also features a sizable port that serves as a base for Japanese patrol boats. Basing on one or more of the southern Ryukyus would clearly be advantageous for the defense of Taiwan; however, it is unclear how much investment would be needed to create adequate facilities (by extending runways, installing munitions storage facilities, and so on).

Whether an expanded or at least southward-shifted USAF base posture in Japan would be feasible from Tokyo's point of view remains to be evaluated. U.S. basing has long been a contentious issue within the Japanese body politic, and any attempt to create new bases—or even COBs—would almost certainly provoke controversy. This might be especially true of requests to use airfields in the Southern Ryukyus, which the Okinawa prefecture wishes to promote as ecologically friendly vacation destinations.

One way to overcome resistance to an initiative to permit U.S. access to the Southern Ryukyus might be either explicitly or implicitly to offer the Japanese government in general—and the Okinawan people in particular—a quid pro quo arrangement. The removal or reduction of U.S. forces elsewhere in the islands, such as the withdrawal of the Marines from Okinawa, could be the currency with which Washington might pay for a foothold in the critical area surrounding the troubled waters of the Taiwan Strait.

---

[21]To be suitable for combat operations, a runway should be at least an aircraft "critical field length." This is the distance an aircraft requires to accelerate to takeoff speed, suffer a serious malfunction, and either stop or get into the air before going off the end of the runway. For an F-15C fully loaded for air-to-air operations and carrying three 600-gallon external fuel tanks, critical field length is between 7000 and 8000 feet, depending on environmental conditions. Thanks to our colleague John Stillion for this information.

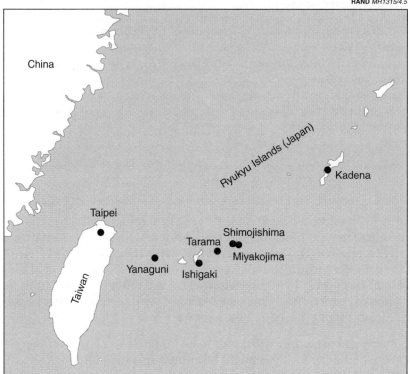

Figure 4.5—Airports in the Southern Ryukyus

Table 4.2

Airports in the Southern Ryukyus

Airport	Runway Dimensions (ft)		Distance from (nm)	
	Length	Width	Taipei	Centerline
Yanaguni	4921	148	150	250
Ishigaki	4921	148	180	280
Tarama	2635	82	210	310
Shimojishima	9843	197	240	340
Miyakojima	6562	148	250	350

Southeast Asia

As discussed in Appendix C, the bulk of the likely scenarios in Southeast Asia concern humanitarian relief, internal instability (as in Indonesia), or international hostilities at a fairly low level of violence (e.g., a Chinese move against the Spratly Islands). In all these cases, the demand for USAF assets and activity would be low, as there does not appear to be a contingency requiring large-scale force application on the planning horizon in this region.

One could envisage a U.S. military mission to help defend the SLOCs in the South China Sea either against one of the Spratlys claimants or, more likely, against pirates (perhaps operating with the tacit support of one of the claimants). Such a mission might resemble that undertaken in 1987–1988 to provide security for the Persian Gulf SLOCs that had come under attack from Iran during the Iraq-Iran war. Alternatively, the U.S. military could be asked to show support for Philippine forces that had come under attack in the South China Sea. Again, this would likely consist primarily of a "presence" mission, albeit one that was undertaken under circumstances in which there was some probability that hostile actions would be taken against the deployed U.S. forces.

Another potential mission for the U.S. military would be humanitarian intervention in Indonesia. As the East Timor crisis demonstrated, unrest in Indonesia can create levels of international concern sufficient to lead to humanitarian intervention. Australia in particular is likely to be very concerned about any unrest in Indonesia that threatened to create a major refugee crisis or that otherwise had the potential to directly affect Indonesia's neighbors. Thus, the U.S. armed forces could be tasked to participate—most likely in conjunction with Australian, other foreign, and perhaps U.N. forces—in a peacekeeping or "peace enforcement" role. In addition, it may be necessary to assist in the evacuation of noncombatants from areas suffering from violence.

These scenarios pose potential problems for the USAF. As in the case with Taiwan, the USAF's current posture in the Western Pacific is less than ideal with regard to projecting power into Southeast Asia. As Figure 4.6 shows, the U.S. base on Guam is almost 3000 nm from

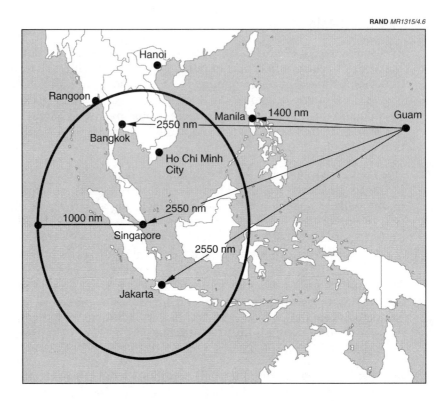

Figure 4.6—Distances from Guam to Southeast Asia

Rangoon (Yangon) and 2500 nm from Bangkok, Singapore, and Jakarta.

The USAF has no permanent combat presence along the Asian rim.[22] However, it maintains contact and conducts a wide range of exercises with a number of countries in Southeast Asia, including Australia, Malaysia, New Zealand, Singapore, and Thailand.[23] These

---

[22]The USAF does maintain a rotational presence in Singapore, with assets deployed there roughly six months each year.

[23]Exercises conducted with Asian partners in recent years have included Cobra Gold (Thailand), Cope Tiger (Thailand, Singapore), Commando Sling (Singapore), Cope Taufan (Malaysia), and Cope Thunder (Philippines, Japan, New Zealand, Australia, Thailand, and Singapore in various years).

activities and similar ones that might be undertaken with or come to include other countries (such as the Philippines and Indonesia, and, in the future, perhaps Vietnam as well) could form the basis of an expanded expeditionary presence in the region on an ad hoc or rotational basis. Since many of the local air forces are engaged in ambitious modernization programs, they are likely to welcome expanded contact with and opportunities to learn from the USAF.

The Philippines may present an especially interesting opportunity to enhance USAF access in the Western Pacific. After reaching their nadir in the mid-1990s, relations between Washington and Manila have recently improved, culminating in the signing of a status-of-forces agreement in 1999. While neither side has expressed any interest in resuming permanent basing of U.S. forces in the islands, the Philippines' key location in the South China Sea could make it an attractive site for future USAF expeditionary deployments.

The United States has a long-standing treaty relationship with Thailand and use of a Royal Thai naval air station at U Taphao. The United States also has an access arrangement with Singapore that offers the USAF a foothold in the heart of Southeast Asia. Looking again at Figure 4.6, it is less than 500 nm from Jakarta and only about 1000 nm from Rangoon. While limited by lack of space, which would impede its ability to support large-scale high-tempo flight operations, Singapore represents an important asset for the Air Force in this region. Guam would play a key role as a staging base and operating location for strategic airlift, ISR platforms, tankers, and bombers, and Singapore could host a small group of fighters as well as C-130s and other mobility assets.

The political dynamics of the region are sufficiently complex that countries willing to support the United States under one set of circumstances could well withhold their assistance under others. Thus, while Singapore is a valuable point of entry into Southeast Asia, the USAF would benefit from diversifying its portfolio of access alternatives there. The United States enjoys good security ties with a number of governments in Southeast Asia, including Australia, the Philippines, and Thailand. Accordingly, expanding or developing access agreements with some of these countries would make for a more robust set of options for the USAF. In the longer term, improving security cooperation between the United States and Malaysia, Indonesia, and perhaps Vietnam could lead to opportunities to work as partners with these countries for some operations in Southeast Asia.

Figure 4.7 presents some basing possibilities. The range-ring circles represent distances of 500 and 1000 nm centered at a location in the South China Sea. As this figure shows, the only adequate airfields within the inner ring are in the Philippines. Other airfields within 500 nautical miles exist in Vietnam but do not meet one or more of the criteria for supporting USAF combat operations. There are, however, many bases between the two range rings that meet all criteria to serve as USAF operational bases.

RAND *MR1315/4.7*

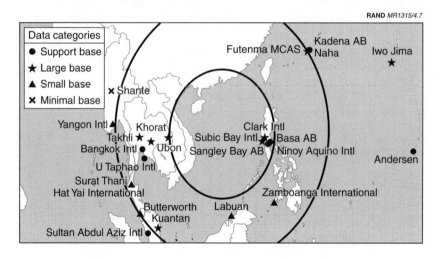

Figure 4.7—Airfields Close to the South China Sea

South Asia

The Indo-Pakistani rivalry is the engine driving the evolution of the South Asian security environment. Like Southeast Asia, the challenges South Asia presents to USAF planners are at least as much political as military. The U.S. objectives of maintaining peace and enhancing stability in the contentious subcontinent will thus require a delicate balancing act, one key component of which will be military-to-military engagement.

U.S. policy toward South Asia was disrupted by the Indian and Pakistani nuclear tests in 1998. After two years, however, it appears to be undergoing a gradual process of improvement. Washington seems to be coming to accept that neither India nor Pakistan is likely to divest its nuclear option regardless of Western pressures; nonetheless, U.S. policymakers hope to cap the competition at some low level and encourage the evolution of a stable equilibrium between the two sides.

In contacts with the Pakistani militaries, emphasis should be placed not just on technical exchanges on topics such as tactics, doctrine, and airmanship but also on professionalism and the proper role of the armed forces in a democratic, modern society. The military coup in Pakistan was the first ever in a nuclear-armed state; it was not an event that we should aspire to see repeated.

Technically, the USAF may be called upon to participate in efforts to help one or both sides develop and deploy robust security and C^2 procedures and systems. Positive control of all nuclear weapons on both sides as well as reliable connectivity to survivable delivery systems can help both minimize the likelihood of inadvertent nuclear use and limit the "use-or-lose" pressures that Indian or Pakistani leaders could confront in a crisis.

In terms of possible scenarios for U.S. military involvement in South Asia, one would seem the most daunting: a large-scale military confrontation between India and Pakistan would cross the nuclear threshold, resulting in enormous civilian casualties in both countries. Under such dire circumstances, the suffering of perhaps tens of millions of civilians could demand a massive and immediate humanitarian assistance effort regardless of whether hostilities had completely terminated. The U.S. military would almost certainly find itself on the leading edge of any such undertaking—a venture that would combine all the stresses of a continental-scale peace enforcement and relief operation with many of the risks of major theater warfare. Given basing and access difficulties, such a task could present Herculean challenges to planners and operators alike.

A second mission in South Asia could be enhanced surveillance. A severe crisis between India and Pakistan or the outbreak of war between them would create high levels of concern with respect to the safety of the two nations' nuclear arsenals and the possibility of their use in the conflict. In this case, it might be desirable to increase reconnaissance activities by sending additional surveillance assets to the area. The U.S. military might be tasked to provide these assets as well as to operate them either from international waters and airspace or over the territory of the combatants—either with or, in an extreme situation, without permission to do so.

USAF basing to support the types of activities discussed above is somewhat limited in this part of the world. Diego Garcia is the permanent U.S. outpost nearest the subcontinent, but we use the term "near" advisedly—for that base lies approximately 2500 nm from Islamabad[24] and 2200 nm from New Delhi.[25] Bangkok is some 1600 nm from the Indian capital and 2000 nm from Islamabad, as are bases in central Saudi Arabia, while Singapore is about 2200 nm and 2600 nm away.

The list of countries that may provide bases for USAF aircraft is scenario-dependent and closely tied to the type of operations conducted. Humanitarian operations will likely yield the longest list of countries that would be willing to support the USAF, while other types of operations would likely yield fewer basing possibilities. The following discussion identifies basing opportunities that could be expected to arise over a wide range of scenarios and operations.

Referring to the map in Figure 4.8, we have identified three major regions to evaluate.

We see limited opportunities east of India in the area of Burma and Bangladesh. First, this is quite far from the Indian-Pakistani border, where we envision the most plausible scenarios taking place. In

---

[24]The base is approximately the same distance from Kashmir, the ever-simmering focal point of Indo-Pakistani tensions.

[25]Incirlik, a quasi-permanent USAF base in Turkey, is considerably closer to both Pakistan and northwestern India. However, aircraft would have to transit nearly 900 nm of Iranian airspace to get there, an unlikely course for any U.S. aircraft. By diverting northward over the former Soviet republics of Central Asia, U.S. jets flying from Turkey could avoid Iran; however, reaching Pakistan would then involve traversing at least the easternmost "finger" of Afghanistan or parts of western China. Getting to India would involve overflying China or Pakistan. The distances saved would still add up to several hundred miles, but the political difficulties involved would under most circumstances be all but overwhelming.

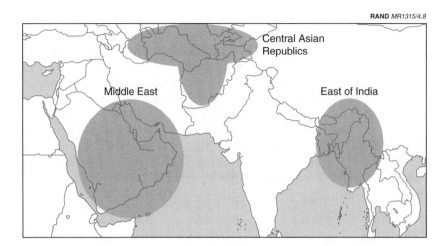

Figure 4.8—Possible South Asia Basing Regions

addition, this region has limited facilities and relations between Burma and the United States are stressed. Finally, given the proximity of this region to China, these countries would likely be reluctant to become too closely aligned with the United States in the event of heightened tensions.

The second region consists of the Central Asian republics. Improved access to South Asia could grow from enhanced relations with these former Soviet republics. Countries such as Uzbekistan and Kazakhstan could serve as valuable entrepôts to this turbulent region presuming that overflight access would be granted by Georgia, Armenia, and Azerbaijan, which lie between them and the USAF's bases in Turkey. At the same time, limited infrastructure and political concerns similar to those of the first region could limit the prospect of using these countries to support USAF operations. The overflight rights needed to deploy to and operate from this region further complicate the issue.

The third region is the Middle East, and it is here that we see the most promise for conducting operations in South Asia. As was shown during the Gulf War, the air base facilities in this region are second to none, and the governments in the region are relatively stable, often with national interests that align with those of the

United States. With regard to geography, Oman is closest to the Indian-Pakistani border—about 500 nautical miles. Relations between the government of Oman and the United States are good, and Oman has shown itself to be a reasonably steadfast ally. In addition, the basing infrastructure in Oman is well developed.[26] Two bases— Seeb International and Masirah Island—are particularly well suited to the conduct of USAF operations. Figure 4.9 shows these bases along with range circles of 500 and 1000 nautical miles from the Indian-Pakistani border; the figure illustrates that both bases are approximately 575 nautical miles from the border. No other country— with the possible exception of Afghanistan—could offer bases in such proximity.

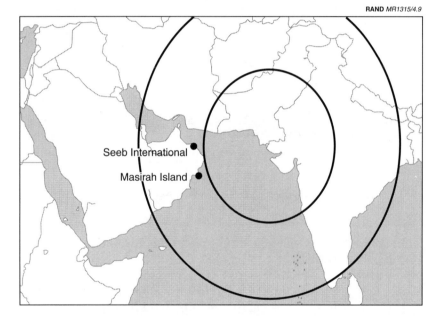

RAND MR1315/4.9

Figure 4.9—Suitability of Bases in Oman to the Support of Operations
Along the India-Pakistan Border

---

[26]The information on bases was taken from U.S. Department of Defense, *High and Low Altitude Europe, North Africa, and Middle East*, DoD Flight Information Publication, Vol. 5, February 27, 1997.

Seeb and Masirah offer very good facilities to support large-scale air operations. The runway at Seeb is more than 11,750 feet long and 148 feet wide, and nearly 5 million ft^2 of ramp space is available for the conduct of virtually any type of USAF operation. In addition, a parallel taxiway is available that could be used as an emergency runway if required. Masirah is also a good facility offering two runways, both 148 feet wide; one is more than 10,000 feet long, while the second is nearly 8500 feet long. Both runways have a parallel taxiway, and the airfield has over 800,000 ft^2 of ramp space.

As always, however, access to these excellent facilities will likely be strongly dependent on the political circumstances surrounding the contingency in question. Pakistan's attitude toward any proposed U.S. action could prove critical in determining the ease with which the USAF secures facilities in Oman.

Finally, there is the critical issue of demarcation. It is at the Indo-Pakistani border that the United States Unified Command Plan (UCP) draws the dividing line between U.S. Central Command (USCENTCOM), which holds responsibility for much of the greater Middle East, and U.S. Pacific Command (USPACOM), which has the brief for Asia. Although this may appear to be an arbitrary and inappropriate division of labor, any geographically based command structure will almost certainly feature one or more such seams. There are, moreover, valid historic reasons for this particular arrangement. Pakistan was, for example, a member of the long-defunct Central Treaty Organization (CENTO) along with Iran and other Middle Eastern countries. In addition, Pakistan's national self-consciousness ties it more to its Muslim neighbors to the west than to the Hindu and Buddhist societies of Asia.

At the same time, however, the tensions between India and Pakistan represent one of the clearest and most dangerous threats to peace in the world today, and there is little reason to believe that this will change significantly in the near term. Given the abiding U.S. interest in maintaining stability between these two nuclear powers, American policy must be well integrated and highly coordinated. Having the U.S. officers responsible for India and Pakistan reporting to different commanders through different chains of command is certainly not helpful in achieving this goal. Thus, both USCENTCOM and USPACOM must be highly sensitive to the potential dangers inherent in this awkward division of labor and must work hard to overcome those dangers. One approach might be to establish a standing coordination committee, perhaps chaired by the deputy commanders-in-chief (DCINCs) of USCENTCOM and USPACOM. Meeting regularly in Honolulu or Tampa and communicating electronically on a daily basis, this group could help ensure that U.S. policy goals and guidance were being interpreted and applied consistently and that military-to-military contacts with both India and Pakistan were being handled in the context of a common framework of objectives and processes.

The next revision of the UCP, however, should consider including Pakistan within the USPACOM boundary; such a reorganization would place both India and Pakistan within the ambit of a single U.S. military command while allowing USCENTCOM to focus its energies and resources entirely on the high-priority challenges associated with Gulf security. Alternatively, a new mechanism might be developed for dealing with countries that, like Pakistan, can logically be placed in one AoR for some purposes and in another AoR for others.

MISSILE DEFENSE

In the long run, the proliferation of ballistic missiles in Asia will pose an increasing threat to U.S. power projection capabilities, U.S. allies, and potentially the U.S. mainland. At present, both China and North Korea field missile forces that are likely to grow in both number and sophistication over time. As part of its strategy for Asia, the United States must therefore address this evolving threat. What is needed is a broad and flexible missile defense capability that takes technical, political, and diplomatic issues into account.

One possible way to deal with the threat to U.S. allies and U.S. forces and assets in the region would involve a theater missile defense (TMD) capability. Assuming that the adversary's missiles had only conventional (or perhaps even chemical) warheads, this TMD capability would not have to be "leakproof"; simply reducing substantially the number of missiles penetrating to their targets would provide an important benefit. On the other hand, if the adversary were willing to escalate to the use of nuclear weapons, the value of a "leaky" defense would be considerably reduced.

The issue of a national missile defense (NMD) for the United States has gained great salience in Washington. At present, the only country in Asia aside from Russia that could threaten the continental U.S. is China, although North Korea is reported to be attempting to develop at least a primitive intercontinental ballistic missile (ICBM) capability. And, not surprisingly, the Chinese have vociferously objected to the notion of missile defense, especially NMD.[27]

Given the small size of China's ICBM force, Beijing has reason to believe that even a "thin" U.S. missile shield would deprive them of their ability to threaten the continental United States and reduce their leverage on the United States in a variety of crises and confrontations. The most obvious Chinese response would be to increase the size of its ICBM force so as to be able to overwhelm American defenses. In addition, the Chinese would presumably attempt to develop various decoys and other penetration aids that would enable them to defeat the U.S. defenses.

As it decides whether to go forward with NMD, the United States should and is likely to consider the impact on Sino-American relations. Several factors will have to inform U.S. calculations. First, should the United States accept that it will remain vulnerable to Chinese missiles even if it could develop the capability to protect itself against them? With regard to the former Soviet Union, the U.S. acceptance of mutual assured destruction was based on the recognition that it was technologically impossible to acquire adequate defenses.

Second, will the United States be militarily worse off given plausible Chinese military responses to a U.S. NMD deployment? If China responds by building up its own ICBM capabilities so as to overwhelm or otherwise defeat the defenses, the United States would remain as vulnerable to a Chinese strategic strike as it is today. This would mean no net change. It is also possible that the United States would become more vulnerable—i.e., that the Chinese would decide to build a strategic nuclear force that would be capable, even in the presence of U.S. defenses, of inflicting more damage on the United States than their current force can. On the other hand, it is not im-

---

[27]With respect to TMD, the Chinese have thus far concentrated their fire on the possibility that a U.S. system could be designed or deployed so as to defend Taiwan.

possible that the Chinese, mindful of America's greater financial and technological capabilities, might decline to enter such an "offense-defense" race.[28]   Would such a race force China to decrease investment in weapon systems that would be more useful in threatening U.S. regional interests?

Third, what would be the political impact of NMD deployment on China's evolution? It could be argued that such action would place China on a hostile trajectory and undermine prospects for the emergence of a more cooperative and democratic China. Alternatively, it might be argued that NMD deployment would have no effect on China's political evolution, which will be determined primarily by internal factors in any case; indeed, deployment of missile defenses might undercut the apparent Chinese belief that China's ability and willingness to absorb large numbers of casualties in pursuit of its goals gives it great leverage against the United States.

Fourth, what would be the effect of a possible Chinese missile buildup on countries like Russia and India? Such activity could induce India to build up its own nuclear and missile capabilities (unless it could be convinced that the Chinese buildup of intercontinental capability was irrelevant to its own security concerns) and cause Russia to be reluctant to further reduce its own offensive forces. This could have some generally negative effects with respect to armament levels and nonproliferation but could also cause these countries to be more willing to cooperate with the United States. Indeed, the possible reactions of its neighbors could moderate any Chinese strategic nuclear buildup undertaken in response to U.S. NMD.

---

[28]During the ABM debate of the late 1960s, it was often argued that missile defense was not cost-effective in the sense that $1 million spent on defense could be effectively countered by a much smaller amount spent on offense. Thus, the side that invested heavily in defense would find that, after its opponent had spent a much smaller sum, it was essentially back where it started from. This argument assumed that the two sides had roughly equal financial resources. In the case of a country whose financial means are much less than those of the United States, however, this argument would not necessarily work. It might turn out that, in the long run, the United States was better able to spend a larger sum on defense than the corresponding smaller sum that its adversary would have to spend on offense.

BOLSTERING OVERALL U.S. POSTURE IN ASIA

Bolstering the overall U.S. posture in Asia will require knitting together a coherent web of security arrangements among the United States and its core partners in Asia—Japan, Australia, and South Korea—that might expand to Southeast Asia as well. This will demand military as well as political steps. Training exercises will need to be expanded to include all the parties; planning forums will need to be established; and some degree of hardware standardization will be necessary to foster human and technical interoperability.[29]

The overall U.S. posture in the Western Pacific would benefit from three additional steps. First, Guam—a sovereign U.S. territory—should be built up as a major hub for power projection throughout Asia. Sufficient stockpiles of munitions, spare parts, and other equipment should be established to support the rapid deployment and employment of a sizable tranche of USAF assets—say, 100 to 150 fighters and up to 50 bombers—anywhere in the region. Within C-130 range of the Philippines, northwest Australia, Malaysia, Indonesia, Singapore, Vietnam, and Thailand, assets could be quickly moved from Guam to FOLS across much of the region.

Second, the USAF and the U.S. Navy should work to develop new concepts of operations that maximize the leverage their combined forces could offer to a joint commander in a future Pacific crisis. With basing for land-based fighters at a premium in much of the region, the USAF and the U.S. Navy should, for example, plan and practice tactics and procedures to enable carrier-based fighters to provide air-to-air and defense-suppression support for Air Force bombers and in turn to be supported by USAF tankers and command, control, communications, computers, intelligence, surveillance, and reconnaissance (C^4ISR) platforms.

Third, the USAF should review its future force structure and consider whether it might not benefit from a mix that places greater emphasis on longer-range combat platforms. In this context, acquiring additional heavy bombers might be one option. Another option that is often discussed is the arsenal plane, an aircraft capable of delivering

---

[29]These steps could provide the political benefit of helping dispel the lingering distrust and animosity between South Korea and Japan.

a large number of smart munitions from a stand-off range beyond the enemy's defensive envelope. A third option would be to develop and deploy a small fleet of high-speed, long-range strike aircraft.[30] Asia is vast, and options for basing large numbers of land-based combat aircraft are few and far between; long range and high speeds have payoffs that might not be evident when looking at contingencies in more compact theaters, such as Korea, Europe, or even the Persian Gulf.

THE LONG TERM

Although any vision of the future by definition grows ever cloudier the further one gazes, three general recommendations can be made to help the United States shape the future Asian security environment in a way that might help avoid the most severe disruptions of regional peace. The first is that the United States should strive to maintain open lines of communication both with and among its Asian partners. The United States should be willing to talk with all parties in the region, even those with which it has a clash of interests, if only to make clear the specific nature and extent of its disagreements. This includes military-to-military contacts, which could help provide vital domesticating influences on powerful security forces in emerging democracies such as Indonesia.

Second, the United States should practice, advocate, and foster increased political-military transparency in Asia. While "calculated" or "strategic" ambiguity may have its place, the United States should make clear its fundamental objectives in the region: that border disputes not be settled by violence, that the China-Taiwan question not be resolved by force, and that democratic and market-oriented governments take deep and secure root. In so doing, the United States

---

[30]By "high speed" we mean roughly Mach-2 supercruise and by "long range" a minimum 2500-nm unrefueled range. If fitted with a dozen or so 250-pound small smart bombs (SSBs), such an aircraft could conduct missions currently executable only by B-1 or B-2 bombers at a sortie rate more comparable to that achieved by current fighter-bombers such as the F-15E or F-117. Preliminary calculations suggest that such a platform would be about the size of an F-4. See John Stillion and David T. Orletsky, *Airbase Vulnerability to Conventional Cruise-Missile and Ballistic-Missile Attacks: Technology, Scenarios, and U.S. Air Force Responses*, Santa Monica, RAND: MR-1216-AF, forthcoming.

can attempt to elicit a similar degree of frankness from Asia's major indigenous powers, even if the main result is to bring to light and clarify those places where disagreements exist.

Finally, hedging against the possibility that all may not turn out for the best in Asia implies that the United States should cast its net broadly in its search for security partners. Not all relationships need to achieve the degree of intimacy that characterizes the U.S.-Japan alliance; contingent access agreements, training rotations, increased foreign access to U.S. professional military education, and other lower-level interactions all offer opportunities for improved bilateral and multilateral relations.

THE CHANGING POLITICAL-MILITARY ENVIRONMENT: NORTHEAST ASIA

Jonathan D. Pollack

MAJOR ISSUES DETERMINING THE NORTHEAST ASIAN SECURITY ENVIRONMENT

Northeast Asia was the predominant if not exclusive pivot of great power rivalry in Asia for much of the 20th century. The region encompasses (1) the military forces of four major powers (the United States, Russia, China, and Japan); (2) a continued military confrontation on the Korean peninsula that in a major crisis would immediately trigger direct U.S. military involvement and would likely entail the use of WMD capabilities; (3) an increasing array of ballistic missile assets; and (4) the latent and quite possibly growing risk of military hostilities in the Taiwan Strait.

Despite the region's extraordinary prosperity and seeming stability, latent threats to peace persist and could increase significantly in the coming decade. A strategic realignment is under way that seems certain to affect U.S. security assumptions and interests in major ways. Depending on the outcome of this realignment, U.S. defense planners could confront a regional strategic future that is reasonably manageable if not benign or one that is much more adverse to long-term U.S. interests.

The principal manifestation of strategic change has been the increasing sophistication of regional military capabilities. Northeast Asia's rapid economic growth has enabled regional states to accelerate the pace of military modernization, with an increasing emphasis on missions and capabilities that extend beyond territorial defense. There has been a pronounced enhancement of air and naval capabilities all along the Pacific Rim, with weapon purchasers able to demand far more sophisticated technologies in an increasingly competitive arms market. Unconstrained by the restrictions and polarities of the Cold War, major weapon exporters from the United States, Europe, and Russia are vigorously marketing more advanced military hardware across the region. As a consequence, Northeast Asia's ascendant military powers (i.e., China, Taiwan, Japan, and South Korea) are in the midst of a far-reaching transformation of their military capabilities. These transitions are occurring against the backdrop of unresolved geopolitical rivalries and potential threats to peace.

The conjunction of economic and technological dynamism, heightened security rivalries, increasingly capable military forces, and the absence of credible regionwide security arrangements has kept the United States a pivotal factor in regional security. At present, support for the forward presence of U.S. air, naval, and ground forces remains largely undiminished among most regional states. Despite contentious issues concerning base consolidation and relocation in Japan and Korea that could impose limitations on U.S. forward-deployed forces, there appear to be few near-term pressures to scale back these forces. If anything, America's Asian allies assert that a reduction of the U.S. presence could portend a larger retrenchment of American military power, a development that none of them favor.

A central question in this analysis is whether these long-prevailing strategic patterns and force deployments will remain undisturbed in the next decade. American policymakers seem persuaded that a robust U.S. forward presence and the U.S. ability to reinforce this presence in a major regional crisis are the critical factors guaranteeing regional stability.[1] In this view, so long as the United States retains its primary role as regional security guarantor, no state will develop the means or incentive to challenge the status quo. Under such circumstances, America's allies and security partners are prepared to leave existing arrangements in place, although these arrangements might be subject to periodic adjustment. The United States therefore expects to continue to address its regional security requirements on a case-by-case basis.

---

[1]Walter B. Slocombe, "Statement of the Undersecretary of Defense for Policy Before the House Committee on International Relations, Subcommittee on Asia and the Pacific," May 7, 1998.

However, some of these assumptions seem increasingly questionable. All regional states recognize that there have been profound changes in the Northeast Asian balance of power over the past decade, entailing economic and politico-diplomatic as well as military change. Regional actors—including America's allies—no longer view their security options and capabilities in exclusively local terms. Military power throughout Northeast Asia is increasingly viewed more in a regional context. Most states believe that severe discontinuities or a major political-military crisis remains unlikely, but all recognize that an armed conflict could prove far more disruptive to the region's economic well-being and infrastructure than the crises of earlier decades.

Changing economic and political dynamics are therefore reshaping (1) power relationships among all regional states; (2) the perceptions of regional actors of American power and policy; and (3) the mix of economic, political, and military capabilities available to each state. Even without a major crisis, regional politics and security planning will be increasingly defined by forces indigenous to East Asia.

The steady enhancement of national-level military capabilities may well prove a pivotal factor in the region's strategic transition. In past decades, the national defense capabilities of various Northeast Asian states were constrained by political and constitutional inhibitions (in the case of Japan); by a singular focus on an immediate military threat (in the case of South Korea); or by economic and technological limitations that precluded the development of more powerful military forces able to extend their reach beyond homeland defense (in the case of China). These constraints now appear far less limiting in all three cases. Even North Korea—now largely bereft of its economic and security subsidies from Moscow and Beijing and ever more dependent on humanitarian, energy, and food aid for its survival as a state—is viewed by the United States and Japan as a regional and (potentially) an intercontinental military threat, given its ballistic missile and WMD programs.

At the same time, changes in military technology are altering national security policy assumptions throughout the region. Defense planning is less premised on a canonical threat. Worries about direct, large-scale attacks have diminished, supplanted by mounting concerns about the application of advanced technologies to new modes of interstate conflict. For example, the compressed warning times associated with ballistic missile attack have rendered geographic distance far less significant and have created far more demanding intelligence and information requirements. The application of information technologies to warfare also appears to be reshaping estimates of gain and risk as well as concepts of offense and defense.

The United States has generally defined its regional security interests in terms of deterring armed conflict and ensuring stability where the possibility of military hostilities persists. These goals seem unobjectionable but may set the bar too low. They posit an essentially static view of Northeast Asia that is belied by the policies and programs of nearly all regional actors. Efforts to preserve the existing pattern of U.S. regional deployments may prove politically and militarily unsustainable as regional military capabilities grow and as various states diversify their longer-term security options.

The national strategies of U.S. allies increasingly entail both enhanced collaboration with U.S. forces where possible *and* the development of indigenous capabilities and policy goals over the longer run. Regional allies see no inherent contradiction in such a dual strategy. Korea and Japan, for example, increasingly believe that the uncertainties and risks to their national interests are too great to warrant relying on U.S. power alone. Tokyo and Seoul also believe that they should acquire a larger voice in alliance deliberations rather than automatically defer to U.S. preferences and needs. These beliefs are driven by a combination of nationalism, domestic politics, bureaucratic self-interest, industrial-technical goals, and simple prudence. All seem likely to be greatly strengthened over the coming decade.

Korean and Japanese policies increasingly entail elements of a hedging strategy. Regional actors believe that competing strategic needs could prompt significant shifts in the future U.S. presence or that the United States may not indefinitely assume a singular role in regional politics and security. Powerful allies deem it necessary to prepare for these possibilities, which also seem likely to shape the attitudes of prospective U.S. political-military rivals. Although inconsistencies in U.S. regional policies over the past decade have contributed to this reassessment of American strategy, larger factors are involved as well.

To varying degrees, all regional actors are making assumptions about the future behavior and national security strategy of the United States. All recognize that the United States has global strategic interests as well as military assets unrivaled by any single state or coalition of states. But Northeast Asia's looming strategic transition cannot be readily fitted within an existing policy template. In addition, latent and potentially growing uncertainties and strategic divergence between both the United States and China and the United States and Russia could leave the larger regional equation increasingly unsettled.

Many changes under way in Northeast Asia represent the culmination of long-term American efforts to encourage its regional allies to assume more responsibility for their own defense. These trends will result in a less subordinate region, with the United States no longer able to assume that its security partners will automatically accommodate to U.S. strategy and policy goals. These changes could ultimately exert an influence on U.S. policy calculations as substantial as changing estimates of military threat.

Thus, the ground is shifting in Northeast Asia. This strategic transition will transform the regional security environment as well as U.S. alliance arrangements, military roles and requirements, and major power relationships. These changes are also redefining future U.S. airpower requirements, the regional assumptions and expectations of the United States, and the incentives of different states to collaborate with American forces. They also reflect the unwillingness of various countries to forgo their separate security identities as well as the increasing role of public opinion in national security debate within various societies.

This chapter will focus on four primary issues that seem likely to shape the future character of the Northeast Asian security environment and of U.S. security policy options: (1) China's political, economic, and strategic transition and how regional states approach long-term relations with China; (2) the future of the U.S.-Japan alliance, in particular the security concerns and goals that are redefining Japan's role as a political-military power; (3) the evolution of the Korean peninsula (in particular, managing future relations with North Korea) and how major change (e.g., unification, a major reduction of the North Korean threat, or an intensification of the threat by further ballistic missile and WMD development) could alter peninsular and regional security; and (4) alternative forecasts for Russia's future, including how different internal political outcomes could affect Moscow's ability and disposition to collaborate with the United States on regional security goals.

Emergence of China

China's economic and political-military reemergence will constitute a defining strategic issue in Northeast Asia in coming decades. Few states (let alone a major power) have achieved as sustained and rapid economic growth as has China over the past two decades.[2] Equally important, China appears intent on narrowing (if not eliminating) the major technological gaps between its military capabilities and those of the major powers, including the United States.[3] These concerns have prompted numerous efforts to define an optimal U.S. strategy toward China that simultaneously addresses the PRC's national security goals and military capabilities and its growing commercial, technological, and institutional weight.[4]

Most proposed U.S. policies toward China have emphasized variants or combinations of engagement and hedging strategies, with few recommending containment, at least in the near to midterm.[5] States

---

[2]Angus Maddison, *Chinese Economic Performance in the Long Run,* Washington, D.C.: Organization for Economic Cooperation and Development, 1998.

[3]James C. Mulvenon and Richard H. Yang (eds.), *The People's Liberation Army in the Information Age,* Santa Monica: RAND, CF-145-CAPP/AF, 1999.

[4]James Shinn (ed.), *Weaving the Net—Conditional Engagement with China,* New York: Council on Foreign Relations Press, 1996; Ezra Vogel (ed.), *Living with China,* New York: American Assembly, 1997; Hans Binnendyk and Ronald N. Montaperto, *Strategic Trends in China,* Washington, D.C.: Institute for National Strategic Studies, National Defense University, 1998; Elizabeth Economy and Michel Oksenberg (eds.), *China Joins the World—Progress and Prospects,* New York: Council on Foreign Relations Press, 1999; Khalilzad et al., 1999; and Philip C. Saunders, "A Virtual Alliance for Asian Security," *Orbis,* Vol. 43, No. 2, Spring 1999, pp. 237–256.

[5]Jonathan D. Pollack, *Designing a New American Security Strategy for Asia,* Santa Monica: RAND, RP-541, 1996.

throughout Asia face comparable policy dilemmas toward China, and without the luxury of distance. On the assumption that the United States will continue to remain a tacit balancer of Chinese power, nearly all are pursuing policies that parallel those adopted by U.S. policymakers.[6] China's neighbors

> must define practicable policies toward Beijing that simultaneously enhance Chinese incentives to pursue collaboration with their neighbors, while preserving options to protect national security should constructive, stable relations prove elusive or unattainable.[7]

Although Taiwan in particular requires a deterrence and defense strategy against China, no regional actor seeks to forgo economic and political opportunities with Beijing. All recognize the potential asymmetries in relations with a major continental and maritime power. Indeed, most major powers are not prepared to acquiesce to what others see as the inevitable preponderance of Chinese power. No state, however, sees a credible alternative to enhanced involvement with China. A mix of collaborative and countervailing capabilities seems a realistic choice for all of China's neighbors and is broadly endorsed by public opinion in most societies.

The tacit strategic consensus favoring closer relations with China has transformed the East Asian political landscape over the past decade. At the start of the 1990s, China (then seriously estranged from the United States following the Tiananmen crisis) did not even have diplomatic ties with South Korea, Singapore, or Indonesia. Ten years later, fueled by a decade of unprecedented Chinese economic growth and a highly resourceful PRC diplomatic and foreign policy strategy, all these relationships have been redefined. Fuller relations with China are deemed an essential component of each country's foreign and defense policy calculations. While these developments have not obviated the need for contingency planning in crises that could in-

---

[6]Jonathan D. Pollack and Richard H. Yang (eds.), *In China's Shadow: Regional Perspectives on Chinese Foreign Policy and Military Development,* Santa Monica: RAND, CF-137-CAPP, 1998.

[7]Jonathan D. Pollack, "Asian-Pacific Responses to a Rising China," in Pollack and Yang (eds.), 1998.

volve China, such changes have had a major effect on prevailing policies toward Beijing.

For example, China now ranks among the ROK's leading trading partners (bilateral trade now approaches $25 billion annually), and there is a rapidly burgeoning set of leadership ties between Seoul and Beijing, including enhanced military-to-military relations. The highest-ranking Chinese official to visit the North during the 1990s (when Beijing notified Pyongyang of its impending plans to recognize the ROK) was the minister of foreign affairs, in October 1992. By contrast, numerous senior Chinese officials visited and traveled extensively within the ROK. Beijing remains mindful of the suspicions of the North Korean leadership whenever the Chinese deal with the South, but it has not allowed such considerations to impede China's compelling interest in fuller relations with the ROK, including political and security discussions. Indeed, North Korea no longer seems able to prevent or intent on preventing such contacts. In January 2000, for example, Chinese Minister of National Defense Chi Haotian visited the ROK—a remarkable development in view of the PRC's alliance relationship with North Korea. Indeed, even in China-Taiwan relations, animosities between Beijing and Taipei have not prevented rapidly burgeoning trade ties (approximately $25 billion at present), investment on the mainland by Taiwanese entrepreneurs and industrialists that in cumulative terms approaches $40 billion, and visitors from the island to the mainland who now number in the millions.

The Chinese leadership recognizes its leverage under such circumstances, provided that China avoids overtly coercive strategies, furnishes individual states realistic incentives to collaborate with Beijing, and does not compel "either-or" choices on the part of its neighbors. The Chinese are also under increased pressure from neighboring states to provide reassurance about China's longer-term national security priorities. Beijing has proposed an alternative approach to regional security that purports to supplant Cold War–era alliances (i.e., policies designed and still pursued by the United States), with particular emphasis on allegedly nonthreatening, more equitable concepts of regional security.[8] The Chinese have also launched increasingly diversified efforts at military diplomacy intended to reduce concerns about China's military modernization and to deflect longer-term suspicions about Chinese strategic intentions.[9]

However, Beijing's "new security concept" remains (1) elliptical about the ultimate goals of China's military modernization; (2) unalterably opposed to concessions or compromises with respect to China's asserted claims to sovereignty (i.e., in the East and South China Seas as well as in relation to Taiwan); and (3) decidedly ambiguous concerning China's longer-term assessment of the legitimacy of the U.S. regional military presence. Absent a major regional crisis or more active attempts by Beijing to undermine support for U.S. forward-deployed forces, this ambiguity seems likely to persist. Indeed, all affected powers seem inclined to avoid or to defer more definitive decisions about national strategies. Chinese military modernization continues to move ahead in this context, although not on a pace or scale that has alarmed Beijing's neighbors.

In the final analysis, regional strategies and policies toward China will be determined by a mix of internal and external factors, in particular China's domestic political evolution, the PRC's external behavior, the capability of the United States to achieve realistic strategic understandings with Beijing, and political-strategic developments along China's periphery. Avoidance of overt conflict in the Taiwan Strait represents a major concern of all neighboring states. Longer-term outcomes on the Korean peninsula, however, also rank high among these concerns, since a "Seoul-centered" unification would mean that a close U.S. ally would then border China, which has a significant Korean ethnic presence in its northeastern provinces.

---

[8]*China's National Defense*, Beijing: Information Office of the State Council, 1998; and David M. Finkelstein, "China's New Security Concept: Reading Between the Lines," *Washington Journal of Modern China*, Vol. 5, No. 1, Spring 1999.

[9]Kenneth W. Allen and Eric A. McVadon, *China's Foreign Military Relations*, Washington, D.C.: Henry L. Stimson Center, October 1999.

This latter possibility highlights the pivotal importance of Korea in regional geopolitics should the half-century division of the peninsula come to an end. The South-North summit of June 2000 has understandably prompted a flurry of speculation about the implications of unification, should it transpire. Many analysts in Seoul, for example, insist that a unified Korea has an inherent incentive to maintain close ties with the United States given the peninsula's location between China and Japan and its proximity to Russia. However, even if the United States seeks to retain an appreciable security presence on the peninsula following unification, Korea's strategic preferences would not automatically favor American strategic interests. For example, a unified Korean government might well seek to conciliate the Chinese by precluding specific U.S. deployments on the peninsula or by circumscribing their location and functions. In addition, the Chinese likely hope to exploit shared historical animosities toward Japan to gain both tactical and strategic advantage with a unified Korea.

Some of these possibilities are already evident in relation to TMD, especially consideration of upper-tier programs. ROK President Kim Dae Jung has repeatedly declined invitations to participate in collaborative TMD programs with the United States. The ROK's stated objections to TMD reflect the inherent threat of North Korean artillery and short-range missiles that cannot be ameliorated by TMD. Seoul also recognizes that as long as U.S. forces are deployed on the peninsula, the United States will pursue the development of TMD with or without ROK support. However, the Korean leadership's cautionary approach to TMD also enables Seoul to curry favor with Beijing, since the Chinese see U.S. concerns about North Korean ballistic missiles as a pretext for larger missile defense programs that could degrade the effectiveness of Chinese missile forces.[10] Yet the ROK and China also share concerns that enhanced TMD programs will greatly heighten U.S. defense linkages with Japan as well as provide Tokyo with new capabilities and responsibilities that others deem threatening to their interests.

---

[10]Luo Jie and Ye Bian, "U.S. 'Missile Defense' Will Bring No End of Trouble for the Future—Sha Zukang on Topics Including [the] International Disarmament Situation and TMD," *Shijie Zhishi (World Knowledge)*, No. 13, July 1, 1999, pp. 8–11.

Redefining the U.S.-Japan Alliance

With the end of the Cold War, the purposes and rationale of the U.S.-Japan alliance—long deemed the centerpiece of U.S. East Asian strategy—were opened anew. The disintegration of the Soviet Union and the Clinton administration's early focus on major imbalances in U.S.-Japanese trade and technology relations resulted in diminished public support for the alliance within Japan and an increased willingness on the part of the Japanese to openly debate the alliance's strategic purposes.[11] The growth of Chinese power and increasing Chinese foreign policy assertiveness reinforced Japan's anxieties about its primacy in American regional policies, especially as Japan remained in a protracted economic slump.[12]

The Japanese believed, however, that they had to reaffirm their alliance with the United States. In the absence of a primary alliance relationship, Tokyo recognized it needed to either undertake a major effort to enhance its strategic autonomy, including much higher levels of defense expenditure and far more robust indigenous military capabilities (perhaps including a nuclear option) or adopt a posture of lightly armed neutrality and reliance on ill-defined multilateral security initiatives, which would have entailed acquiescence to Chinese strategic predominance in East Asia. Neither option seemed palatable to Japan.

Reinvigorating the alliance with the United States presupposed a revised understanding of the alliance's strategic purposes. Japanese strategists had long been mindful of the highly asymmetric character of their defense ties with the United States. Constitutional restrictions on the use of military power beyond the defense of the Japanese home islands, territorial waters, and airspace (i.e., the constraints imposed by the "no war" provision of Article IX) had kept Tokyo in a highly subordinate position throughout the Cold War,

---

[11]David L. Asher, "A U.S.-Japan Alliance for the Next Century," *Orbis*, Vol. 41, No. 3, Summer 1997, pp. 343–374; and Michael J. Green and Patrick M. Cronin (eds.), *The U.S.-Japan Alliance—Past, Present, and Future*, New York: Council on Foreign Relations Press, 1999.

[12]Michael J. Green and Benjamin L. Self, "Japan's Changing China Policy: From Commercial Liberalism to Reluctant Realism," *Survival*, Vol. 38, No. 2, Summer 1996, pp. 35–58.

with the United States assuming major responsibilities for the defense of Japan, but without Japan incurring corollary obligations on behalf of the United States. Japan's provision of bases, U.S. access to Japanese port facilities, and extensive host-nation support for U.S. forces were deemed an acceptable outcome for both countries; most security disputes were relegated to periodic negotiations over technology transfer, burden-sharing allocations, and policy coordination.[13]

But accumulated tensions and frictions during the past decade revealed the potential for major strategic divergence across the Pacific. The Gulf War in particular proved a galvanizing event. Although U.S. arm twisting ultimately compelled Tokyo to contribute nearly $15 billion to the war effort, the Japanese were at first highly equivocal in their responses. Tokyo's initially lukewarm response reflected poorly on Japan and placed major strains on its relationship with the United States, highlighting as it did the country's inability to define a broader approach to international security beyond a narrow concept of Japan's self-interest. Japan therefore began to move toward a more active international security role, beginning with the deployment of Japanese minesweepers to the Gulf following the coalition victory in Operation Desert Storm.

By mid-decade, however, the sense of drift in alliance relations was palpable, with senior U.S. defense officials particularly attuned to the risks and consequences.[14] Washington and Tokyo undertook detailed strategic reviews, culminating with the publication of a Joint Security Declaration in April 1996. The joint declaration obligated both governments to revisit the U.S.-Japan Security Guidelines of 1978. The revised guidelines, first published in September 1997 and formally approved by the Japanese Diet in the spring of 1999, formalized major transformations in the U.S.-Japan alliance. They also ini-

---

[13]Daniel I. Okimoto, *The Japan-America Security Alliance: Prospects for the Twenty-First Century,* Stanford, CA: Asia/Pacific Research Center, Stanford University, January 1998.

[14]Yoichi Funabashi, *Alliance Adrift,* New York: Council on Foreign Relations Press, 1999.

tiated a larger process of change in Japanese defense policy that will be increasingly evident over the next decade.[15]

The Japanese also viewed these changes through the prism of U.S.-China relations. The signing of the Joint Security Declaration occurred in the immediate aftermath of the PLA's live fire exercises and missile tests near Taiwan. But Washington and Beijing were simultaneously engaged in efforts to renew high-level strategic consultations. These discussions ultimately led to Jiang Zemin's state visit to the United States in the fall of 1997 and to President Clinton's reciprocal visit to China in the summer of 1998, replete with mutual pledges to advance a Sino-American "collaborative strategic partnership." Although this label seemed more a political slogan than an explicit strategic design, it engendered renewed suspicions in Tokyo that Japanese interests might be compromised by U.S. dealings with China. Senior U.S. officials argued that the joint security review was partly intended to reassure Tokyo about Japan's pride of place in U.S. regional security calculations.[16] But latent Japanese suspicions of U.S. efforts to balance its separate ties with Tokyo and Beijing seem likely to persist.

Given the efforts to augment the U.S.-Japan alliance and the major strains evident in U.S.-China relations in recent years, it is possible that Tokyo's suspicions about U.S. policy have somewhat eased. Indeed, the Security Guidelines review will reconfigure the alliance relationship, entailing independence as well as interdependence. The Japanese believe that their enhanced role and responsibilities should entail a much fuller process of defense and strategic consultations. Tokyo also believes that it will now be better able to deflect efforts by Beijing to deny Japan a larger long-term role in regional security.

The new guidelines focused on four pivotal considerations: (1) the political-strategic logic of the U.S.-Japan security relationship after the demise of the Soviet Union; (2) the policy guidelines associated with adaptations in the U.S.-Japan security framework; (3) modifications in long-standing constraints on Japan's national defense roles and responsibilities, in particular Japan's potential role in major re-

---

[15]U.S.-Japan Security Consultative Committee, "Joint Statement," Washington, D.C.: U.S. Department of Defense, September 23, 1997.

[16]Funabashi (1999).

gional crises and its development of indigenous military capabilities less integrally tied to those of the United States; and (4) planning, programming, and acquisition strategies appropriate to Japan's projected future security requirements.

The new terms of reference in the U.S.-Japan alliance commit Tokyo to a much more active involvement in regional security affairs. The Self-Defense Forces are now authorized by law to execute an array of new roles and missions embedded in the revised Security Guidelines. Although Japan has continued to forswear any combat role beyond the defense of Japanese territory, the guidelines mandate a much broader spectrum of operational responsibilities and procedures in a future crisis. For the first time, Tokyo is obligated to provide much fuller assistance to U.S. military forces in the event of unspecified emergencies in "the areas surrounding Japan."[17] These include active logistical support for U.S. forces, amply strengthened U.S. access agreements to bases and military facilities in Japan in the event of a major regional crisis, increased Japanese responsibility for non-combatant evacuation operations (NEOs), and an array of related operational responsibilities. Japan would therefore no longer be a bystander in a major regional crisis.

These changes have provoked intense concern on the part of neighboring states, especially China and Korea. Beijing has repeatedly cautioned Tokyo that any Japanese involvement in emergencies "in the areas surrounding Japan" threatens to embroil Japan in matters related to Chinese sovereignty (i.e., contingencies involving Taiwan). The Chinese continue to emphasize that Japan should "strictly confine the scope of [security] cooperation to the Japan-U.S. bilateral framework." Japanese "clarifications and explanations" (published verbatim in the Chinese press) have emphasized that the new security guidelines "are not targeted at any third country, including China." By the same logic, "situations in surrounding areas refer to situations that could have a major impact on Japan's security in ar-

---

[17]U.S. Department of Defense, *The United States Security Strategy for the East Asia-Pacific Region*, Washington, D.C., November 1998, p. 21.

eas surrounding Japan, and do not represent a geographical concept."[18]

These disclaimers are inherently ambiguous and to the Chinese are unpersuasive. Indeed, numerous Japanese observers acknowledge in private discussions that, in the event that the United States were to defend Taiwan in a major crisis, the new guidelines would almost certainly obligate Japan to assist U.S. forces. This is not a circumstance and choice that Tokyo would welcome, and this judgment leaves unstated the precise role Japan would assume under such circumstances. Given the extreme sensitivities associated with U.S. contingency planning for a Taiwan scenario, this lack of Japanese specificity seems doubly understandable. But Japanese observers speak with uncharacteristic clarity on this issue.

The Security Guidelines review presumably reassured many in Japan about Tokyo's pivotal position in American regional policy calculations. The explicit focus on "emergencies in the areas surrounding Japan" reiterated the U.S. commitment to ensuring regional stability—i.e., that the United States would respond to any overt use of force in Japan's vicinity and that Washington would not permit any disruptive imbalance of power to develop within the region. The prevailing focus, however, was on U.S.-Japanese behavior in a major regional crisis, not on longer-term transitions in the regional balance of power.

The revised guidelines highlight a significant shift in Japanese public opinion and policy debate. As a consequence of the new legislation, senior Japanese officials have far more latitude in committing the country's armed forces to regional responsibilities. Quite apart from more active consultations with the United States, the sphere of action for Japanese forces has also expanded significantly. Japanese planners intend to use these new political circumstances to restructure and upgrade their defense capabilities, to include areas lying outside the immediate purview of the U.S.-Japan alliance.

Some especially pertinent examples are found in the areas of PKO, disaster relief, and humanitarian operations. Japan has increasingly

---

[18]Sakaturo Tanino, Japanese Ambassador to China, "Statement to Chinese Ministry of Foreign Affairs," *BBC Selected World Broadcasts—Far East,* FE/3241/63, May 29, 1998.

identified such areas as fitting within the domain of its enhanced international responsibilities. As Paul Giarra (a former Office of the Secretary of Defense official responsible for U.S.-Japan relations) has noted, such operations were originally part of the revised Security Guidelines but they "quietly disappeared" from the final declaration. According to Giarra, the decision to omit these activities from the final accords in part reflected Japan's experience in the Rwanda refugee crisis of 1994, when the United States did not provide the needed transport aircraft for Japanese medical and transport teams. As a consequence, Japanese peacekeepers were transported to Rwanda on chartered Russian aircraft. The "lessons learned," Giarra suggests, will find the Japanese seeking more self-sustaining capabilities in this area:

> PKO and its extensions—disaster relief and humanitarian operations—will become a major operational and force-building rationale. Almost certainly, the next Mid-Term Defense Plan will increase emphasis on the kinds of amphibious and air support capabilities for the [Maritime Self-Defense Forces], airlift for the [Air Self-Defense Forces], and deployment potential for the [Ground Self-Defense Forces] needed to support such missions.[19]

Thus, even though support in Tokyo for the U.S.-Japan alliance remains strong, with the Japanese prepared to facilitate U.S. security goals, they are also enhancing indigenous capabilities. The guideline revisions and PKO activities have provided Japan with a rationale and political cover for the acquisition of new capabilities and for an increased focus on longer-term Japanese policy directions.

Tokyo has also redefined some of the operational parameters of its national security planning, including actions it is prepared to undertake if Japanese security is judged at risk. North Korea's test of the Taepo Dong missile in August 1998 had a particularly galvanizing effect.[20] The test took place without advance notice and demonstrated

---

[19]Paul Giarra, "Peacekeeping: As Good for the Alliance As It Is for Japan?" *Japan Digest,* February 9, 1999.

[20]*East Asian Strategic Review, 1998–1999,* Tokyo: National Institute for Defense Studies, 1999; and Barbara Wanner, *Mounting Anxiety over North Korean Security Threat Fuels Defense Debate in Japan,* Washington, D.C.: Japan Economic Institute, Report No. 33A, August 27, 1999.

North Korea's technological capability to launch a multistage missile. Even more jarring to Tokyo, it flew directly over Japanese territory, and some Japanese officials expressed quiet displeasure at what they deemed inadequate warning from the United States. Indeed, various Japanese observers characterized the Taepo Dong launch as equivalent to the Sputnik launch of 1957, since it jolted Japanese public opinion from a sense of complacency and presumed technological superiority. The test also helped tip the balance in internal opinion, with Japan for a time deferring approval of its $1 billion contribution to funding of the light-water reactor project under way in the North.

The implications for Japanese technological development and military R&D strategies could, however, prove especially significant. Despite Tokyo's long-standing *political* concurrence with U.S. regional defense policies, major Japanese industrial firms have long sought to enhance their technological edge and autonomy, to include numerous military areas.[21] This process has frequently entailed highly ambitious indigenous technological goals and programs and in other instances has justified active collaboration with the United States in areas where the United States possessed ample technological advantage.[22] These will over time enhance Japan's indigenous defense industrial base, and not always in ways that will enhance alliance interoperability.[23] Indeed, Japanese officials remain wary of providing the Department of Defense unconstrained access to proprietary industrial technologies, since Tokyo believes that this would complicate an array of commercial development efforts.

One such area is theater missile defense.[24] In the aftermath of the Taepo Dong test, Japan decided to accelerate TMD research collaboration with the United States. A memorandum of understanding

---

[21]Richard J. Samuels, *Rich Nation/Strong Army: National Security and the Technological Transformation of Japan,* Ithaca, NY: Cornell University Press, 1994.

[22]Mark Lorell, *Troubled Partnership: A History of U.S.-Japan Collaboration on the FS-X Fighter,* Santa Monica: RAND, MR-612/2-AF, 1995.

[23]Gregg A. Rubinstein, "U.S.-Japan Armaments Cooperation," in Michael J. Green and Patrick M. Cronin, *The U.S.-Japan Alliance—Past, Present, and Future,* New York: Council on Foreign Relations Press, 1999; and Sheryl WuDunn, "In Arms Sales, Japan Coddles Its Own," *New York Times,* June 24, 1999.

[24]Giarra (1999) and Green and Cronin (1999).

(MOU) signed in July 1999 commits both countries to collaborative research undertakings geared principally toward missile interceptor development for the Navy Theater Wide (NTW) program.[25] Although these R&D activities remain at a highly exploratory stage and are many years removed from any deployment decisions, heightened collaboration has already prompted increased discussion in Tokyo of command relationships should the program progress to operational capabilities. Indeed, Masashi Nishihara, a leading Japanese defense specialist, has already noted that joint U.S.-Japanese command of such a missile force would be indispensable to Tokyo's concurrence with such a project, and his views seem broadly shared within Japanese strategic circles.[26] The Japanese recognize that it is not too early to begin raising highly sensitive issues related to command and control.

Within weeks of the Taepo Dong test, Tokyo also announced plans to launch four reconnaissance satellites as part of a nascent monitoring capability for detecting missile launches. The intensity of Japanese reactions to the missile test may well have contributed to the speedy U.S. approval of these satellite programs—at $1.6 billion, the largest U.S.-Japan collaborative defense effort since the troubled FS-X fighter project of the 1980s. The Taepo Dong test afforded an opportunity to propose activities that Japanese industry had hoped to pursue for some time; there seems no other explanation for the uncharacteristic alacrity and speed with which Tokyo tabled its satellite requests. Unlike the aviation codevelopment program, the United States viewed the satellite project principally as an indigenous Japanese effort that American companies would facilitate rather than insisting on a dominant portion of U.S. content in the program.[27] If the program proceeds according to schedule, Japan will have manufactured and launched all four satellites by FY 2002. Even assuming that Japan would meet such ambitious program objectives, this

---

[25]John Donnelly, "U.S., Japan to Ink Missile-Defense Deal," *Defense Week*, July 26, 1999, pp. 1 and 12–13; and Calvin Sims, "U.S. and Japan Agree to Joint Research on Missile Defense," *New York Times*, August 17, 1999.

[26]Don Kirk, "U.S. Plans New Missile in Project with Japan," *International Herald Tribune*, August 7–8, 1999.

[27]Robert Wall, "Japanese Recce Program Wary of FS-X Missteps," *Aviation Week & Space Technology*, August 23, 1999, p. 44.

would constitute only the initial building blocks of a national-level reconnaissance capability.[28]

Thus, the larger effects of the Taepo Dong test reinforced Japan's sense of vulnerability. Indeed, in addition to the single Taepo Dong test, North Korea has already deployed approximately 20 Nodong missiles, a single-stage missile whose range (1300 km) posed a direct threat to most Japanese territory. Although North Korea represents the clear and present danger, some Japanese quietly raise concerns about the missile threat that could be posed by a unified Korea as well. Other Japanese observers regard heightened missile surveillance and defense programs as a longer-term defensive measure against Chinese ballistic missile threats. Regardless of the explanation, the Japanese have undoubtedly crossed a critical security threshold. Indeed, in the aftermath of the Taepo Dong test, the Japan Defense Agency (JDA) unequivocally reiterated Japan's inherent right to self-defense either against a missile attack or in the event of unambiguous warning of an impending attack. As stated in Japan's Defense White Paper:

> We can never think that the basic principle leads us to wait for death doing nothing in case there is an imminent and illegitimate act of aggression against Japan and . . . ballistic missiles are used for attacking our country . . . it is legally speaking within the limit of the right of self defense to attack the bases for launching missiles, and such attack is constitutional.[29]

The increasingly forceful tone of Japanese policy statements is paralleled by a vigorous military modernization program. Acquisition plans include aerial refueling capabilities for combat aircraft (purportedly for enhancing Japanese response capabilities in peacekeeping operations); AWACS aircraft for the Air Self-Defense Forces; additional intelligence and reconnaissance assets, particularly for detecting and tracking missile launch activities; and increased maritime reach, including amphibious capabilities. Although defense planners justify these acquisitions in the context of circumscribed

---

[28]"Japan Opts for Domestically Made Spy Satellites," Nikkei, reprinted in *Nihon Keizai Shimbun*, September 28, 1999.

[29]*Defense of Japan—1999*, Tokyo: Japan Defense Agency, 1999.

roles and missions (i.e., those deemed legitimate under Article IX of the Japanese Constitution), these programs constitute the building blocks of a much more capable military force.

Actions taken by the Diet will also enhance Japan's capacity to act more decisively in the event of a major regional crisis. Having approved measures to facilitate assistance to U.S. forces in "regional emergencies," the ruling coalition is seeking parallel authorization for the Self-Defense Forces should Japan come under attack.[30] Such legislation would place more authority in the hands of the Cabinet and the prime minister to expedite the use of domestic facilities during wartime without necessitating extensive bureaucratic consultations. The stimulus for this legislation derived both from the Taepo Dong test and from the March 1999 intrusion of several North Korean spy ships into Japanese territorial waters.[31] Some observers, however, believe that this legislation runs the risk of fracturing the ruling coalition, one of whose parties (Komeito) remains wary of Japan assuming a more active national defense policy. No matter what the outcome of these legislative deliberations, the days of Japanese strategic passivity are drawing to a close.

In the near to midterm, however, budgetary constraints may limit some of Tokyo's defense modernization plans. Japan's total defense expenditures and acquisition programs are determined according to Mid-Term Defense Programs, each of which runs for five years. Japan's extended recession long antedated the financial turmoil that swept much of Asia during 1997 and 1998, appreciably slowing the rate of annual budgetary increases registered during the 1980s. For example, during the FY 1981–FY 1985 plan, the average annual increase in defense expenditure was 4.4 percent; for the FY 1986–FY 1990 program the average increased to 5.4 percent. During the FY 1991–FY 1995 plan, however, the annual increases diminished to 2.1 percent, and the same rate is projected for the FY 1996–FY 2000 program. The even deeper slump at the end of the 1990s yielded (in

---

[30]"Crisis Laws Needed, Obuchi Tells SDF," *Japan Times,* July 15, 1999.

[31]Sayuri Daimon, "New Defense Role: Next Step Is to Free Up SDF," *Japan Times,* May 25, 1999.

FY 1999) a net *decrease* in defense expenditure of –0.2 percent.[32] In August 1999, however, rising tensions with North Korea led the JDA to submit a budgetary request for FY 2000 totaling 4.99 trillion yen (U.S. $45 billion), the first real increases in defense expenditure since 1997–1998.[33]

Economic uncertainties as well as unease in some political circles could impose additional limitations on procurement decisions proposed for the next Mid-Term Defense program, slated to begin in FY 2001. For example, the JDA's planned acquisition of midair refueling aircraft (for which it had hoped to earmark initial funds in FY 2000) may be deferred for both political and budgetary reasons.[34] Despite these near-term uncertainties and complications, the consensus favoring an augmented defense effort appears sufficiently robust to overcome these internal differences.

Japan's enhanced defense profile also extends to a growing range of military-to-military contacts with its Northeast Asian neighbors. For example, Japanese–South Korean military consultations, which proceeded only tentatively as recently as the 1980s, accelerated appreciably in the 1990s, especially in the aftermath of the North Korean nuclear crisis of 1993–1994. But the Taepo Dong test and the North's provocative maritime operations in Japanese waters helped prompt information exchange and emergency communication channels between Tokyo and Seoul as well as enhanced personnel exchanges. In August 1999, Japan and the ROK conducted exercises in the East China Sea, the first such joint training in the past half-century.[35]

The increasing bilateral and trilateral consultations among the leaders of Japan, the ROK, and the United States have lent added mo-

---

[32]"Japanese Budget in Brief—1998," Ministry of Finance, Government of Japan, available at http://www.mof.go.jp/english/budget/bib004.PDF, 1998; and "Major Budget Item—Defense," Ministry of Finance, Government of Japan, available at http://www.mof.go.jp/english/genan11/sy001n3.htm, 1998.

[33]Teruaki Ueno, "Japan, Fearing North Korea, Seeks Bigger Defense Budget," Reuters, August 31, 1999.

[34]"Appropriation Sought for Refueling Aircraft," *Yomiuri Shimbun,* July 22, 1999; and "Defense Agency to Delay Request for Airborne-Refuelling Aircraft," Kyodo, reprinted in *BBC Selected World Broadcasts—Far East,* FE/3604, August 4, 1999, p. E/1.

[35]Toshi Maeda, "Japan, South Korea Hold First Joint Naval Drill," *Japan Times,* August 5, 1999.

mentum to these developments and have diminished previous opposition to such exchanges on the part of Seoul.[36] At the same time, the Chinese have not criticized these consultations as long as they have remained limited to discussions about North Korea. As a leading defense specialist in Tokyo has observed:

> The Japanese have achieved a new level in their awareness that an event involving North Korea could directly involve Japan . . . . The recent shocks by North Korea have merely awakened the latent knowledge from its hibernation of fifty years . . . . Tracing back through history, we find that . . . nearly all the sparks of war threatening the independence and safety of Japan have involved the Korean Peninsula.[37]

So construed, the immediacy of North Korea's missile threat to Japan provided a focus to Japanese planning that has been absent since the demise of the Soviet Union. But Japan now has the capabilities and political will to assert its interests that it lacked during the Cold War.

Japan's efforts to achieve a "normal nation" status and defense profile extend to China and Russia, as well. Despite continued Chinese suspicions of Japanese defense collaboration with the United States and repeated warnings from Beijing that Japan must heed "the lessons of history," the two countries resumed military-to-military ties in September 1999 after a several-year hiatus.[38] The ties were then upgraded to the vice-ministerial level during a November visit to Beijing by JDA Vice Minister Seiji Ema.[39] Such steps, although modest and potentially subject to reversal, highlight Chinese incentives to explore (or at least not to preclude) a normal defense relationship with Japan. The Chinese, however, continue to combine such initiatives with harsh warnings about the implications of U.S.-

---

[36]Victor D. Cha, "What Drives Korea-Japan Security Relations?" *Korean Journal of Defense Analysis,* Winter 1999, pp. 69–87; and Howard W. French, "Seoul Drawing Closer to Tokyo as Anger Fades," *New York Times,* September 20, 1999.

[37]Hideshi Takesada, "Korea-Japan Defense Cooperation: Prospects and Issues," *Pac Net,* November 1999.

[38]Hisani Masake, "Japan, China Consider Upgrading Security Forum," September 14, 1999.

[39]"Chief of General Staff Meets Japanese Defense Official," Xinhua, November 23, 1999.

Japanese collaboration over missile defense, which Beijing characterizes as intended "to establish [U.S.-Japanese] military superiority over other nations . . . . With the development of military technology today, offensive and defensive systems are interchangeable . . . [and] will have an extremely big impact on maintaining the global strategic balance."[40] Should missile defense collaboration advance significantly, the Chinese might well opt to limit future defense interactions with Tokyo—but Beijing has yet to specify its fuller potential responses to such possibilities.

The advancement of Japan's military-to-military relations with Russia has been much more substantial and cumulative. Notwithstanding the still-extant abnormalities in bilateral relations (including the absence of a peace treaty more than 50 years after the Pacific War), both countries recognize shared incentives to enhance defense collaboration. Russian-Japanese security ties, formally initiated in March 1996, have proceeded vigorously ever since and have included increased consultations, security and confidence-building measures, ship visits and formal ministerial exchanges, and joint search-and-rescue exercises. Many of these activities are without precedent, including during Tsarist Russia.[41] When then–Russian Defense Minister Igor Rodionov visited Tokyo in May 1997, he stated that Russia no longer opposed the U.S.-Japan alliance or objected to pending modifications of the U.S.-Japan Security Guidelines. Although some Russian officials have since cautioned Japan about collaboration with the United States on TMD and others have expressed concerns that the revised Security Guidelines could also be used to infringe on Russian sovereignty, both Moscow and Tokyo see reasons to further advance their security collaboration.

From Japan's perspective, these ties confirm Russia's acceptance of the legitimacy of Japan's role as a major power and quietly impart to Beijing that Tokyo's relations with Moscow can serve as a tacit balance against Chinese predominance in Northeast Asia. The Japanese also see enhanced military relations with Russia as allowing for a

---

[40]"Commentary on U.S.-Japan Relations and the ABM Treaty," *Jiefangjun Bao (Liberation Army Daily)*, November 14, 1999, p. 5.

[41]Chitose Harada, *Russia and North East Asia,* London: International Institute for Strategic Studies, Adelphi Paper No. 310, July 1997, pp. 57–58.

fuller regional security role without all these activities being integrally tied to Tokyo's alliance with Washington. More broadly, these policy initiatives reflect Japan's wider international legitimacy and enhanced regional stature, diversifying Tokyo's policy options without placing its core relationship with the United States at risk.

Without question, security debate in Japan has advanced well beyond its prior conceptual and policy restraints. Although the potential fragility of the ruling political coalition remains a limiting factor, it has not inhibited the development of more innovative Japanese policies. The Japanese see both incentives and opportunities to diversify and deepen their political and security relationships across Northeast Asia while simultaneously enhancing technology programs and operational-policy linkages with the United States. These efforts portend the development over the next decade of a more active, indigenously derived security strategy. Current acquisition plans and development programs will also bear fruit in Japanese defense capabilities throughout the next decade. Thus, even though Japanese actions appear embedded in the prevailing framework of the bilateral alliance with the United States, the evidence of shifting directions is palpable. American policymakers as well as Japan's neighbors will increasingly deal with a leadership far more willing and able to chart its own course, with a far clearer concept of Japan's long-term national interests.

Evolution of the Korean Peninsula

Although U.S. security strategy in Northeast Asia entails elements of deterrence, defense, and reassurance, preparing for a second Korean war has long been the primary determinant of U.S. regional defense policy. Korea remains the final Cold War frontier, where the threat of large-scale armed conflict directly involving U.S. forces remains essentially undiminished from decades past. The North Korean conventional and WMD threat constitutes the principal rationale in planning for a major theater war (MTW) in East Asia; it also continues to underlie Department of Defense global military planning, as outlined in the Quadrennial Defense Review.[42]

---

[42]William S. Cohen, Secretary of Defense, *Report of the Quadrennial Defense Review,* Washington, D.C.: U.S. Department of Defense, May 1997.

North Korea's political, economic, and military prospects therefore assume central importance in Northeast Asian geopolitics and in U.S. regional defense planning. Should the regime in Pyongyang undergo significant internal change, the consequences for Northeast Asia as a whole and for U.S. regional strategy would be profound. Such internal change—long anticipated but never realized—now seems a more tangible possibility, although it is far from assured. For close to a decade after the end of the Cold War, and notwithstanding the loss of its long-term economic and political benefactors in Moscow and Beijing, North Korea grimly upheld its own version of dynastic politics and strategic autarky even as its dependence on the outside world for energy, food, and other forms of humanitarian aid increased vastly. Decades of ideological rigidity and self-imposed isolation had left the North ever more impoverished and ever more militarized. North Korea continues to operate according to political norms and expectations that apply to no other state. Its pretensions to serve as the sole legitimate embodiment of Korean nationalism—including continued propagation of ideologically driven formulas for unification—ring increasingly hollow: regime survival has superseded all other policy objectives.[43] These urgent needs have also led the North to rely on missile sales as a primary source of revenue, now augmented by growing economic, energy, and humanitarian assistance furnished by the international community.

Faced with such dire and pressing needs, the North has had to adjust its half-century of ideological and military hostility directed against the ROK, which Pyongyang had always treated as an illegitimate appendage of American power. Indeed, the North's claims to legitimacy rested on characterizations of South Korea as an American client state. This made genuine normalcy and stability on the peninsula all but impossible. Pyongyang's unwillingness to consider peaceful coexistence with the ROK or any moves toward military threat reduction ensured continued U.S. and ROK attention to deterrence and defense.

ROK President Kim Dae Jung's historic visit to North Korea in June 2000 and the anticipated reciprocal visit by North Korean leader Kim

---

[43]David Reese, *The Prospects for North Korea's Survival*, London: International Institute for Strategic Studies, Adelphi Paper No. 323, November 1998.

Jong Il to the South portend the first meaningful if far from definitive change in five decades of peninsular confrontation. Although Kim Jong Il continues to insist that North Korean military power will remain the fundamental underpinning of the regime's strength, he also sees an opportunity to secure substantial assistance from the South and other countries to help resuscitate the North's moribund economy. He additionally seeks to challenge the fundamentals of the U.S.-ROK alliance, insisting that the United States can no longer deem North Korea a military threat if Washington is seriously intent on improving relations with the North. The primary question is whether the South-North accommodation process will be matched by verifiable reductions in North Korea's military threat to its immediate neighbor and by the elimination of its missile threat to the region. There are grounds for ample skepticism on both counts—even as President Kim Dae Jung claims that Kim Jong Il supposedly asserted that he no longer objects to the presence of U.S. forces either before or after unification.

However, the accommodation between South and North—even one dominated by the open-ended provision of external assistance to the North and (perhaps) excessive exuberance on the part of the ROK— could well portend the largest changes on the peninsula since the Korean War. This does not make either a "soft landing" or a "hard landing" inevitable. With sufficient external assistance from all major powers as well as from the ROK, it is possible that North Korea might stave off extinction without having to undertake major internal reforms or without moving toward substantial threat reduction toward the ROK. On balance, however, the latter scenario does not seem indefinitely sustainable, although it is impossible to predict when and how large-scale internal change in the North might ultimately transpire.

Whether or not Korean unification occurs, national sovereignty concerns will undoubtedly constitute a pivotal factor in South Korean strategic calculations. In the event of unification, much would depend on how it occurred; ROK leadership attitudes toward the future of U.S. military deployments on the peninsula at the time of transition to unification would also play a pivotal role.[44] It is possible to imagine that all involved major powers might convene with a unified Korean government to discuss the peninsula's future, but any Korean leadership will insist that its sovereign rights be upheld by all of its neighbors. This would extend to the United States and the future role of U.S. forces on the peninsula even though the ROK's national interests would likely dictate the retention of close U.S.-ROK security ties.

Even in the absence of unification, there are potential strains between the United States and the ROK. Korean officials have long chafed at the asymmetric character of U.S.-ROK alliance relations and have repeatedly pushed for a shift in the U.S. position from a "leading" to a "supporting" role. Issues of command relations (in particular, matters pertaining to operational control [OPCON] of South Korean military forces) have proven extremely contentious for the military commanders of both countries, with American officials ultimately concurring in the ROK's assumption of peacetime OPCON for the Ground Component Command (GCC). The original C^2 arrangements were based on judgments concerning the high degree of Korean dependence on U.S. military capabilities. The United States also sought to ensure effective integration and coordination of U.S. and ROK forces. Although some of these considerations still influence U.S. and ROK combined defense planning, many have been alleviated over the years as Korean capabilities and responsibilities have grown. Over the longer run, it therefore seems inevitable and appropriate that the ROK ultimately assume more of a lead role in defense of its own territory.

The "Koreanization of Korean defense" thus remains integral to ROK national security thinking and will continue to shape longer-term Korean expectations of U.S. policy.[45] Such change could also prove pivotal in any effort to induce the North to negotiate threat reduction and arms control agreements directly with the ROK. North Korea still hopes to bypass the ROK through bilateral negotiations with the

---

[44]Robert Dujarric et al., *Korea: Security Pivot in Northeast Asia,* Indianapolis: Hudson Institute, 1998; and Jonathan D. Pollack and Chung Min Lee, *Preparing for Korean Unification: Scenarios and Implications,* Santa Monica: RAND, MR-1040-A, 1999.

[45]Hwang Byong Moo et al., "Fifty Years of National Security in South Korea," *KNDU Review—Journal of National Security Affairs,* Vol. 3, 1998, pp. 5–180.

United States on a peace treaty—a move to which the United States and ROK remain resolutely opposed. Meaningful, verifiable threat reduction in the absence of unification presupposes direct, equitable political relations between North and South. Thus, a less subordinate ROK position in its national defense strategy would better reflect realities on the ground and would facilitate the larger goals of U.S. strategy on the peninsula.[46]

Additional corollaries flow from Korea's stated desire to pursue an "independent" or "self-reliant" national defense posture.[47] These include expectations of enhanced access to an array of advanced defense technologies and weapon systems (not only U.S. technologies but European and Russian as well). Korea is also seeking to develop a larger indigenous defense industrial base, thereby reducing its dependence on foreign weapon suppliers.[48] A major consolidation and rationalization of the Korean aerospace industry is under way, that, it is hoped, will allow Korea a more cost-effective entry into civilian as well as military aviation markets, with primary emphasis at present on defense programs.[49] Korea also expects to continue to acquire leading-edge weapon systems beyond the capabilities of its own industry. For example, the Defense Ministry anticipates a mid-2001 decision on the purchase of the next generation of an advanced strike aircraft; the leading contenders are thought to be the F-15K and the Rafale. A program buy of 40 aircraft is expected to total $3.5 billion.[50]

Korean planners also hope to reduce the size of the standing army and to strengthen navy, air force, and intelligence capabilities to address "the strategic environment of the future."[51] Current plans, for example, project a decline in military manpower levels from 690,000

---

[46]William T. Pendley, *Restructuring U.S.-Korea Relations and the U.S. East Asia Strategy for the Twenty-First Century,* Honolulu: East-West Center, March 1999.

[47]*Defense White Paper, 1998,* Seoul: Ministry of National Defense, Republic of Korea, 1999, pp. 74–75 and 155.

[48]Op. cit., p. 248.

[49]Don Kirk, "Seoul Melds Rivals into a Contender," *International Herald Tribune,* June 12–13, 1999.

[50]"FX Program Ready to Soar," *Korea Newsreview,* June 12, 1999, p. 8.

[51]*Defense White Paper, 1998* (1999), pp. 170–172 and 239.

to between 400,000 and 500,000 in 2015, with ground force personnel reduced from 81.2 percent to 71 percent of the total force.[52] These goals are still kept somewhat in check by continued concerns about the North Korean threat, but they would accelerate should unification take place or if the current threat eroded significantly.

Force structure and modernization plans will also be influenced by the ROK's economic recovery from the acute financial downturn of 1997–1998. At first, many modernization priorities were placed on hold, and purchases of some "big ticket" items (e.g., AWACS aircraft) were deferred.[53] However, unusually rapid economic recovery during the latter months of 1998 and throughout 1999 renewed and extended many of these earlier modernization plans. In early 1999, a Ministry of National Defense (MND) official revealed that the ROK's next five-year defense plan anticipated a total expenditure of nearly $70 billion with annual increases of between 4 and 6 percent, presumably depending on economic conditions.[54] Accelerating economic growth by mid-1999 led the MND to lobby for far larger increases in the year 2000.[55]

Korea's modernization plans are highly ambitious. The five-year plan includes funding for new attack helicopters, Aegis destroyers, the next-generation fighter aircraft, AWACS aircraft (delayed from 2001 to 2004), and aerial refueling aircraft, also by 2004. Contractors from France, Russia, and the United States have been invited to bid on a major contract for Korea's next generation of surface-to-air missiles.[56] In addition, there are also plans (under the Agency for Defense Development) for indigenous development of the ROK's first reconnaissance satellite, scheduled for completion by 2005.

In the near to midterm, Korea is embarked on a transition strategy of selectively addressing potential military deficiencies in relation to the

---

[52]Yoo Yong Weon, "MND to Reduce Manpower," *Chosun Ilbo,* August 20, 1999.

[53]Paul Mann, "Asia's Recession Holds Korean Arms Hostage," *Aviation Week & Space Technology,* November 9, 1998, pp. 35–36.

[54]"South Korea to Spend $69.3 Billion in Five Year Defense Plan," Reuters, February 12, 1999.

[55]"12.1% Increase Sought for Nation's Arms Budget," *Korea Herald,* June 9, 1999.

[56]Lee Sung Yul, "U.S., Russia, France Compete for Seoul's Missile Program," *Korea Herald,* September 21, 1999.

North while building capabilities for the postunification era. Despite the declared intention to achieve overall equality in the military balance with North Korea by 2010, the rationale of equality with the North seems somewhat contrived. The ROK is aware that major dimensions of North Korean combat capabilities have continued to degrade. Moreover, many of the ROK's impending weapon purchases are dual capable (i.e., they are relevant to both preunification and postunification defense planning). ROK defense planners clearly posit the continued existence of the North Korean state, but they do not want to invest too much in a threat that could well diminish over time and that might disappear altogether.

Over the next decade, therefore, the peninsular focus of Korean national security policy will be increasingly supplanted by more of a regional orientation. The ROK will need to assess its longer-term security requirements in terms of the evolving framework of major-power relations in Northeast Asia and of Korea's opportunities and needs within this framework. This will place a premium on sustaining alliance ties with the United States, enhancing policy collaboration with Japan where feasible, and exploring the possibilities for closer relations with Russia and China. These considerations reflect the realities of Korea's size, geographic location, and economic and political interests.

But the ROK does not want simply to subordinate itself to the strategic designs of others. This is supported both at a leadership level and in terms of Korean public opinion.[57] The growth of Korean air and naval capabilities will be a natural corollary of this process. Viewing Korea in the regional power equation assumes diminished attention to a territorial defense function and ultimately a less decisive position for the ground forces. This will encompass the increasing growth and sophistication of the Korean air force and navy, although future air and maritime doctrine remains under continued review.[58]

---

[57]Norman D. Levin, *The Shape of Korea's Future: South Korean Attitudes Toward Unification and Long-Term Security Issues,* Santa Monica: RAND, MR-1092-CAPP, 1999.

[58]Moon Chung In and Chung Min Lee (eds.), *Air Power Dynamics and Korean Security,* Seoul: Yonsei University Press, 1999; and Jonathan D. Pollack et al., *Chinese and Japanese Naval Power and Korean Security,* Taejon, South Korea: ROK Navy Headquarters, 1999.

Optimizing Korea's future strategic opportunities will not rest on military power alone, but future possibilities cannot be realized without such power. This could pose some potentially contentious issues in U.S.-ROK alliance management as leaders in Seoul pursue political and strategic paths that the United States may deem detrimental to larger U.S. interests.

President Kim Dae Jung repeatedly insists that Korea intends to maintain close security ties with Washington following unification. This provides needed assurance to the United States that the ROK attaches priority importance to the U.S.-Korean alliance with or without a North Korean threat. But what kind of alliance might be envisioned in the future? This would depend not only on the preferences and interests of both countries but also on their respective visions of Northeast Asia over the longer term. All concede that the regional security structure would undergo major change, but this leaves unresolved its dominant characteristics and contours. It seems reasonable to infer that U.S. strategy assumes that the Korean peninsula will remain divided. Statements from the Korean leadership seem more contradictory, perhaps reflecting Seoul's unease in contemplating a "messy" unification process as well as its continued efforts to reassure Pyongyang that the ROK does not challenge the North's legitimacy as a state or threaten its existence.

In innumerable statements, the Korean leadership has emphasized that it is seeking to define a new regional peace structure or mechanism to supplant the arrangements of the Cold War. At one level, this is a natural outgrowth of U.S.-ROK efforts to move beyond the current situation of neither peace nor war. The Korean War ended with an armistice, not a peace agreement. The strategic divergence in this area remains fundamental: The United States, the ROK, and China all seek a formal agreement that would ratify the end of the Korean War, whereas North Korea seeks a bilateral peace agreement with Washington that would provide Pyongyang the separate security guarantees it seeks from the United States. Absent North Korea's willingness to definitively treat the ROK as an equal sovereign state and to sharply reduce its military threat to the South, it is difficult to see how these views can be reconciled.

But ROK statements also look to the longer term—i.e., to regional rather than the peninsular security—and in this regard, there is a revealing symmetry in Chinese and ROK policy pronouncements. Both countries emphasize their desire to move beyond the Cold War arrangements—i.e., to supplant a threat-based security structure in which U.S. bilateral alliances have predominated. Numerous observers deem such formulas largely cosmetic and intended principally for political effect, and hence not a realistic reflection of Korea's true national security interests. Many find it inconceivable that the ROK would even tacitly signal that it might revisit some of the prevailing assumptions underlying its security alliance with the United States. Indeed, some believe that ROK policy is designed principally to propitiate Beijing in an effort to enlist more active Chinese efforts to restrain North Korea. Seoul may also hope to engage China more fully in managing potential crises on the peninsula—for example, a major humanitarian crisis or serious instability in the North that threatened to spill outward.

However, major controversy was also aroused by the comments of Defense Minister Cho Sung Tae in August 1999, during the first visit of a senior South Korean defense official to China. In response to a question following a speech at the Chinese National Defense University, Cho purportedly stated that the future status of U.S. forces in Korea would be decided "in consultation with neighboring countries."[59] These remarks were immediately disowned by other ROK officials, who insisted that they did not reflect official government policy. The defense minister also expressed "regret [for] creating misunderstanding," insisting that he believed that neighboring countries (i.e., China) would be prepared to concur in the continued presence of U.S. forces on the peninsula following unification.[60] He also stated, however, that "the USFK [U.S. Forces Korea] is essential to the security of the Korean peninsula as long as North Korea's military threats exist," implying that in the absence of such a threat the U.S. presence would no longer be needed. Further compounding the confusion, however, he also insisted that continued U.S. deploy-

---

[59]"Defense Minister's Remarks Cause Controversy," *Chosun Ilbo* (Internet version), August 26, 1999.

[60]Yoo Yong Weon, "Defense Minister 'Regrets' Comments on U.S. Troops," *Chosun Ilbo,* August 28, 1999.

ments on the peninsula following unification remain "essential for the regional security of Northeast Asia."[61]

Regardless of the explanation of the minister's remarks, they do suggest that the United States and Korea do not have an agreed-upon strategic concept for the longer term. At the same time, this episode suggests that some in the ROK believe Seoul should more explicitly seek to conciliate Beijing on the future U.S. military presence on the peninsula. Although hardly giving China veto power over future ROK policy, such statements implicitly concede that the realities of unification will reshape Korea's security perceptions and expectations. This will make Korea increasingly mindful of Chinese security concerns, but unless addressed carefully by Seoul, such statements could be construed as strategic deference toward Beijing.

ROK planners also believe that the country must rectify perceived strategic asymmetries with the missile capabilities of neighboring states. Plans include fuller development of an indigenous missile (the Hyonmu) with a range of 300 km—i.e., one that approaches but does not exceed guidelines under the Missile Technology Control Regime (MTCR), to which the ROK is not yet a signatory. Korean officials assert that such a missile would provide essential equivalence with the North's extant SRBM capabilities and better serve ROK interests than participation in U.S. TMD programs.[62] Indeed, Koo Sang Hoi, a former senior official in the Agency for Defense Development, which oversees the missile project, has stated, "We must regain our missile sovereignty and push ahead for independent development."[63] Koo's argument seeks to revisit a 1979 U.S.-ROK MOU that limited the ROK to missile tests of less than 180 km. South Korean officials argue that a shorter-range system would be unable to retaliate against Pyongyang in the event of a North Korean missile attack, thereby leaving the South disadvantaged in relation to the North.

---

[61]"Defense Minister Regrets 'Diplomatic' Remarks on U.S. Forces Korea," Yonhap, August 29, 1999, in *BBC Selected World Broadcasts,* FE/3626, August 30, 1999, p. D/3.

[62]Don Kirk, "Seoul Seeks U.S. Backing for Missile Development," *International Herald Tribune,* July 2, 1999.

[63]Hoon Shim Jae with Shawn W. Crispin, "Different Drummer—South Korea Prefers a Homegrown Missile Program," *Far East Economic Review,* July 1, 1999, p. 26.

The United States, however, has voiced concern that a more capable South Korean missile could hugely complicate ongoing efforts to induce the North to cease development of its longer-range missiles. Other U.S. officials worry that the Hyonmu would possess an inherent capability to extend its range beyond MTCR guidelines (i.e., 300 km), creating the prospect of a dedicated ROK offensive military capability in the future. Indeed, quite apart from Seoul's expressed concerns about the North's missile capabilities, an enhanced indigenous program could ultimately produce a more capable missile that would be deployable following unification, with potential relevance to China and Japan. South Korean officials have strenuously denied U.S. press reports that the ROK has failed to disclose the full dimensions of its missile R&D program to the United States.[64] Continued U.S.-ROK negotiations are clearly intended to secure ROK compliance with MTCR guidelines in exchange for enhanced access to U.S. missile technology, and the United States now seems somewhat more prepared to accommodate to some of the ROK's expectations.

However, developments in the North will have a pivotal effect on regional strategy. Marginalization or elimination of the North Korean threat would be a reconfiguring development of lasting strategic consequence. So long as an antagonistic North Korean threat remains, planning for military contingencies with the North will still retain central importance in U.S. and ROK defense planning and would presumably limit Seoul's pursuit of a more autonomous defense posture. Thus, should North Korea prove capable of defying external importunings to forgo its missile programs, this outcome would help sustain the inherited security policy framework of the Cold War. An enhanced North Korean ballistic missile capability would also remove many of the constraints on fuller pursuit of missile defense programs elsewhere in Northeast Asia.[65] This would tend to draw the ROK into heightened collaboration with the United States and potentially with Japan, with diminished attention to initiatives toward Beijing. In the final analysis, leaders in Seoul would need to

---

[64]James Risen, "South Korea Seen Trying to Extend Range of Missiles," *New York Times,* November 14, 1999; and Son Key Young, "Seoul Denies Longer-Range Missile Bid," *Korea Times,* November 15, 1999.

[65]However, North Korean advances in this area could also spur the ROK's missile development efforts, thereby creating tensions between it and the United States.

decide how to balance the competing pulls in their regional strategies, presumably seeking to preserve as much flexibility as security
circumstances would allow.

The Future of Russia

The severe decline of Russian power over the past decade, including
economic and military capabilities, is quite possibly without precedent in the history of major states. The degradation of Russia's combat capabilities in East Asia has been especially marked. This decline
reflects systemic failures and the loss of a strategic logic for large-
scale military deployments throughout the Asia-Pacific region, including what had been a growing power projection capability.[66]

The conjunction of such an abrupt decline with the substantial ac-
cumulation of power by neighboring powers (especially China)
would seem to create an acute risk of regional political-military instability. Given the backwardness, underpopulation, and geographic
remoteness of the Russian Far East relative to the rest of the Russian
Federation, this possibility would seem even more worrisome. Thus
far, however, it has not materialized. Paradoxically, Russia's weakness has provided Moscow with more effective policy options toward
all regional actors,[67] which Russian foreign policy and defense planners have successfully sought to exploit.

Although Russian power may no longer be a dominant security factor
in Northeast Asia, the consequences of its involvement are measur-
ably affecting the calculations of other powers in the region. Even in
its diminished state, Russia has not been standing still in terms of
diplomacy and arms sales. Russian initiatives include (1) sustained
efforts to cultivate closer economic, political, and military ties with
China, including negotiated border agreements and bilateral and
multilateral confidence-building measures; (2) the resumption of
significant arms sales to China after a three-decade hiatus; (3) rene-
gotiation of treaty ties with North Korea and continued pursuit of

---

[66]Felix K. Chang, "The Unraveling of Russia's Far Eastern Power," *Orbis,* Vol. 43, No. 2,
Spring 1999, pp. 257–284.

[67]Gennady Chufrin (ed.), *Russia and Asia: The Emerging Security Agenda,* New York:
Oxford University Press, 1999.

economic, political, and military-to-military relations with the ROK; and (4) a quasi-normalization of relations with Japan despite the absence of a peace treaty and resolution of long-standing territorial disputes. Hence the paradox: Moscow may lack the military weight it possessed during the Cold War, but a nonconfrontational strategy toward its Asian neighbors has allowed for more meaningful Russian political influence throughout the region. Forgoing its previous imperial role has contributed to a much more fluid geopolitical picture in regional geopolitics. The United States, relieved of its earlier defense requirements in East Asia related to Russian military power, has played a minimal role in this realignment.

Over the longer run, Russia's regional position would seem likely to depend on achieving increased internal political stability and effecting a parallel economic and institutional recovery. Russia's new president, Vladimir Putin, envisions a longer-term rebuilding of Russian national power, including its military power. Despite some improvement in the Russian economy, the larger decline of the power of the Russian state has yet to be arrested. Absent demonstrable achievements in altering this overall picture, Russia will find itself increasingly disadvantaged in relation to China. At the same time, Russia would prove unable to achieve a political-economic breakthrough with Japan crucial to resource and energy development in Siberia and the Russian Far East—regions that have largely had to fend for themselves over the past decade. The inability of Russia and Japan to reach a territorial settlement during President Putin's September 2000 visit to Tokyo does not augur well in this regard, although both sides still seem intent on reaching such an agreement.

In a more pessimistic scenario, Russia's inability to halt the steady decline of its power in the Far East might leave the regional provinces weaker and even more vulnerable to encroachment. Russian policymakers, however, believe they can achieve meaningful understandings with neighboring states that will ensure the country's national security interests. These initiatives do not depend on close relations with the United States. If anything, the increasing divergence between Moscow and Washington further enhances Russian incentives to collaborate more actively with China.

Future Russian-Chinese relations represent an important factor in regional geopolitics as well as potentially entailing major consequences for American security interests. Despite earlier Russian expectations of a more comprehensive economic and energy relationship with the Chinese, military sales and defense industrial collaboration have become the dominant factors in bilateral ties. They attest to the increasing complementarity of Russian and Chinese strategic interests that both leaderships appear determined to enhance in future years. Neither side views these transactions as invalidating U.S. economic aid to Russia, U.S. assistance for Russian denuclearization, and U.S. trade and investment ties with China. There is, however, a clear convergence of bureaucratic and national interests between Russia and China that has given momentum and direction to the security component of bilateral relations.

Russian arms transfers to China began somewhat tentatively and fitfully in the early 1990s, but they have broadened in scale and scope in subsequent years.[68] Annual sales during the mid- to late 1990s have most likely ranged between $1 billion and $1.5 billion. Although these transactions have been subject to repeated rumors and endless speculation, the cumulative results of officially reported transactions are nonetheless revealing. They include sales of several different versions of military helicopters, Su-27 and Su-30 fighter aircraft, T-72 tanks, S-300 surface-to-air missiles, Il-76 transports (the platform that was to have been used in Israel's recently canceled AWACS project with the Chinese), Kilo-class submarines, and Sovremenny-class destroyers outfitted with Sunburn anti-ship cruise missiles.[69] There has also been a progressive shift from sales to technological and industrial collaboration (for example, licensed coproduction of 200 Su-27 aircraft, the prospect of a separate coproduction agreement for the Su-30, and the reputed involvement of significant numbers of Russian R&D personnel in Chinese weapon programs).

Russian weapon sales and military technology transfer reflect the endangered status of Russia's defense industries: Sales to China (and

---

[68]A. A. Sergounin and S. V. Subbotin, *Russian Arms Transfers to East Asia in the 1990s,* SIPRI Research Report No. 15, Oxford: Oxford University Press, 1999.

[69]Allen and McVadon (1999), p. 62.

also to India) are essential to continued employment of the workforce and to the industry's longer-term survival. On the Chinese side, given the shortcomings of its indigenous defense industrial base, the pace of its military modernization (especially in air and naval power) appears to depend heavily on Russia's willingness to transfer higher-end weapon systems to Beijing. As the results of this defense collaboration grow, they could ultimately extend to technology transfer in more sensitive defense programs.[70]

Defense planners in Beijing were initially uneasy about renewed dependence on a nation that had been both ally and adversary, and their counterparts in Moscow were equally discomfited by enhancing China's military capabilities as their own power declined. Russia also recognizes, however, that these agreements lock the Chinese into long-term collaborative relations. The Russians likely believe that they can control the flow and scope of these transactions, with Russian industry retaining control over specific technologies vital to the performance of various higher-end weapon systems. At the same time, the pace of deliveries in most areas still entails a highly protracted process, in part reflecting constraints on production rates in Russian facilities.

But the strategic context of Russian-Chinese collaboration warrants closer attention. Convergent interests in Central Asia (e.g., shared concerns about stability in vulnerable border areas) and the incentives of both states to diminish their long-standing rivalries in East Asia (thereby enabling each to concentrate on more pressing security priorities) ultimately altered their respective political and security calculations.[71] Leaders in Moscow have concluded that the enhancement of Chinese military power will not seriously endanger Russian national security interests. Although some Russian analysts continue to express longer-term anxieties about the consequences of the growth of Chinese power,[72] the operative consensus at present does not presume a serious Chinese national security threat.

---

[70]Yi Jan, "Prospects for Sino-Russian Military Cooperation," *Ching Pao*, No. 264, July 1, 1999, pp. 90–91.

[71]Mark Burles and Abram N. Shulsky, *Patterns in China's Use of Force: Evidence from History and Doctrinal Writings*, Santa Monica: RAND, MR-1160-AF, 2000.

[72]Dmitri Trenin, *Russia's China Problem*, Washington, D.C.: Carnegie Endowment for International Peace, May 1999.

Moscow's prevailing assumption is that China's defense moderniza-tion is directed at more pressing Chinese security concerns to the east—i.e., a primary focus on Taiwan, the longer-term military role of Japan, and the predominant power and position of the United States in the West Pacific.

Shared concerns about U.S. strategic domination and its longer-term consequences have lent momentum and direction to Sino-Russian bilateral relations. Russia's increasing strategic marginalization and its ever more intense preoccupation with instability in the Caucasus have produced a much more assertive nationalism in which the Russian armed forces are playing a pivotal role. The step-by-step cementing of the Sino-Russian accommodation has diminished the prospects of a multifront security problem for Moscow. The Chinese have signaled that they will collaborate with Moscow in Central Asia rather than contest Moscow's dominant position in border areas, where both fear the implications of unrest among ethnic minorities. In exchange, the Russians have tacitly conceded China a predomi-nant position in border areas in the Russian Far East where Moscow long sought to assert its claims.

Sino-Russian relations are also focusing more explicitly on shared security concerns and on the willingness of both states to support the other's asserted sovereign interests. The joint statement of the Rus-sian and Chinese presidents at the December 1999 "informal sum-mit" made these understandings more explicit, with both sides pledging "coordinated actions to oppose damage to [global strategic] stability," including shared pledges of support related to Taiwan and Chechnya.[73] The capacity for unilateral intervention by U.S. forces in Yugoslavia and of unchallenged U.S. air supremacy were worrisome portents for both leaderships, and these shared concerns have persisted in the aftermath of the NATO victory. Neither Beijing nor Moscow appears intent on creating a formal coalition to oppose U.S. global strategy, but both hope to utilize expanded ties as a constraint on U.S. actions directed against either state's vital interests. Thus, as permanent members of the U.N. Security Council, both see advan-tages in an informal political coalition that can stymie moves di-rected against the interests of either or both states.

---

[73]ITAR-TASS: Russian-Chinese Statement, FBIS-SOV-1999-1210, December 10, 1999.

Russia also continues to envision closer relations with other East
Asian neighbors as a means to diminish U.S. regional dominance and
to enhance its regional political and security role. As noted earlier,
these policies have led to a substantial improvement in Russian-
Japanese defense relations, even if a larger political breakthrough
with Tokyo continues to elude both leaderships. The larger issue for
the longer term is the extent to which regional states such as Japan
see realistic opportunities for more active collaboration on infras-
tructural and energy development with Russia given the scale of the
capital requirements. The choices in this regard vary among different regional states. As the immediate neighbor of Russia and the
Central Asian republics, China has inherent incentives to ensure stability in its inner Asian frontiers as well as to more vigorously pursue
joint development of energy resources.[74] Tokyo and Seoul seem
likely to remain more cautious, both because the economic returns
are more problematic and because the political and security risks are
greater. But neither wants to preclude more active collaboration
with Russia over the longer run, especially if Russia's internal situation should stabilize.

However, the growing strategic divergence between Russia and the
United States could have direct as well as indirect consequences for
Northeast Asia. If these differences portend a more unstable region
or imply the possibility of renewed polarization between continental
and maritime Asia, then Russia's longer-term policy opportunities in
East Asia could be significantly diminished. A more active and explicit coordination of Russian and Chinese policy positions, especially if combined with a more vigorous Sino-Russian defense collaboration designed to accelerate the PLA's modernization, could
make Tokyo and Seoul more wary of closer relations with both
Moscow and Beijing.

In the final analysis, domestic factors seem most likely to prove decisive to Russian regional policy and the determination of its strategic
interests. The "Russia factor" in Asian security derives principally
from Russian weakness rather than from Russian strength. But even
a much-diminished Russian state is still able to affect the Asian bal-

---

[74]Gaye Christoffersen, *China's Intentions for Russian and Central Asian Oil and Gas*,
Seattle: National Bureau of Asian Research, Vol. 9, No. 2, March 1998; and Burles
(1999).

ance of power in important ways, especially should the collaboration between Russia and China be further enhanced in the coming decade. In the near to midterm, the implications for U.S. defense planning may not prove especially significant inasmuch as neither China nor Russia appears prepared to directly contest U.S. regional predominance.

IMPLICATIONS FOR U.S. POLICY AND THE USAF

Northeast Asia remains in the midst of a major strategic transformation. Notwithstanding innumerable pledges of U.S. engagement and a continued commitment to regional stability, major uncertainties persist concerning the region's dominant political and strategic characteristics and America's place in it. Thus, the region's longer-term strategic alignments seem far from settled, and U.S. policymakers need to assess the likelihood and consequences of alternative futures that are not simply marginal adjustments to the status quo.

At present, no nation or coalition of states in Northeast Asia appears inclined or able to contest American predominance. Since the end of the Cold War, most have regarded the United States as a nonthreatening great power with unrivaled technological capabilities, military power, commercial prowess, and financial clout. (However, increased U.S. strategic dominance may be leading China and Russia to somewhat modify this largely benign assessment.) Given these overall circumstances, U.S. policymakers believe that the United States should continue to enjoy ample leverage within the region. Indeed, the United States is not alone in deeming the status quo (even a somewhat uneasy status quo) as preferable to any strategic alternative that seems discernible at present. The question, therefore, is how U.S. policymakers seek to advance American long-term interests while they possess such a strong hand.

Regional attitudes toward U.S. power are not immutable. For example, numerous states assume that the United States will remain the principal balancer of a more powerful China, but this is not necessarily the decisive factor influencing regional attitudes to collaborate with the United States. Some regional futures are potentially less hospitable to U.S. interests. Under some circumstances, for example, U.S. allies might seek to redefine the ground rules for the future U.S. regional military presence; a unified Korea might represent one such case. The United States must nonetheless retain the capability for alternative courses of action should future political or strategic developments put American interests at risk or should larger changes in the regional distribution of power necessitate major alterations in U.S. policy.

Over the longer run, there will also be an increased need for a more integrated regional strategic concept that is less geared to separate bilateral relationships. This concept would ideally address the full spectrum of policy concerns, including (1) the purposes of U.S. regional alliances; (2) deterrence and defense requirements in the next century; (3) the management of looming power transitions; and (4) influencing technology and weapon acquisition decisions throughout the region. Such an approach would be far more likely to elicit sustained support from America's regional allies while also clarifying U.S. expectations and goals in relation to China, Russia, and North Korea.

However, the nascent strategic transitions discussed in this chapter are unmistakably transforming the security environment in which the United States and the USAF will operate in the future. The ultimate effects will most likely result in a very different mix of U.S. forces, some of which may no longer be regionally deployed on a continuous basis. It was far easier for the United States to justify a major regional presence in a higher-threat environment or when the region as a whole was highly unstable.

At the present time, most efforts to devise a long-term strategy for the USAF are configured to a set of global requirements, reflecting the Air Force's designated roles, responsibilities, capabilities, and distinctive technological advantage. These seem predicated on the Air Force's retention of a full spectrum of capabilities in the service of a global engagement strategy.[75] All posit a dominant role for U.S. airpower in specific crises.

---

[75]John T. Correll, "On Course for Global Engagement," *Air Force Magazine,* January 1999, pp. 22–27; Elaine M. Grossman, "Air Force's 'Strategic Vision' to Include 'Global Vigilance,'" *Inside the Pentagon,* December 2, 1999; and John A. Tirpak, "Strategic Control," *Air Force Magazine,* February 1999, pp. 20–27.

In Northeast Asia, for example, Air Force global engagement strategies would be most relevant under the following conditions: (1) in a Korean contingency; (2) in an environment where internal vulnerabilities resulted in increased regionwide instability that local actors were unable to manage; (3) in a renewed high-threat environment—for example, should Chinese power pose a larger risk to U.S. security interests as well as threatening the interests of a core U.S. regional ally; or (4) in a much more starkly competitive regional security environment, with the United States assuming an arbiter role. Only the first of these conditions retains immediate relevance to current Air Force planning. The question, therefore, is the appropriate balance between current security requirements and what might be realistic and prudent to plan for over the longer term.

Although the potential threats to Northeast Asian security remain uncertain, some essential factors seem beyond dispute. First, the global threat posed by the Soviet Union has evaporated, and no remotely comparable Russian threat looms on the horizon. Second, the North Korean threat, although still tangible, could either diminish over time or shift toward more asymmetric capabilities that would potentially require a different mix of skills. Third, China has yet to challenge the United States directly or warrant mobilization of a regional coalition against it, although the latent possibilities of a serious U.S.-China crisis persist in relation to Taiwan and in a North Korean endgame scenario. Fourth, America's allies are building indigenous capabilities to better ensure their own interests.

Thus, in the absence of movement toward a regionwide security structure, national-level interests and strategies will increasingly dominate the security agendas of all principal actors. This does not make existing alliance arrangements irrelevant or unimportant, but regional actors are seeking to diversify their political-security options rather than depend exclusively on the United States or assume the forward deployment of U.S. military power in perpetuity. Basing arrangements may prove a particularly troublesome issue, posing the question of whether projecting U.S. power (as opposed to in-theater deployments) will prove more viable over the longer run. The United States therefore faces a threefold challenge with respect to the future role of airpower in Northeast Asia:

- It seeks to remain the security "partner of choice" for its regional allies on terms that are complementary, reciprocal, and mutually acceptable;

- It wants to ensure that the maturation of regional air capabilities does not degrade U.S. comparative advantage and that duplicative or redundant capabilities are avoided;

- It wants to retain sufficient capabilities (in theater or rapidly deployable to the region) to protect core U.S. security interests.

The larger challenge is how the United States seeks to shape and adapt to a much more militarily capable region. In essence, American policymakers confront five overall policy challenges:

- The United States wants its regional allies to "do more," but without triggering instability or strategic realignment;

- The United States also seeks to maintain alliance interoperability, base access, and (to the degree possible) commonality in strategic goals;

- The United States also hopes to ensure that the growth of Chinese military power does not transform the regional balance of power in unanticipated ways;

- The United States needs to retain sufficient capabilities for near-term crisis response while it assesses alternative deployment modes in the longer run; and

- The United States must also define new terms of reference if and when Korean unification takes place or if there is a major deterioration either in future U.S.-China relations or in future U.S.-Russian relations.

Although the momentum of East Asia's military modernization was somewhat slowed by Asia's financial upheaval, the basic trend favoring more sophisticated capabilities remains unchanged.[76] Indeed, in the aftermath of the Kosovo campaign, all regional powers recog-

---

[76]Frank Umbach, "Financial Crisis Slows but Fails to Halt East Asian Arms Race," *Jane's Intelligence Review,* August 1998, pp. 23–27 (Part One), and September 1998, pp. 34–37 (Part Two); and Tim Huxley and Susan Willett, *Arming East Asia,* London: International Institute for Strategic Studies, Adelphi Paper No. 329, July 1999.

nized the need to reassess the relevance of their military strategies. For example, the Kosovo campaign enhanced Chinese and Russian incentives for increased consultation and technology exchanges and will likely accelerate the pace of various collaborative programs.

The unification of Korea would be certain to generate a major reassessment of U.S. regional defense strategy and the forces deemed necessary to fulfill it. It is therefore only prudent for the Air Force to begin to assess its postunification requirements in Northeast Asia, in particular the potential challenge confronting "alliance interoperability" as regional capabilities and security identities mature.

Perhaps the ultimate irony in U.S. Northeast Asian strategy is its declared commitment to regional stability. Stability is defined as "the quality, state, or degree of being fixed and unchanging." This may pertain to U.S. regional *interests*, but it cannot apply to conditions, circumstances, and relationships within Northeast Asia or to U.S. policy goals in the region. These will have a dynamic all their own to which the United States must seek to adapt as well as to shape. The United States, including the USAF, must begin to assess alternative strategic futures in a region of enduring importance to U.S. global interests, but where current policies may prove far less relevant in future years.

THE CHANGING POLITICAL-MILITARY ENVIRONMENT: CHINA[1]

CHINA'S EMERGENCE AS A GREAT POWER

The preeminent geopolitical factor in Asia for the next several decades would appear to be the emergence of China as a great power. In most discussions of the region's future, this assertion is all but taken for granted, although some observers have dissented. Those who accept this assertion can point to the following realities and trends.

Economic Growth

First and most fundamentally, China has enjoyed rapid and sustained economic growth since 1978, when Deng Xiaoping initiated the current era of economic reform. Indeed, before the Asian economic crisis erupted in 1997, this growth was so rapid that some analysts, using optimistic but not unrealistic assumptions, predicted that China's GNP—evaluated in terms of purchasing-power parity—would surpass that of the United States by 2006.[2] Yet while China

---

[1]This appendix draws on Khalilzad et al. (1999) and on project contributions by Jonathan D. Pollack.

[2]See Charles Wolf, Jr., K. C. Yeh, Anil Bamezai, Donald P. Henry, and Michael Kennedy, *Long-Term Economic and Military Trends 1994–2015: The United States and Asia,* Santa Monica: RAND, MR-627-OSD, 1995, p. 9. Although more recent work by most of these authors reduces Chinese GNP estimates slightly, it does not contradict the earlier prediction that, under the "stable growth scenario," Chinese GNP will

has escaped the immediate brunt of the region's financial crisis, the Asian economic slump has exposed and highlighted some weaknesses in the Chinese economy as well as in the "Asian model" of economic development in general.

Despite large "pump-priming" efforts by the government over the past several years, the Chinese growth rate has been slowing down. According to some measures, prices have been falling as well, which suggests the existence of excess productive capacity. China also faces serious economic challenges not only with respect to its state-owned enterprises (SOEs), many of which have been losing money as they encounter increased competition from the private sector and from imports, but also with regard to its banking sector, which is burdened with the large nonperforming loans that are required to keep many of the SOEs afloat. Thus, the key question for the immediate future is whether the private sector can grow fast enough to absorb those workers who would inevitably be laid off in the course of restructuring China's SOEs and reforming its banks. This reform process is likely to be accelerated when China is admitted to the WTO, thereby bringing matters to a head more quickly.

China's economic prospects for the next decades thus depend largely on whether its leadership has the political will to back economic reforms that are in the short run likely to lead to the bankruptcy of some SOEs or, alternatively, whether China will opt instead for a Japanese-style policy of putting off hard decisions. In the first two decades of economic reform, the Chinese leadership exhibited a talent for "muddling through"—i.e., for implementing enough reform to keep the economy moving forward while for the most part avoiding major shocks to the political system. However, the urban inflation of the late 1980s, which was closely linked to the public dissatisfaction underlying the 1989 Tiananmen protests, offered one instance in which the leadership's ability to strike this balance was sorely tested and ultimately found lacking. Whether China's leadership will prove capable of juggling these competing economic and

---

surpass U.S. GNP (in terms of purchasing-power parity) by the end of the first decade of the 21st century. (The latter work does not contain new estimates of future U.S. GNP.) See Charles Wolf, Jr., Anil Bamezai, K. C. Yeh, and Benjamin Zycher, *Asian Economic Trends and Their Security Implications*, Santa Monica: RAND, MR-1143-OSD/A, 2000.

social/political requirements remains an open question. This analysis proceeds on the assumption that it will, but it must be recognized that China's economic prognosis may be less optimistic than it now appears.[3]

Technological Modernization

China's economic reform program of the past 20 years has included rapid if selective technological modernization. Nevertheless, China's level of technological sophistication is likely to prove a more significant obstacle to its achievement of great-power status than its overall economic development. Starting as it has from a very low level, China's technological progress—while relatively rapid in some areas—has a long way to go.

In eight of nine technologies deemed critical for military purposes,[4] Chinese production capabilities have been found to be significant yet limited. The exception is biotechnology, with respect to which China has good basic research but poor production capability.[5] Although China has access to "all but the most advanced dual-use technologies" and is able to assemble many high-tech products, it remains largely dependent on imported high-tech equipment. Nevertheless,

> [c]urrent capabilities . . . reflect a significant improvement over the past two decades. When China's economic reform program began in the late 1970s, Chinese industrial technology was universally obsolescent. Now, while China is hardly a high-tech powerhouse, some sectors are relatively modern.[6]

The key question for the future is the extent to which China will be able to develop a technological base sufficient to support advanced weapon production. Although China purchases some advanced

---

[3]The analysts cited above believe that even in a less optimistic "disrupted growth scenario," China's GDP will increase by about 50 percent between 1999 and 2015. See Wolf et al. (2000), pp. 34–39.

[4]The nine areas are microelectronics, computers, telecommunications equipment, manufacturing, nuclear power, biotechnology, chemicals, aviation, and space.

[5]Roger Cliff, *The Military Potential of China's Commercial Technology,* Santa Monica: RAND, MR-1292-AF, 2001. This section draws heavily on this work.

[6]See Cliff (2001).

weapon systems on the international market, primarily from Russia, Chinese leaders are unlikely to remain content to base their military power entirely on imported equipment. Indeed, on two occasions— in 1960 and 1989—China suffered an abrupt cutoff of foreign arms transfers from the Soviet Union and the West. Thus, putting aside questions of national prestige, China will not want to remain dependent on foreign suppliers in the future.

A RAND assessment of China's future technological capability insofar as it affects the country's military potential asserted that

> China's prospects for technological progress are moderate. . . . By many measures China's potential for technological progress looks comparable to that of South Korea or Taiwan in the 1970s. In terms such as absolute numbers of scientists and engineers or total spending on R&D, however, China already vastly surpasses smaller countries like South Korea or Taiwan. Thus, average technological levels in China in 2020 are likely to be comparable to those of South Korea or Taiwan today, but China's greater size suggests that the number of areas in which China possesses state-of-the-art capabilities will be larger than is currently true in those countries.[7]

It was thus concluded that

> [w]hile China can expect to make significant technological progress in coming years, it is impossible that China will catch up to, much less "leapfrog," the United States . . . for the foreseeable future. By many measures, China's prospects ... appear comparable to those of Taiwan or South Korea in the 1970s. . . . Thus, it seems likely that, by 2020, *average* technological levels in China will be roughly comparable to those in Taiwan and South Korea. There may be a difference, however, due to China's scale. . . . [South Korea and Taiwan] have become very competitive in particular technological niches. If China follows a similar development path, its huge size . . . means that the number of these niches will be far greater. Thus, while China will on average still be significantly behind the United States . . . technologically, its technological capabilities could be very competitive in a significant number of areas by 2020.[8]

---

[7]Ibid.

[8]Ibid. (italics added).

Depending on the strategic insight with which China chooses these niches and the competence with which the relevant R&D is conducted, China could build a technological base sufficient for the development of a military force that could pose some severe challenges to the United States. To be sure, such a military force would not be the equal of that of the United States and might not be designed to defeat U.S. forces in an all-out battle—but by exploiting various asymmetric strategies, it could be used to further Chinese political interests in Asia, even against some U.S. opposition.[9]

Military Modernization

Previous RAND research has dealt with Chinese military modernization in detail[10] and has concluded that by 2015 China could emerge as a *multidimensional, regional competitor* to the United States—i.e., as a military power that, while not a peer of the United States, could nonetheless assert itself in its immediate region so as to thwart U.S. political-military objectives. In particular, it has been asserted that China could credibly:

- exercise sea denial with respect to the seas contiguous to China;

- contest aerospace superiority in a sustained way in areas contiguous to China's borders;

- threaten U.S. operation locations in East Asia with a variety of long-range strike assets;

- challenge U.S. information dominance; and

- pose a strategic nuclear threat to the United States.[11]

Of course it is by no means a foregone conclusion that the Chinese military will reach this level of capability within the second decade of the 21st century. Aside from the caveats expressed in the preceding sections concerning China's economic and technological develop-

---

[9]For a discussion of how China might decide to fight U.S. military forces even while recognizing their overall military superiority to the forces available to China, see Burles and Shulsky (2000).

[10]See Khalilzad et al. (1999), Chapter Three.

[11]This list is taken from Khalilzad et al. (1999), pp. 59–60.

ment, China would probably have to significantly increase its defense spending, continue to trade quantity for quality, and ensure
that the PLA opens itself to doctrinal, operational, and tactical innovation in order to do so. Assuming that its economy continues to
grow, however, China would not find it difficult to increase defense
spending to a sufficient extent to meet this objective; indeed, merely
keeping defense spending constant as a percentage of GNP would in
all likelihood suffice. In recent years, real defense spending in China
has been growing faster than GDP, although it is unclear whether this
trend represents a policy shift or a confluence of other factors (e.g.,
the unexpectedly rapid drop in inflation and "compensation" to the
PLA for relinquishing its control of many business enterprises to
other governmental entities).[12]

Nationalism and Geopolitical Ambition

Finally, the argument for China's growing strategic importance also
rests on the country's strong sense of nationalism and geopolitical
ambition, which could bring it into conflict both with its neighbors
and with the United States. Although these variables are not the only
determinants of Chinese national security policy, they do tend to dis-

---

[12]Estimating the size of China's defense budget is a notoriously difficult and
contentious problem. Although the official budget figures certainly understate
spending, it is unclear what if any meaning should be attributed to the year-over-year
changes. Assuming for the moment that such comparisons are meaningful, we note
that the official defense budget (in nominal RMB) rose 12.5 percent, 11.9 percent, 12.7
percent, and 12.7 percent in 1997, 1998, 1999, and 2000. Given that inflation was low
or nonexistent in those years (the GDP deflator is calculated at 1.0 percent for 1997;
1998 and 1999 saw consumer price *decreases* of 0.8 percent and 1.3 percent, after
which deflation gave way to price stability in the first quarter of 2000), it is clear that
these increases surpass GDP growth (8.8 percent, 7.8 percent, and 7.2 percent for 1997,
1998 and 1999). These calculations are based on several sources. The official defense
budget for 1996 and 1997 was taken from *China Statistical Yearbook*, Beijing: China
Statistical Publishing House, 1998, p. 276. The official defense-budget increase for
1998 is taken from *The Military Balance 1998/99*, London: International Institute
for Strategic Studies, October 1998, p. 178. The official defense-budget increase for
1999 is from "Senior Officer Says Defense Budget Remains at 'Low Level,'"
FTS1999030800024, reprinted from Xinhua, March 8, 1999. The 2000 official defense-
budget increase is from "China Military Budget Up 12.7% for 2000" (2000). The real
GDP growth and deflator for 1997 are taken and calculated from *China Statistical
Yearbook* (1998), pp. 55 and 58. The real growth for 1998 and 1999 and the data on
consumer prices are taken from *Country Report: China and Mongolia,* London:
Economist Intelligence Unit, 1999, p. 6, and 2000, pp. 6 and 7.

tinguish China from other countries—most notably Japan—that are more content with the international status quo and that no longer harbor major ambitions beyond the enhancement of their security and prosperity within the current international order.[13]

Figuring prominently in this context is the fact that China claims possession of territories that it does not currently control—most notably Taiwan but also the South China Sea. In 1972, China agreed to shelve the Taiwan issue in the interests of forming a quasi-alliance with the United States against the Soviet Union. By the late 1980s, however, the ground had shifted. In 1972, the U.S. "acknowledgment" that Chinese on both sides of the Taiwan Strait agreed that there is only one China was for the most part accurate, at least with respect to the leaderships on both sides of the strait. This assertion became less accurate, however, as the leadership of Taiwan's ruling party, the Kuomintang (KMT), passed into the hands of native Taiwanese rather than mainlanders who had fled the Communist takeover in 1949—and it grew even less valid with the victory of the Democratic Progressive Party (DPP) in 2000. Thus, China faced the possibility that an indefinite delay in recovering Taiwan could lead to a consolidation of the island's de facto independence in ways that would make eventual unification difficult if not impossible.

China's response to this situation has been bifurcated. On the one hand, it has sought to entice Taiwan by offering seemingly favorable terms for reunification under the rubric of "one country, two systems".[14] On the other, it has been willing to engage in saber rattling efforts to warn Taiwan against seeking an enhanced international standing.

As cited in Chapter Two, China has similarly been willing to use military force to assert its claims in the South China Sea.[15] Until 1995, many believed that China would use force only against Vietnam, as it

---

[13]For a thorough discussion of the determinants of Chinese national security behavior, see Khalilzad et al. (1999), Chapter Two, on which this section draws heavily.

[14]This formula was initially proposed by Deng Xiaoping in the late 1970s, when the PRC may have believed that the U.S. derecognition of the Republic of China offered a favorable opportunity for reunification.

[15]The South China Sea issue is discussed in greater detail in the last section of this appendix.

had done in 1974 and 1988. In February 1995, however, China stationed armed vessels at—and built permanent structures on— Mischief Reef, an islet claimed by and relatively close to the Philippines. Yet, in general, China has attempted to defer questions of sovereignty with respect to the South China Sea while promoting the idea of bilateral "joint development" of the region's resources. Such a stance is intended to preserve China's claims while deferring any decisive confrontation, presumably until such time as China is in a better position to vindicate its claims against its rivals.

Despite this relative moderation in terms of policy (at least compared to the past nationalism of other rising powers, such as Germany from the 1860s to World War II), some observers have noted a rising tide of nationalist sentiment among Chinese officials, particularly in the PLA, as well as among some segments of the public.[16] This has no doubt been fueled by China's economic dynamism and by its successful reincorporation of Hong Kong. The sense that China has finally found the right formula for modernization and that it is not condemned to weakness, backwardness, and national humiliation has in all likelihood fed the idea that China can indeed become a great power.

More broadly, China regards the current system—in which the United States, as the only "superpower," often acts in a "hegemonic" manner—as inherently unsatisfactory. At the beginning of the 1990s, many Chinese observers predicted that the predominance of the United States would erode, allowing for the emergence of a multipolar international system. To some extent, this claim was based on the notion that Japan and Germany were outperforming the United States economically, in part because the United States was "overextended" by virtue of its higher defense burden and global security commitments. However, this view of the fragility of the U.S.

---

[16]In a review of a Chinese book that claimed that China would "become the leading power in the world by the third decade of the next century," John W. Garver notes that "[t]his book is representative of recent nationalist tracts designed to fan and profit from patriotic ardour in contemporary China" and that "[t]here is a profitable market in China today for books that contain forceful and proud patriotic rhetoric—they are popular with the reading public." Garver then expresses his "hunch" that the book "does reflect the thinking of at least some Chinese officials." Interestingly, the book was banned shortly after it appeared. See John W. Garver, "China as Number One," *China Journal*, No. 39, January 1998, pp. 61–66.

position was subsequently belied by world events, and Chinese analysts have thus come to view the shift to multipolarity as a longer-term proposition.

In the long run, Chinese policy retains the ostensible objective of replacing of the current "unipolar" system with a multipolar one in which China will be one of several relatively equal great powers. Thus, in 1996–1997, when Sino-U.S. relations grew strained, the Chinese successfully incorporated statements favoring "multipolarity" into the communiqués of President Jiang Zemin's summit meetings with President Boris Yeltsin of Russia and Jacques Chirac of France.[17] More generally, China appeared to be strengthening its contacts with Western European nations in order to broaden its options for economic and technological development.

There is substantial debate about the significance of such high-level strategic assessments to China's national security policy in the post–Cold War period.[18] Nevertheless, the very existence of such assessments highlights Chinese reservations about the current international system as well as China's desire to be able to do something about that system.

Does China Matter?

In late 1999 the noted scholar Gerald Segal argued that China's geopolitical significance has been greatly exaggerated. Segal maintained that

> until China is cut down to size in Western imaginations and treated more like a Brazil or an India, the West stands little chance of sustaining a coherent and long-term policy toward it.[19]

---

[17]"Joint Statement by the People's Republic of China and the Russian Federation on the Multipolarization of the World and the Establishment of a New International Order," *Beijing Review*, May 12–18, 1997, and *"Text" of Beijing-Paris Declaration*, FBIS-CHI-97-095, reprinted from Xinhua, May 16, 1997.

[18]The question of importance of multipolarity for Chinese national security policy is discussed in Khalilzad et al. (1999), pp. 10–11.

[19]Gerald Segal, "Does China Matter?" *Foreign Affairs*, Vol. 78, No. 5, September/October 1999, p. 36.

According to Segal, the importance many attribute to China is due not to the underlying realities but to China's ability to disguise them:

> China is a second-rank middle power that has mastered the art of diplomatic theater: it has us willingly suspending our disbelief in its strength.[20]

This critique challenges the more commonly accepted view of China's importance along three different dimensions: economic, military, and political.

Economic Significance. China's economic importance may be questioned in light of the recent slowdown in its growth rate and in view of the Asian growth model's typical drawbacks, which China too is experiencing. These include poor allocation of capital, excessive debt, overcapacity, and political interference in decisions more properly left to the market ("crony capitalism"). In particular, China may be facing a massive crisis in its banking system as it tries to clean up bank balance sheets by transferring bad loans to newly created entities similar to the Resolution Trust Corporation (RTC) created in the United States to handle the savings-and-loan problem.

Although China is still a relatively minor participant in world trade,[21] the important question is whether this will remain so in the future. There is no doubt, as Segal claims, that China faces major economic challenges, but it is also true that during the two decades of the economic reform period, China's leadership has proven itself quite adept at innovating and maneuvering so as to preserve the economy's forward momentum. Hence, it is likely that China will continue to become a more important factor in the world economy. In addition, continued growth would provide the basis for a more powerful military force. Thus, while economic failure could derail China's emergence as a great power, it seems prudent to assume that China will continue its upward trajectory, albeit at a slower pace.

---

[20]Op. cit., p. 24.

[21]For example, China was the 9th-largest merchandise exporter in 1998 (representing 3.4 percent of total global exports) and the 11th-largest importer (2.5 percent). With respect to trade in commercial services, China's ranks and percentages were 15th/1.8 percent (for exports) and 11th/2.2 percent (for imports). World Trade Organization press release, April 16, 1999, available at http://www.wto.org/intltrad/ internal.htm.

Military Strength. Militarily, Segal similarly notes that

> China is a second-rate military power—not first-rate, because it is
> far from capable of taking on America, but not as third-rate as most
> of its Asian neighbors.[22]

Such a "static" comparison does not, however, get to the heart of the
matter, which is whether China could use its admittedly inferior military power to achieve a significant geopolitical objective even in the
face of U.S. opposition. On the most important potential conflict,
Segal—using the Kosovo conflict of 1999 as a guide—thinks not:

> If the Taiwanese have as much will to resist as did the Serbs, China
> will not be able to easily cow Taiwan.[23]

Although China would in this scenario have less advanced weapons
to bring to bear than did the United States and NATO, this comparison is inapposite. In fact, many of the more sophisticated aspects of
U.S. systems were employed precisely to increase the accuracy of
bombing attacks—i.e., to limit collateral damage to civilian targets.
An attack that used less sophisticated weaponry and that was less
constrained by political factors could thus do much more civilian
damage and thereby have a greater political effect on the target's will
to resist. In addition, Taiwan, as an island, could perhaps be sub-
jected to a more effective economic blockade than was Serbia given
that the latter could engage in widespread smuggling across its land
borders with less hostile neighbors. Thus, despite its "second-rate"
character, the Chinese military is and will likely continue to be a
major geopolitical factor.

Political Factors. Politically, Segal correctly notes that China no
longer exerts the attraction that it did when it could put forward
Maoism as an ideological model. It is also true that China's emphasis on sovereignty and on maintaining its freedom of action implies
that for a large country it is relatively bereft of allies or friends. Nevertheless, China is by no means isolated; indeed, one could argue
that it has never been *less* isolated. In recent years, for example, it

---

[22]Segal (1999), p. 29.
[23]Ibid.

has improved its relations with Russia; formed a close relationship with the three bordering Central Asia states (Kazakhstan, Kyrgyzstan, and Tajikistan); reinvigorated its ties to North Korea; and increased its influence in Burma.

More generally, China has championed the cause of multipolarity as an antidote to what it sees as excessive U.S. influence in the international system. However seriously this is intended to be taken, it provides China with a possible way to bid for international influence and allies. Realist international theory suggests that a possible if not probable outcome of the current "unipolar" situation would lie in the development of an anti-U.S. coalition.[24] If this is the case, China is one of the most likely candidates to lead such a coalition.

TRENDS IN CHINESE POLICY

Beijing's strategic deliberations and military modernization goals reflect continued internal debate about current and future strategy toward the United States. Although there appears to be a working consensus underlying current Chinese policy, the priority of defense modernization relative to other policy goals remains a potentially contentious issue for the longer term. Estimates of current and future U.S. defense capabilities are at the core of this internal debate. Having anticipated diminishing American power and influence relative to other major powers, the Chinese now confront increasingly robust U.S. capabilities and a growing trend toward U.S. unilateralism, which some deem a potential direct threat to vital Chinese interests.[25]

Thus, American strategic dominance remains an inescapable fact of life for Chinese defense planners, with American military power

---

[24]In the words of Christopher Layne, using "neorealist theory to analyze the implications of unipolarity": "States balance against hegemons, even those like the United States that seek to maintain their preeminence by employing strategies based more on benevolence than coercion." See Christopher Layne, "The Unipolar Illusion: Why New Great Powers Will Rise," *International Security*, Vol. 17, No. 4, Spring 1993, p. 7.

[25]David M. Finkelstein and John Unangst, *Engaging DoD: Chinese Perspectives on Military Relations with the United States,* Alexandria, VA: CNA Corporation, CRM-99-0046.90, October 1999.

continuing to advance the frontiers of military innovation. For the Chinese, the operative question is whether and how to diminish this singular U.S. advantage. Some military planners believe that this requires a more credible Chinese ability to counter U.S. power projection capabilities. A Taiwan scenario represents the preeminent Chinese concern, although it seems unlikely that a credible denial capability will be realized at any time soon. Some strategic observers argue that China could rely on exploiting contradictions and rivalries between the United States and its major allies in order to inhibit U.S. political-military response options in a future international crisis.[26] Most seem convinced, however, that China must ultimately be able to raise the perceived costs and risks to U.S. forces deployed close to Chinese territory. Enhancing such capabilities seems likely to remain among the primary factors shaping China's military modernization strategy in the coming decade. Few see options for a "quick fix" to the country's potential military vulnerabilities.[27]

Some Chinese observers believe that the U.S. regional presence (especially under conditions of an augmented U.S.-Japan alliance) infringes on China's "strategic space." The primary objection to the future U.S. security role may be less to the forward deployment of U.S. power per se and more (given Washington's open encouragement of an enhanced Japanese security role) to the possibility that China could be faced in the future with a regional security system that would sharply limit if not exclude Chinese influence. Some Chinese strategists, for example, characterize a transformed U.S.-Japan relationship as a bilateral version of NATO enlargement; they see the logic of the alliance as moving well beyond the confines of a bilateral relationship focused on the defense of Japan.[28]

---

[26]Sa Benwang, "The Impact of the Kosovo War on International Situations," *International Strategic Studies*, No. 4, Serial No. 54, October 1999, pp. 1–9.

[27]Mark A. Stokes, *China's Strategic Modernization: Implications for the United States*, Carlisle Barracks, PA: Strategic Studies Institute, U.S. Army War College, September 1999.

[28]Yang Bojiang, "Why [the] U.S.-Japan Declaration on [the] Security Alliance?" *Contemporary International Relations*, Vol. 6, No. 5, May 1996, pp. 1–12; and Yang Bojiang, "Closer Alliance with Washington: Tokyo's Strategic Springboard for the New Century," *Contemporary International Relations*, Vol. 9, No. 6, June 1999, pp. 9–19.

Given the regional implications of the enhanced U.S.-Japan alliance, officials in Beijing are seeking common cause with other Asian states wary of a greatly strengthened Japanese security role. The Chinese also likely view enhanced political and economic relations with neighboring states as a cost-effective means to mitigate some of the potential strategic consequences of an expanded U.S.-Japan alliance framework.

On the other hand, a U.S.-led security coalition also helps maintain Japan's nonnuclear status by undercutting the arguments of those Japanese who distrust the durability of the alliance with the United States. This poses a dilemma for Chinese security planners. China's repeated advocacy of multipolarity is intended to promote the dilution of U.S. predominance. As discussed in Chapter Two, however, the logic of multipolarity would encourage a major power like Japan to assert its policy independence and would imply that both Japan and India could emerge as autonomous great powers in Asia. China's longer-term view of the U.S.-Japan alliance may depend on whether such collaboration is seen as maintaining Japanese subordination to the United States or as facilitating the growth of an independent Japanese military capability. In this context, the key question would be whether the United States was constraining Japanese political-military capabilities or providing Japan with military protection and political cover to augment its indigenous strength and assert its own interests.

An alternative approach to China's national strategy emphasizes China's longer-term economic potential and advancement. This view retains few illusions about China's ability to compete credibly with American military power, and its proponents see little reason to attempt it. A more effective long-term strategy would enmesh China (especially the dynamic coastal regions) financially, commercially, and technologically both with the United States and with Beijing's East Asian neighbors. As a consequence, coercive options would presumably lose much of their potential relevance both for China and for its potential rivals in Northeast Asia.

This alternative strategy, although muted at times of heightened nationalism and increased suspicions about U.S. strategic intentions toward China, may yet emerge as a more credible policy option in Beijing. Despite China's distinct displeasure with U.S. interventions abroad (most recently in Kosovo), most Chinese strategists believe it is neither feasible to rapidly accelerate military modernization nor necessary to mobilize a political coalition to oppose the exercise of American power.[29]

The Chinese remain sobered and perhaps somewhat frustrated by American global dominance and by the prospect of increased U.S. unilateralism. Absent a direct U.S. threat to core Chinese strategic interests, however, few see major gains in an overt challenge to American power. This calculation might change at some point in the future, but it is likely to do so only when China believes it possesses the economic and technological wherewithal to contest American regional strategic predominance—and only if U.S. actions are deemed a direct threat to China's vital national security interests. Thus, even a more fully developed China would not automatically re-sult in a heightened challenge to the United States; it could depend as much or more on perceived challenges posed by U.S. military power to Chinese vital interests.

U.S. involvement in a major crisis in the Taiwan Strait undoubtedly ranks uppermost among Chinese strategic anxieties. Despite the rapid growth of economic ties and people-to-people relations be-tween China and Taiwan, Beijing has been unable to forestall the is-land's democratization and its increased political identity apart from the mainland.[30] In the aftermath of China's March 1996 ballistic missile tests near Taiwan's major ports, the United States enhanced military relations with Taiwan to include increased arms sales and more regular exchanges with Taiwanese defense officials. These military ties could also lead to heightened collaboration on missile defense (for example, provision of early warning radars) that could under some circumstances renew more direct U.S. defense linkages with Taiwan. The Chinese, however, repeatedly insist that any overt

---

[29]Chu Shulong and Wang Zaibang, "Thoughts on [the] International Situation and China's Response," *Contemporary International Relations,* Vol. 9, No. 9, September 1999, pp. 1–13; and Yan Xuetong, "The International Environment and Our Foreign Policy," *Contemporary International Relations,* Vol. 9, No. 9, September 1999, pp. 14–24.

[30]Bernice Lee, *The Security Implications of the New Taiwan,* London: International Institute for Strategic Studies, Adelphi Paper No. 331, October 1999; and Yu-shan Wu, "Taiwanese Elections and Cross-Strait Relations," *Asian Survey,* Vol. 39, No. 4, July/August 1999, pp. 565–587.

declaration of independence by Taiwan would automatically trigger Chinese military actions. Beijing is not specific about its strategic, operational, or tactical objectives should it use force against Taiwan, but major SRBM attacks would likely be a primary component of any military campaign directed against the island.

The Chinese also recognize, however, that the United States is almost certain to respond to an unprovoked attack on Taiwan, thereby fulfilling U.S. security obligations to the island under the Taiwan Relations Act. American deployment of two carrier battle groups east of Taiwan during China's live-fire exercises and missile tests imparted to Beijing the risks of undertaking major military actions. The Chinese also recognize that a major attack against Taiwan would likely lead to renewed repolarization in East Asia and to a huge setback in China's plans for economic development. Thus, China's "lessons learned" from the 1996 crisis appear to inhibit outright Chinese coercion against the island in the near term while spurring accelerated Chinese efforts to secure the capacity to preempt or preclude U.S. involvement in a Taiwan contingency over the longer run.

Beijing therefore continues to pursue a multipronged strategy toward Taiwan, combining elements of political pressure with heightened military preparations to warn Taipei about the possible consequences of overt moves toward independence. As one Chinese military analyst has concluded, "[T]he strategy we should pursue is one of sustained high-intensity deterrence or pressure combined with political or diplomatic efforts . . . . [W]e are going to have to endeavor to keep . . . deterrence believable while doing all possible to draw our bows without shooting and keeping the pressure on without fighting, to keep the danger and huge cost of large scale military conflict between mainland China and Taiwan and between China and the United States within limits that we can commonly stand."[31] The Chinese thus recognize that they cannot exclude significant U.S. reactions to any use of force against Taiwan, underscoring the latent possibilities of an even larger and far riskier U.S.-China crisis. While not a guarantee of Chinese restraint, it induces a large element of sobriety into Chinese military strategy toward Taiwan.

---

[31]Shi Yinhong, "Difficulties and Options: Thoughts on the Taiwan Matter," *Zhanlue Yu Guanli (Strategy and Management)*, October 1, 1999, pp. 1–4.

POLITICAL-MILITARY IMPLICATIONS FOR THE UNITED STATES[32]

Assuming that China does prove increasingly pivotal to the long-term balance of power in Asia, it is crucial to assess the various political-military challenges the country could pose to the United States. The discussion in this section proceeds from the most concrete to the most speculative; its purpose is not to predict future Chinese behavior but to facilitate consideration of the implications of China's emergence as a great power for the U.S. armed forces in general and the USAF in particular.

Vindicating Claims to Territory or Territorial Waters

Like any other state, the People's Republic of China can be expected to use force to maintain its territorial integrity. Unlike most contemporary states, however, the PRC claims as rightfully belonging to it territories that it does not physically control. Of these territories, the most important by far is Taiwan.

Taiwan. As discussed previously, China explicitly reserves the right to use force to vindicate its claim to Taiwan. This could come either in response to some action by Taiwan or others that threatens to make eventual reunification less likely or even impossible (such as a Taiwanese declaration of independence) or at China's own initiative should it decide that the underlying political, social, and economic trends are unfavorable to peaceful reunification and are unlikely to be reversed.

Whatever China's political motivation, Chinese military action could entail a wide variety of more immediate objectives. In order of increasing seriousness, Chinese military operations could encompass:

- saber rattling for political effect;
- harassment designed to cause minor cost or inconvenience for political effect (e.g., interfering with shipping or air routes or causing detours or delays);

---

[32]This section draws heavily on Khalilzad et al. (1999), pp. 27–36.

- occupation of one of the offshore islands, Jinmen (Quemoy) or Mazu (Matsu), or some other island under Taiwanese control;[33]

- serious interference with shipping or air routes in efforts to cause serious economic loss and/or financial panic;

- blockade and/or missile bombardment designed to induce Taiwan's surrender; and

- direct assault and occupation of Taiwan.

The occupation of Taiwan would seem to lie beyond China's current military capabilities even if the United States were not to become involved.[34] However, some of the other operations cited above would seem to be well within the realm of possibility, although their utility would depend heavily on political factors—specifically on Taiwanese domestic political unity and strength of will—as well as on the nature and extent of any support Taiwan received from the international community in general and the United States in particular.

South China Sea and the Spratly Islands. China claims (as do Taiwan and Vietnam) all the islands, reefs, and rocks in the Spratly Islands that lie above sea level. Malaysia, the Philippines, and Brunei also have overlapping claims on many of these islands. In addition, China claims (as does Taiwan) almost the entire South China Sea, including areas that other nations consider parts of their continental shelves. The area is important for several reasons. For one, it is thought to contain significant oil and natural gas deposits, although estimates of the size of these deposits have varied widely;[35] some Chinese authors also emphasize its potential importance as a fishing area. In addition, crucial sea routes between the Middle East and

---

[33]For example, although Taiwan occupies Itu Aba (Taiping) Island in the South China Sea, it is not clear whether the PRC would have any interest in taking that island. Politically, removing this symbol of Taiwan's "Chineseness" would seem unwise. On the other hand, Itu Aba is the largest island in the Spratlys, and the ROC has soldiers stationed there; hence, the PRC might be motivated to take it by virtue of its potential usefulness as a military base. See Mark J. Valencia, *China and the South China Sea Disputes*, Oxford: Oxford University Press for the International Institute for Strategic Studies, Adelphi Paper No. 298, 1995, pp. 6 and 39.

[34]Shlapak et al. (2000).

[35]Valencia (1995), p. 10, gives a range of 1 to 17.7 billion tons (approximately 7 to 125 billion barrels).

East Asia pass through the area; hence, any interference with freedom of navigation would have important economic repercussions.

Each of the claimants in this area except Brunei has taken some action (e.g., occupying an island) to assert its claims. In addition, various clashes have occurred over the years, most notably in 1974, when the Chinese evicted South Vietnamese forces from some of the Paracel Islands, and in 1988, when the Chinese drove Vietnamese troops away from Johnson Reef in the Spratlys. In 1995, the Chinese established some permanent structures on Mischief Reef, which is also claimed by the Philippines. In the future, China may again use force to vindicate its claim to the South China Sea and its islands.

Other Territorial Claims. China claims (as does Taiwan) eight uninhabited islands (known in Chinese as Diaoyu and in Japanese as Senkaku) located about 100 miles north of Taiwan that are currently controlled by Japan. The area may contain some oil, and the islands' location could also be strategically significant as part of the "first island chain" that separates China from the open areas of the Pacific Ocean.[36]

Over the years, a number of minor incidents have taken place in which activist groups of the claimant countries have taken action to assert their countries' claims. China has acted in a restrained manner in the course of these incidents. Were China to deem it advantageous to raise tensions with Japan, however, it might well use force with respect to these islands.[37] While the United States does not take a position with respect to these claims,[38] it could not ignore any Chinese attempt to exert military pressure against its Japanese ally.

---

[36]Robert G. Sutter, *East Asia: Disputed Islands and Offshore Claims—Issues for U.S. Policy*, Washington, D.C.: CRS Report for Congress 92-614S, July 28, 1992, p. 7.

[37]The Japanese 2000 Defense White Paper notes that "in recent years, Chinese research vessels have been operating in water zones including Japan's territorial waters." See "Summary of 2000 Defense White Paper," *Sanbei Shimbun*, July 28, 2000, p. 2, reprinted as *Paper Carries Gist of Japan's FY2000 Defense White Paper*, FBIS-CHI-2000-0802.

[38]The United States controlled these islands after World War II but returned them to de facto Japanese control at the time of the reversion of Okinawa (1971). In a press conference on April 9, 1999, U.S. Ambassador to Japan Thomas Foley stated that the United States does not take a position in the territorial dispute concerning the islands but that the islands are "part of Japanese-administered territory." He ducked a

China does not formally recognize the McMahon Line separating northeastern India from Tibet, claiming that the Tibetan officials who agreed to that line in 1914 were not authorized to do so. Instead, Chinese maps show the boundary along the foot of the hills some 50 miles to the south, thereby claiming some 35,000 square miles of territory currently ruled by India as part of the Northeast Frontier Agency (NEFA). In September 1993, China and India agreed to "maintain peace and tranquillity" along the existing line of control.[39] However, they still disagree in principle about the status of the McMahon Line.

On December 30, 1999, China and Vietnam signed a treaty on their land border, bringing to an end a dispute that had figured prominently in China's justification of its invasion of Vietnam in 1979.[40] However, disagreement over the maritime boundary in the Gulf of Tonkin and the South China Sea remains unresolved.

To Deal with a Separatist Threat

China faces a series of threats to its territorial integrity from separatist movements in its non-Han-dominated areas, particularly Tibet, Xinjiang, and Inner Mongolia. For geopolitical or ethnic/religious reasons, support for these separatist movements could come from the regions' neighbors—i.e., India, the Central Asian states (primarily Kazakhstan and Kyrgyzstan), and Mongolia.

In the past, China has accused India of supporting Tibetan resistance to Chinese rule (for example, by providing sanctuary for the Dalai Lama following the 1959 revolt). There has also been serious Uighur opposition in Xinjiang that in recent years resulted in a series of violent actions. China has obtained pledges of "good behavior" on the part of the neighboring Central Asian states, which have valued cooperation with China above ethnic or religious solidarity with the

---

question concerning the applicability of the U.S.-Japan Security Treaty by saying that "[w]e do not believe . . . that these islands will be the subject of any military conflict."

[39]Malik (1995).

[40]"La Kha Phieu Meets with Tang Jiaxuan," Xinhua, December 31, 1999, reprinted in FBIS-CHI-1999-1231.

Uighurs.[41] With the exception of Kyrgyzstan, whose president was a democratically minded dissident during Soviet times, most of these states are ruled by Soviet-era *apparatchiki*. If future governments were headed by leaders who take their countries' Muslim and/or national identities more seriously, however, they might be willing to run some risks vis-à-vis China. If separatist activity were to become more serious and if neighboring states were to become important bases of support, then China could threaten the use of force to deter those states from supporting separatism and/or to disrupt or destroy separatist bases on the territory of neighboring states.

Finally, there is an ethnic affinity between the Mongolians who live in China (in Inner Mongolia) and those who populate independent Mongolia. In the context of a general loosening of political controls by Beijing, there could be agitation for greater autonomy by the Mongol population of Inner Mongolia, which would raise the question of support from their brethren across the border.

To Prevent the Emergence of a New Threat to China

With Gorbachev's rise to power in the Soviet Union, the PRC entered a new and unprecedented situation in which it believed that it no longer faced a mortal foreign threat to its existence either from the United States or from the Soviet Union. Looking forward, however, China must consider whether a new threat might not emerge, perhaps from Japan or India. If so, is it conceivable that China might use force to prevent or deflect a potential opponent from posing a serious threat? Although the United States would be compelled to react to the use of force against its Japanese ally, any U.S. involvement in a Sino-Indian dispute would depend on the circumstances at the time.

Present-day Japan presents the anomalous case of an "economic superpower" that remains a subordinate factor on the world political-military stage. Nevertheless, the Chinese remain intensely suspicious of Japanese intentions, reacting strongly to even minor shifts in Japanese policy or practice that might presage a stronger world

---

[41]See Burles (1999), p. 56.

role.[42] China might resort to the threat or use of force against Japan in a situation in which the U.S.-Japan alliance had broken down in some fashion or had for some reason been transformed into an alliance of equals, and Japan appeared poised to radically break with its past policies and adopt a much more active political-military role.[43] China might believe that it could use force in such a way as to humiliate and discredit those Japanese who favored a more militarist course while alarming and energizing their opponents, thereby averting the threatened change in Japan's behavior. Alternatively, China might seek to secure the disputed islands before Japan became militarily strong enough to contest them.[44]

Of course, China would need to carefully assess the risk that any such threat or use of force might prove counterproductive by stimulating rather than restraining Japanese nationalism and rearmament. The key point would be not so much what military objective China sought to obtain by its use of force as the anticipated political effect of the incident on internal Japanese opinion and politics. The characteristics of such a use of force—especially the emphasis on achieving surprise and producing a major psychological shock— would be consistent with past Chinese uses of force.

India, by contrast, is an economically, militarily, and, generally speaking, technologically weaker power than China. Nevertheless, it has been an active political-military player in South Asia that, as its nuclear test program makes clear, is intent on increasing its military capabilities to deal with China on more equal terms. At least some Chinese observers have questioned whether India has fully accepted the incorporation of Tibet into China.[45] More generally, in the af-

---

[42]For a discussion of Chinese attitudes toward Japan, see Thomas J. Christensen, "Chinese Realpolitik," *Foreign Affairs*, Vol. 75, No. 5, September/October 1996, pp. 40–45.

[43]This assumes that the U.S.-Japan alliance had broken down in some fashion or had for some reason been transformed into an alliance of equals.

[44]Christensen (1996), p. 44, asserts that if it appeared that the U.S.-Japan security relationship were foundering, there would be a "widening consensus among Chinese analysts that China should quickly build up its military power and settle various sovereignty disputes in the *East* and South China seas, by force, if necessary" (italics added).

[45]"The five nuclear test explosions have laid bare the lies and schemes of the Indian authorities. China has never invaded India, but India has occupied Chinese territory.

termath of the 1998 nuclear tests, Chinese military writers accused India of seeking hegemony in South Asia as well as "great-power status in the international community."[46] For example, China might feel compelled to react militarily in the event of a future Indo-Pakistani war, especially if it appeared that India was on the verge of a major victory. The border dispute could provide the justification to act, much as border tensions and incidents provided the pretext for the Chinese invasion of Vietnam in 1979; the real motive had to do with Vietnam's attempt to gain "regional hegemony" by invading Cambodia and installing a friendly government in Phnom Penh.

To Protect Ethnic Chinese Populations

The PRC has not used force to protect the ethnic Chinese population in neighboring countries. The Chinese complained about the mistreatment of ethnic Chinese in Vietnam in the late 1970s, but the real motive for the Chinese invasion of 1979 must be sought elsewhere: The Chinese remained allied to the Khmer Rouge rulers of Cambodia, who treated Chinese residents of Cambodia far worse than did the Vietnamese. The PRC did not go beyond expressing its concern to help Chinese victims of anti-Communist massacres in Indonesia in 1965 (although, given the distance involved, there was probably little it could do had it wished to). Similarly, China did not go beyond a protest expressing its concern to help protect the Chinese merchants who were the primary victims of the Indonesian riots caused by the economic crisis of 1997–1998.

India has taken advantage of the Tibetan issue to interfere in China's internal affairs." Quote from Dong Guozheng, "Hegemonist Ambition Is Completely Exposed," *Jiefangjun Bao (PLA Daily)*, May 19, 1998, p. 5, reprinted in FBIS-CHI-98-140. Prior to the PRC military occupation of Tibet in 1950, Tibet had, while recognizing formal Chinese "suzerainty," enjoyed varying degrees of autonomy relative to the central government. In addition, Great Britain, when it ruled India, had maintained quasi-diplomatic direct contacts with Tibetan authorities; upon gaining independence in 1947, India retained the last British representative in Lhasa, Tibet, as its own representative there. See Neville Maxwell, *India's China War*, New York: Random House, 1970, p. 68.

[46]Zhang Changtai, "It Would Be Hard for the Indian Government to Get Out of Its Dilemma by Conducting Nuclear Tests," *Jiefangjun Bao (PLA Daily)*, May 20, 1998, p. 5, reprinted in FBIS-CHI-98-140.

This pattern of restraint could, however, change in the future. First, the PRC regime may depend even more heavily on nationalism as a source of its legitimacy; this may make it more difficult to ignore the fate of fellow ethnic Chinese in neighboring countries. Second, the process of opening up the Chinese economy has resulted in increased ties between China and the overseas Chinese, who have become important sources of investment, trading opportunities, and expertise. As the idea of "Greater China" (the mainland, Hong Kong, Taiwan, and the overseas Chinese in Southeast Asia) becomes more important in economic terms, the PRC may have a greater interest in defending ethnic Chinese elsewhere in the region.

To Protect Chinese Business Interests

The Chinese have begun to invest in oil production and transportation facilities in Central Asia as an important means of satisfying their growing need for energy. This may create a large economic interest in those neighboring countries, which the Chinese may be willing to protect by force if necessary.

To Secure Deference from Regional States

As China becomes economically and militarily stronger, it will seek to be treated with greater deference by its less powerful neighbors. In particular, China will hope to influence the closeness of the relationship that neighboring countries enjoy with external powers, especially the United States.

China might thus seek a role in a regional state's decisions concerning U.S. military bases or other forms of military access to its territory. For example, the issue of whether U.S. troops would continue to be based on the Korean peninsula after the country was unified could lead to a crisis and to a potential threat or use of force by China. Similarly, U.S. basing in Vietnam—if such an eventuality is conceivable—might be seen by China as particularly threatening.

CONCLUSION

None of the possibilities discussed in this chapter is carved in stone. For many reasons, China may not emerge as a great power in the next two decades—and if it does, it remains unclear what kind of great power it will be. The processes of reform and globalization that have facilitated China's rise may well soften its nationalism and restrain or dilute its geopolitical ambitions. Whether the Communist Party will be able to maintain its monopoly of political power or whether it will be forced to accommodate to a more democratic and pluralistic form of rule is among the major uncertainties that cloud our view of China's future.

Nonetheless, China will be a central focus of political-military deliberations and actions in Asia over the next decades. In the accompanying appendices, we examine how the nations of Northeast, Southeast and South Asia view China; where concerns about China fit in their overall geopolitical outlook; and how these views might affect their interest in engaging in political-military cooperation both with the United States in general and with the USAF in particular.

THE CHANGING POLITICAL-MILITARY
ENVIRONMENT: SOUTHEAST ASIA

Angel Rabasa

Southeast Asia derives its geopolitical importance principally from its location at the crossroads between the concentration of industrial, technological, and military power in Northeast Asia to the north, the Indian subcontinent and the oil resources of the Middle East to the east, and Australia to the south. A high proportion of the trade of Japan, the Republic of Korea, Taiwan, and Australia, including much of their oil imports, transits the straits and SLOCs in Southeast Asia.[1] From a military perspective, these sea lanes are critical to the movement of U.S. forces from the Western Pacific to the Indian Ocean and the Persian Gulf.

With a population of more than 500 million, a wealth of natural resources, and economies growing at rapid rates before the 1997–1998 economic crisis, the region is also important in its own right as a component of the Asian and global balance of power as well as a market for the United States. From 1993 to 1997, Southeast Asia was second only to Japan and well ahead of China and Hong Kong in terms of U.S. exports to the Pacific Rim.[2] U.S. exports to the region fell about 20 percent in the immediate aftermath of the Asian financial crisis, but trade is expected to resume its robust level of growth when the region emerges from that crisis. Southeast Asia was also an

---

[1]Shipping transiting the region must pass through one of three or four chokepoints: the straits of Malacca, Sunda, or Lombok, or possibly the straits east of East Timor. See John H. Noer, *Chokepoints: Maritime Economic Concerns in Southeast Asia,* Washington, D.C.: National Defense University, 1996.

[2]U.S. Department of Commerce, *Statistical Abstract of the United States,* No. 1323, 1998, p. 801.

important destination of U.S. direct investment, having surpassed Japan and Brazil by 1997.[3]

Southeast Asia is, moreover, the cultural as well as geographic cross-roads of Asia, where Sinitic, Hindu, Islamic, and Western civilizations have met and interacted for almost a millennium.[4] The struggles that play out in the region therefore resonate well beyond the region. For instance, how Indonesia—the world's largest Muslim majority country—deals with the issues of democracy and political and religious diversity could well influence the course of events in Asia and the larger Islamic world.

A DYNAMIC REGIONAL SECURITY ENVIRONMENT

The Asian economic crisis and the associated political upheaval in Indonesia knocked out the underpinnings of the Southeast Asian security system and brought about dynamic changes in the region's security environment. This study seeks to identify key factors shaping the regional security environment and to postulate potential geopolitical events that the interplay of these factors might produce. Finally, we will examine the implications of these scenarios for the political stability and security of Southeast Asian countries and U.S. interests in the region.

There is no question that the economic crisis of 1997–1998 was a transformational event in Southeast Asia and that the forces set in motion by this event have not yet played themselves out.

First, the Asian economic crisis seriously weakened the cohesion and regional security role of ASEAN. The crisis also coincided with two other developments that, taken together, further reduced ASEAN's ability to function as a regional security organization. One such development was the political crisis in Indonesia. With Indonesia—

---

[3]U.S. Department of Commerce, Bureau of Economic Analysis, *Survey of Current Business*, July 1998, Table 3.2.

[4]Trade routes linking peninsular and insular Southeast Asia to China and India began to emerge in the first century A.D. Islam had become entrenched in the Malayan peninsula and Sumatra by the 13th century and spread widely in Southeast Asia from the 14th to the 17th centuries. European colonization began with the Portuguese capture of Malacca, center of the most important Malay state, in 1511, and the Spanish settlement of Manila in 1571.

historically the center of gravity and de facto leader of ASEAN—beset by grave domestic problems and with its very future uncertain, Jakarta has been unable to exercise its customary regional leadership. ASEAN therefore has been left to drift, as was demonstrated by its passive role during the East Timor crisis of 1999. The other development was ASEAN's decision to expand its membership by incorporating Vietnam, Laos, Cambodia, and Burma. The inclusion of these far less developed states, with their rudimentary market economies and more authoritarian and, in some cases, neo-communist political cultures, diluted the ASEAN consensus and further paralyzed its decisionmaking process.[5]

Second, and of more immediate concern to defense planners, the economic crisis put a severe strain on defense budgets throughout the region. Military modernization programs in all Southeast Asian countries, with the notable exception of Singapore, have been canceled or postponed, as shown in Table C.1. Readiness has been affected as militaries have been forced to cut back on training and exercises and become more focused on internal security.

Table C.1

Impact of the Economic Crisis on Procurement of Major Air Systems by ASEAN Countries

Country	System	Status
Indonesia	12 SU-30 MK aircraft	Canceled
	8 Mi-17 helicopters	Canceled
Thailand	8 F/A-18 aircraft	Canceled
	16 F-16A/Bs	LOA[a] requested
Malaysia	Additional F/A-18 aircraft	Suspended
Philippines	New multirole aircraft	Uncertain

[a]LOA = letter of offer and acceptance.

Third, economic hardships increased political volatility and ethnic and religious tensions in a number of Southeast Asian states. Indonesia is the starkest case. The collapse of the rupiah and the consequent financial and economic crisis brought down the 32-year

---

[5]See James Clad, "Fin de Siècle, Fin de l'ASEAN?" Center for Strategic and International Studies, Pacific Forum CSIS, *Pac Net Newsletter*, March 3, 2000.

Suharto regime and sparked anti-Chinese riots in major Indonesian cities. The collapse of the Suharto order led to the separation of East Timor, the growth of armed separatist movements in other Indonesian provinces, massive religious violence on the eastern islands, and a loss of central authority over the provinces. In the Philippines, there has been an intensification of both communist and Islamic insurgencies, and in Malaysia the growth of Islamic fundamentalism is a potential factor of instability.

The strategic implications of these changes in the regional security environment center on a diminished ability on the part of the ASEAN states to counter security threats. The unstable regional security environment presents unprecedented opportunities for internal and external actors—whether political dissidents, religious extremists, separatists, or prospective hegemons—seeking to overturn the status quo. In particular, it could present a rising China with opportunities to extend its presence and influence in the region.

This is a dynamic security environment. The only certainty is that it could and likely will evolve rapidly over the next decade. The interplay of several key factors will define the security problems in Southeast Asia and the range of demands and constraints likely to be imposed on the United States and the USAF during this time frame. These factors are the Southeast Asian states' economic and political evolution, China's economic and military strength and its interaction with Southeast Asia, the regional states' success in maintaining their national cohesion and in dealing with ethnic and religious conflicts, and the course of regional integration. The United States and Japan—the key extraregional actors—represent additional and potentially decisive factors. Australia and the European Union can also play smaller but important roles in defining the future Southeast Asian security environment.

SOUTHEAST ASIAN THREAT PERCEPTIONS—GENERAL

For some of the Southeast Asian states, concerns about national cohesion trump external threats. In Indonesia, nothing less than the survival of the state is at stake. Although not to the same extent as Indonesia, the Philippines also faces issues of national stability and cohesion—issues that in a way go back more than 400 years to the Spanish colonization of the Philippines and to Manila's efforts to assimilate the Muslim-majority areas of the southern Philippines. In all Southeast Asian countries, there is a sense of the interrelatedness of these trends. The ripple effect of political tremors in Sumatra is felt across the strait in Singapore and Malaysia. In both the Philippines and Thailand, there is concern about the demonstration effect of Muslim separatism in Indonesia on their own Muslim minorities.

Transnational threats have been magnified by chaotic conditions in the region. Piracy has been on the increase, particularly in waters around Indonesia and the Philippines. In the first nine months of 1999, 66 actual or attempted pirate attacks took place on Indonesian waters—representing 67 percent of the total for Southeast Asia—and double the number of incidents for the same period in 1998.[6] Illegal migration is increasingly viewed as a security problem. There are hundreds of thousands of illegal Indonesian migrants in Malaysia, including many Acehnese suspected of links with Acehnese secessionist organizations. In April 1998, in an effort to avoid deportation, several dozen Indonesians forced their way into a number of embassies and the U.N. compound in Kuala Lumpur. The operation was apparently orchestrated by the Acehnese separatist organization GAM. Narcotics trafficking has long been an endemic problem as well, particularly in mainland Southeast Asia, but of late it has taken on some new dimensions. The Thais consider the smuggling of methamphetamines from Burma a major security concern.

Turning to external threats, the primary potential threat from the standpoint of a number of Southeast Asian states is China—but Southeast Asian perceptions of China are far from monolithic. These perceptions are shaped by the power asymmetries between China and the Southeast Asian countries; expansive Chinese claims to the South China Sea; the development of Chinese power projection capabilities; historic fears of Chinese domination on the part of some regional states, especially Vietnam; and fear of Beijing's manipulation of the ethnic Chinese communities in a number of Southeast Asian countries.

Over the years, relations between the ASEAN states and China have gone through several stages. Throughout the 1960s and early 1970s,

---

[6]See *Piracy and Armed Robbery Against Ships: Report for the Period 1 January–30 September 1999*, London: International Maritime Bureau, p. 3.

fear and suspicion of China were pervasive in Southeast Asian capitals because of Beijing's support for communist insurgencies in several countries and its involvement in the attempted 1965 coup in Indonesia. Beginning in the 1980s, a thaw emerged in China's relations with the ASEAN countries, largely as a result of growing trade and investment links spurred by China's economic reforms, the declining role of ideology in Beijing's policies toward the region, China's determined drive to improve relations with the ASEAN states, and ASEAN's support of China as a counterweight to Vietnam. Since the late 1980s, however, a more ambivalent attitude toward China has emerged. On the one hand, relations between most of ASEAN and China improved markedly, reflecting a common desire to achieve economic growth through expanded trade and investment as well as the belief in ASEAN circles that as China's power grows it may have to be accommodated. On the other hand, many in ASEAN, particularly in the insular states, remain apprehensive of China's intentions.[7]

At the same time, China is not the only perceived external threat. In some countries, there remains considerable residual suspicion of Japan, which derives from unpleasant memories of the Japanese occupation during World War II. Among nationalist circles in Indonesia and Malaysia in particular but in other countries as well, there is also a distrust of Western powers. During the East Timor crisis of 1999, for instance, the view that the West and Australia were conspiring to keep Indonesia weak received widespread credence in Jakarta. Finally, despite ASEAN's success in managing disputes among member states (which was in fact the original *raison d'être* of the organization), there is considerable potential for intra-ASEAN conflict.

SOUTHEAST ASIAN THREAT PERCEPTIONS—INDIVIDUAL COUNTRIES

The Philippines

Filipinos view Chinese expansionism as the main long-term threat, with insurgencies, communist and Islamic, in second place. In dis-

---

[7]For a more detailed analysis, see Sokolsky et al. (2000).

cussions with senior Philippine military officers in Manila in November 1999, our interlocutors not only spoke of potential Chinese hegemony but maintained that China was already well on its way to establishing its hegemony on the South China Sea.

In 1995 the Chinese occupied an outpost on Mischief Reef, which lies only 150 miles from the Philippines and well within the Philippines' Exclusive Economic Zone (EEZ), and built what were alleged to be fishermen's shelters. Manila's strategy for dealing with China's encroachment was to rely on diplomacy. The Philippines and China held two rounds of bilateral discussions in 1995, resulting in agreement on a code of conduct. According to the Philippines, however, China has violated this code of conduct, moving military assets in and out of the area without informing Manila and upgrading its facilities on Mischief Reef.[8] Between November 1998 and January 1999, the Chinese substantially expanded these structures, adding electronics communication and surveillance equipment and building multistory buildings on concrete platforms large enough to serve as landing pads for helicopters and manned by Chinese military personnel.[9]

After decades of defense efforts concentrated on the internal communist and separatist threats, the Mischief Reef incident galvanized the Philippine government into a decision to launch a modernization plan focused on capabilities (e.g., naval combatants and combat aircraft) that would allow the Philippine armed forces to better defend its claims in the Spratlys and its 200-mile EEZ. Unlike other ASEAN states, the Philippines' economic ties with China are relatively modest and therefore less of an inhibition on Manila's willingness to confront China over its aggressive behavior in the South China Sea. This military modernization plan—originally proposed by then–Vice President Fidel Ramos in 1990—has foundered on a lack of resources and political will. The Philippine government is currently exploring alternative ways of meeting its defense needs, but

---

[8]Ian James Storey, "Creeping Assertiveness: China, the Philippines, and the South China Sea Dispute," *Contemporary Southeast Asia*, Vol. 21, No. 1, April 1999; and B. Raman, "Chinese Assertion of Territorial Claims: The Mischief Reef, a Case Study," Chennai, India: South Asia Analysis Group Papers, 1999.

[9]Ian James Storey, "Manila Looks to USA for Help over Spratlys," *Jane's Intelligence Review*, August 1999, p. 47.

there do not appear to be any practical proposals for funding major military equipment purchases.[10]

The Filipinos identify two distinct internal threats: communist insurgents and Islamic separatists. According to Philippine security officials speaking at the end of 1999, communist revolutionaries pose the more serious threat. The New People's Army, the military arm of the Communist Party of the Philippines (CPP), has been waging an armed struggle for more than 30 years. It reached the peak of its strength in 1986, with more than 20,000 armed fighters, declined to about 5000 by the mid-1990s, and strengthened to about 9000 in 1999. At present, the communists are divided into several factions: three factions broke away from the CPP in 1992 and another split took place in 1998. The largest faction is led by Netherlands-based CPP founding chairman Jose Maria Sison. There have been on-and-off negotiations with the communists for several years, but the communists broke off talks after the Philippine Senate ratified the VFA with the United States in May 1999. Since then the Sison faction has escalated its attacks—some in connection with demonstrations by leftists protesting higher oil prices. Philippine security officials believe that the communists may be seeking to take advantage of the economic crisis to regain their strength.

Islamic separatism centers on the islands of Mindanao and the Sulu archipelago, historically Muslim areas in which the ethnic and religious consciousness of the Muslim population has been sharpened by decades of assimilationist policies and Catholic transmigration from the northern Philippines. There are three main Islamic separatist movements, all active in the majority Muslim regions of Mindanao and the Sulu archipelago in the Southern Philippines.

The Moro National Liberation Front (MNLF), the largest of the Islamic rebel movements, has not been considered a threat since the peace agreement signed with the Ramos government that established the Autonomous Region of Muslim Mindanao. The MNLF leadership, which includes individuals educated in the University of

---

[10]In a discussion with the chairman of the Philippine Senate Defense Committee, Senator Biazon, in November 1999, the senator suggested reactivating the U.S.-Philippines Military Assistance Agreement, through which the Philippines received most of its military equipment from 1947 to 1992.

the Philippines, has a more secular outlook than do the other Moro organizations and is primarily interested in the implementation of the government's economic aid package. The agreement between the government of the Philippines and the MNLF provides for economic incentives to the region, and the government is seeking to comply within the constraints of a difficult economic and budgetary situation. Philippine authorities are aware that failure to meet the government's commitments could affect the credibility of the MNLF and the viability of the peace agreement.

The Moro Islamic Liberation Front (MILF) has a stronger Islamic identity than the MNLF and a base of support among the Islamic religious establishment (*ulema*) of southern Mindanao. The MILF's current strength is about 10,000 fighters, trained by Afghan war veterans. On-and-off negotiations are taking place with this group, but so far no agreement has been reached. The MILF advocates an Islamic state on Mindanao, but in the view of Philippine security officials it may be willing to settle for an autonomous region. The MILF suffered a severe blow when Philippine government forces captured its headquarters, Camp Abubakar, in May 2000, but despite this defeat the MILF retains its military capabilities. Military operations in Mindanao will increase pressure on the Philippine budget and may not bring a political settlement any closer.

Abu Sayyaf is the third and most radical group. It advocates the establishment of a fundamentalist Islamic state and sees its struggle linked to a worldwide Islamic movement. Abu Sayyaf was in the news in 2000 over the kidnapping of tourists in Malaysia. According to Philippine authorities, it has an estimated 1000 fighters in the Sulu archipelago and includes veterans of the Afghan war and individuals identified with the bin Laden network. Abductions of elementary-school teachers and children on the island of Basilan and of foreign tourists at a resort in Malaysia by Abu Sayyaf in the spring of 2000 provoked large-scale Philippine military operations against the group in its stronghold of Jolo and Basilan.

The communist and Islamic rebel movements, of course, have different agendas and are driven by different dynamics, but there appear to be tactical linkages between the underground Communist Party of Jose Maria Sison and the MILF.

Singapore

Singapore is concerned primarily about the situation in Indonesia, secondarily about Malaysia, and only tangentially with China. During the Suharto era, Singapore shared with Jakarta an interest in upholding regional order and stability. As the Indonesian economic and political order began to collapse, Singapore played an important role in international efforts to stabilize Indonesia. Senior Minister Lee Kuan Yew has agreed to serve with Henry Kissinger and others on a board of distinguished international advisers to Indonesian President Wahid. Nonetheless, the Singaporeans are exceedingly careful not to be perceived as interfering in Indonesia's internal affairs; they are conscious of both the limitations of their influence and the potential for a nationalist backlash, especially if they are perceived as pressing unpopular or painful policies on the Indonesians.

By and large, Singaporean analysts are not optimistic about Indonesia's future prospects. They believe that the Wahid government is unfocused, particularly on economic policy, and that the security situation is worsening. In their view, some radical Muslims are fostering violence in the Moluccas as a warning to Jakarta not to ignore Islamic interests. From their perspective, the most likely prospect for Indonesia is a succession of short-lived governments. Other scenarios, such as Islamization and fragmentation, are also seen as possible, with dire consequences for the security of Singapore and the region.

Malaysia is seen as a smaller problem but remains a priority. The Singaporeans are carefully watching Malaysia's political evolution, especially the growth of the Islamic Party of Malaysia (PAS). They believe that the problem, from the standpoint of Malaysia's stability, is that the Malays themselves are divided. Many rank-and-file members of the Malaysian ruling party, the United Malays National Organization (UMNO), realize that their leadership under Prime Minister Mahathir is not prepared to accept change and are thus defecting to the Islamic Party. The Singaporeans do not believe that a Malaysian political crisis is at hand and do not expect the Islamic Party to come to power without non-Malay support. They also believe, however, that the fact that only the Chinese and Indian vote kept Mahathir and UMNO in power in the last election is an ominous indication of the state of Malay politics.

With regard to China, Singapore's approach is prudential. As a small, predominantly ethnic-Chinese state in the proverbial sea of Malays, and as an entity dependent on international trade for economic survival, Singapore cannot afford to antagonize a major regional power. Singapore is also one of the largest investors in China and has developed close economic ties with China, although some of Singapore's major investments, such as the industrial township in Suzhou, have fallen far short of expectations.

On the other hand, Singaporeans, like their neighbors, fear the long-term threat a hegemonic China could pose to their country's independence and look to the United States as the indispensable "balancing" power in Asia. For this reason, Singapore strongly supports a continued U.S. military presence in the region and hosts a broad spectrum of U.S. military activities. At the same time, Singaporeans are not uniformly confident of U.S. resolve. As one Singaporean scholar noted, the United States might decide to withdraw from the region, but Singapore will always have to live with China.

On Taiwan, the Singaporeans have struck a balance between Beijing and Taipei, maintaining strong commercial and informal political ties with Taiwan while advising Taipei against any action that might precipitate a PRC military response. They do not want a conflict with China even if China were to attack Taiwan (although they do not expect this to happen unless there is a Taiwanese declaration of independence), and they recognize that a conflict between the United States and China would create a painful policy dilemma for them.

In Singapore's thinking, ASEAN's security space extends well beyond the immediate Southeast Asian region and includes the evolution of the situation in Northeast Asia, particularly on the Korean peninsula. In their view, Russia has disappeared as a factor in Southeast Asian security, but the agreements on peace cooperation and the arms supply relationship with China place Russia on the Chinese side. India was not yet seen as a factor in Southeast Asia in a strategic, economic, or military sense, although this perception might change following the Indian naval exercises with Vietnam and the visit of Indian Defense Minister Fernandes in the spring of 2000.[11]

---

[11]The above analysis of Singaporean views on regional security issues is based on discussions with Singapore Defense and Foreign Ministry officials and defense experts

Indonesia

As discussed in Chapter Two, the most important question about Indonesia's future in the post-Suharto era is whether that country will survive in its present configuration or whether it will splinter in the manner of Yugoslavia or the former Soviet Union. Other pivotal issues are the fate of Indonesia's democratic transformation and the future role of the armed forces.

Jakarta's disarray and the separation of East Timor have, as discussed, encouraged secessionist movements in the key provinces of Aceh, Riau, and Irian Jaya. In addition, religious and ethnic violence has been escalating in eastern Indonesia. Taken together, these factors are creating stresses that Indonesia may not be able to endure.

Most Indonesians view the Aceh insurgency as the gravest challenge to Indonesia's territorial integrity. The resurgent Acehnese Liberation Movement, GAM, is reported to have more than 800 armed fighters—four times as many as there were in the early 1990s. They are well funded by sympathizers abroad and are armed through a pipeline extending from the mainland of Southeast Asia—which reportedly extends to the Tamil Tigers in Sri Lanka and to the Muslim separatist guerrillas in the Philippines.[12]

The Wahid government's strategy in Aceh is to address the political and economic demands of the Acehnese, short of granting independence. There are two key demands that analysts agree would have to be satisfied for Jakarta to gain the confidence and trust of the Acehnese:

* Greater local control, especially control of the province's economic resources. This demand could be met through measures that have been passed or are under consideration by Parliament that would give Aceh control of 70 percent of the revenues from

---

at the Institute of Defence and Strategic Studies at Nanyang Technological University, held in February 2000, and on publicly available materials, particularly *Defending Singapore in the 21st Century*, Singapore: Republic of Singapore Ministry of Defence, 2000; and Andrew T.H. Tan, "Singapore's Defence: Capabilities, Trends, and Implications," *Contemporary Southeast Asia*, Vol. 21, No. 3, December 1999, pp. 451–474.

[12]"Indonesia: Worse to Come," *Far Eastern Economic Review*, July 29, 1999, p. 16.

extractive industries and extensive local autonomy, including the introduction of Islamic law for the province.

- Accountability for human rights violations by the security forces during the Suharto period. Jakarta has tried to accommodate this demand through investigations of alleged human rights violations, which led to the trial of soldiers accused of participating in the killing of civilians in Aceh. In May 2000, 24 soldiers and one civilian were convicted of the massacre of 57 Aceh villagers.

The Indonesian government and the GAM agreed on a temporary cease-fire in May 2000 and agreed to withdraw some combat elements from the province. The question that remains is whether the government's concessions will satisfy Acehnese demands. Currently neither the government nor the insurgents are strong enough to defeat the other, so an accommodation that permits significant autonomy for Aceh within Indonesia may well be viewed by both sides as the best possible outcome. Yet a perceived weakening of Jakarta's authority or political will might stimulate demands for full independence.

In the view of one senior Indonesian military officer, the insurgency in Irian Jaya—a region that did not become part of Indonesia until 1963 and that therefore shares few cultural or social characteristics with the rest of Indonesia—might prove even more dangerous than that in Aceh. This view holds that the rebels in Irian Jaya are Christian and are therefore more likely to garner Western support than are the Muslim rebels in Aceh. It also maintains that the border with Papua New Guinea might afford the insurgents the possibility of cross-border sanctuaries.

The eastern islands of Indonesia have also seen large-scale violence between Muslims and Christians, centering on Ambon and other islands in the Moluccas and in Sulawesi. A variety of theories have been put forth in Indonesia on who is behind this sectarian violence, with some pointing to Muslim radicals and others to Indonesian army factions. Although the possibility of political manipulation cannot be eliminated, the most likely trigger was the collapse of authority following the fall of Suharto, which unleashed tensions between the region's original Christian inhabitants and Muslim immigrants from Java who had moved in under Suharto's resettlement program. It is postulated that these tensions developed into an economic and religious civil war.

Given the gravity of these internal threats, external threats have not been accorded priority in Indonesian defense thinking. President Wahid's government has initiated a policy of rapprochement with China that represents a departure from that of the Suharto government. Citing the distance from Chinese operating bases to Indonesian waters and the fact that Indonesians expect the Philippines and Vietnam to block China's southern expansion, senior Indonesian military officers do not believe that China poses a direct military threat to Indonesia in the near to midterm. Nevertheless, they do see China as a long-term threat. They are particularly concerned about China's potential ability to intervene in domestic Indonesian politics.

At a time when the Indonesian military is confronting some of its most demanding challenges since the mid-1960s, it is itself in a process of transformation. Even senior military officers acknowledge that the armed forces suffered a severe loss of reputation and credibility as a result of its association with the Suharto regime. The armed forces are retreating from their traditional political role— which included corporate representation in the Parliament and a territorial structure that reached down to the village level—and are developing a new doctrine that shifts the focus from internal security to external defense.[13]

Thailand

With a long and continuous history as an independent state and the institution of the monarchy as a unifying factor, Thailand does not have the severe national cohesion problems that other regional countries face. Nonetheless, radical Islamic groups are active in the

---

[13]The above discussion on Indonesia is based on discussions with senior Indonesian military officers and defense academics in Jakarta in March 2000. Particularly valuable were the discussions with Dr. Hadi Soesastro, Executive Director, Centre for Strategic and International Studies (CSIS); Brigadier General (retired) Soedibyo, Senior Fellow, Institute for Strategic Studies of Indonesia; and Dr. Indria Samego, Center for Political and Regional Studies, Indonesian Institute of Sciences. The analysis also benefited from presentations and discussions at the international seminar on Indonesia's future challenges and implications for the region, sponsored by the Council for Security Cooperation in the Asia Pacific in Jakarta on March 8–9, 2000.

four southernmost provinces of Thailand. The two principal militant Islamic groups in southern Thailand are the Pattani United Liberation Organization (PULO) and the New PULO, a dissident faction that broke away from PULO in 1995. The various militant groups have close links with their ethnic kin in the northern Malaysian state of Kelantan—an Islamic stronghold and the only Malaysian state governed by the PAS—and reportedly operated in the early 1990s with tacit support from Kelantan's PAS government. In 1997, however, the Malaysian government sanctioned a crackdown on Thai separatists in northern Malaysia, depriving them of sanctuary and support. Since then, separatist activity in southern Thailand has declined. Although these groups do not pose an immediate threat, Bangkok is concerned about the demonstration effect of Islamic insurgencies elsewhere in the region and is keeping a watchful eye on their southern provinces.[14]

As discussed in Chapter Two, the Thais do not see China as a threat. Thailand is not party to the South China Sea dispute, and in contrast to the Southeast Asian states to the south, the ethnic Chinese community in Thailand is well integrated into Thai society. Moreover, the Thai-Chinese relationship has a strategic component based on common opposition to Vietnamese designs in Indochina in the 1970s and 1980s. After the Vietnamese invasion of Cambodia, Thailand cooperated with China as well as with the United States in opposing Vietnamese regional hegemony and became a conduit for logistical support of the anti-Vietnamese forces in Cambodia.

Vietnam's withdrawal from Cambodia and its entry into ASEAN, combined with the withdrawal of Russian forces from Vietnam, diminished the strategic rationale for Thai-Chinese security cooperation. There are stirrings of Thai uneasiness with Chinese intentions and capabilities on the South China Sea. Of more direct concern to Bangkok are China's expanding military ties with Burma and the possibility that the Sino-Burmese relationship could lead to Burma's acquisition of offensive weapons. Border tensions between Thailand and Burma, in the view of some Thai analysts, have the potential to escalate into armed conflict. The Thais are also concerned about reports of Chinese use of Burmese facilities on the Indian Ocean—a

---

[14]PULO has a website at http://pulo.cjb.net/.

development that could turn the Bay of Bengal into an arena of strategic competition between India and China.[15]

Malaysia

Malaysia's defense policy is based on national resilience—a concept also found in the defense strategies and doctrines of other Southeast Asian states—and conventional deterrence.[16] It considers itself to be a "front-line" state on the South China Sea dispute and has stationed small garrisons on islets on the southern Spratlys claimed by China and the Philippines. Malaysia also has boundary disputes with Indonesia in Borneo as well as a long-standing dispute with the Philippines over ownership of the Malaysian state of Sabah. Strains in Malaysia's relationship with Singapore and the possibility, however improbable, of a conflict between the two also affect Malaysia's security environment.

Many Malaysians, especially among the Malay elite and the military establishment, harbor deep suspicions about China's long-term intentions. These attitudes are due to some extent to the historic legacy of China's support for the predominantly ethnic Chinese guerrillas during the insurgency of the 1950s and 1960s. At a deeper level, Malaysian attitudes toward China are also influenced by the interplay of ethnic politics at the core of the Malaysian political system. Although Malaysia has been governed by coalitions of parties representing all the major ethnic groups since independence from Great Britain in 1957, the politics of the Malay majority has been driven by the Malays' fear of losing their dominant position in the state. Singapore's forced separation from the Malaysian Federation in 1965 was an outcome of this dynamic, as were the Kuala Lumpur race riots of May 1969.

The political and economic power-sharing arrangements in place for the last 30 years satisfied the Malays' demand for political control

---

[15]The above discussion of Thai security concerns is based on discussions in Bangkok with Thai military officials and defense academics in November 1999. I am particularly indebted to Professor Surachart Bamrungsuk of Chulalongkorn University.

[16]Charles E. Morrison (ed.), *Asia Pacific Security Outlook 1999*, Tokyo: Japan Center for International Exchange, 1999, p. 118.

and the preservation of their special privileges and gave the Chinese and Indian minorities a role as junior partners in the governing coalition. Taken together with the high rates of economic growth Malaysia experienced during much of this period, these arrangements have prevented a recurrence of ethnic strife. Yet a protracted economic contraction could lead to the recurrence of ethnic tensions and could spill over into Malaysian-Singaporean and Malaysian-Chinese relations.

For the moment, however, Kuala Lumpur is firmly embarked on a policy of rapprochement with Beijing. The Mahathir government has expanded economic and political ties with China. Both Mahathir and China have found common ground against alleged Western economic domination and so-called international speculators supposedly responsible for precipitating the Asian economic crisis. On the South China Sea dispute, the Mahathir government has also chosen to "bandwagon" with China rather than join an ASEAN front, as proposed by the Philippines, and has even emulated Chinese tactics in its own dealings with the Philippines.[17]

Vietnam

The security environment in mainland Southeast Asia was transformed by the Vietnamese withdrawal from Cambodia in 1989, the subsequent settlement of the Cambodian civil war, and Vietnam's accession to ASEAN. Despite the periodic breakdown of fragile internal political arrangements in Cambodia, the U.N.-sponsored settlement in Cambodia ended the strategic competition between Vietnam and the coalition opposed to the Vietnamese presence in Cambodia. It enabled Vietnam to break out of its isolation within the region yet maintain sufficient influence in Cambodia to protect its interests, which include preventing Cambodia's alignment with a potentially hostile power and protection of the Vietnamese ethnic minority.

---

[17]In June 1999 the Philippines protested Malaysia's occupation of two uninhabited locations in the Investigator Shoal in the Spratlys and construction of a concrete platform, helipad, and two-story building featuring a radar facility. In a private conversation, a senior Philippine official noted that the Malaysian construction, at a site also claimed by China, did not bring about a Chinese protest and thus wondered if there was collusion.

Despite its normalization of relations with China in 1991 and expanding bilateral trade, Vietnam continues to see China as a significant external threat and remains suspicious of China's intentions and ambitions. China casts a large shadow over Hanoi's strategic outlook for several reasons. First, the bitter and violent legacy of Vietnam's historic relationship with China—including several Chinese invasions and armed confrontations, most recently the 1979 border war—has engendered deep and abiding mistrust. Second, Vietnam is one of the main protagonists in the Spratlys dispute, and the two countries have had armed confrontations in 1974 and 1988 over the Paracel Islands and the Spratlys, respectively. A third source of tension was removed with the signing of a land border agreement in Hanoi in December 1999. In December 2000, Vietnam and China signed an agreement demarcating maritime territory in the Gulf of Tonkin and issued a joint statement outlining a comprehensive program of future cooperation.

The current reconciliation between Vietnam and China remains fragile, however, and further belligerent Chinese actions in the South China Sea could revive Vietnam's fear of China and lead to a more hostile and confrontational posture. That said, the Vietnamese are keenly aware of their own vulnerabilities vis-à-vis China and remain preoccupied with addressing the country's economic and social development through expanded foreign trade and investment. At least for the moment, therefore, Vietnam's strategy for dealing with China emphasizes continued normalization of relations, solidarity and integration with ASEAN, and expanding economic and political ties with outside powers, especially the United States and Japan.

Vietnamese military capabilities declined sharply with the end of Soviet support in the late 1980s. Nevertheless, the Vietnamese have pursued a program of military modernization with Russian equipment. The centerpiece of this program is the planned acquisition by Vietnam of Russian Su-27 air superiority/ground attack aircraft with a combat radius that will enable Vietnam to contest for air superiority over disputed areas of the South China Sea. The Russian Navy still maintains several hundred personnel attached to the Pacific Fleet's 15th Operational Squadron at Cam Ranh Bay. Russia has a

25-year lease on the Cam Ranh base that expires in 2004 and that Moscow reportedly seeks to extend.[18]

MOTIVES AND OBSTACLES TO REGIONAL COUNTRIES' COOPERATION WITH THE UNITED STATES AND THE USAF

Since the withdrawal of the British from Southeast Asia, the United States has played the indispensable role of regional stabilizer. However, because of both historic reasons and sensitivities in some countries about the U.S. presence, there have been substantial differences in ASEAN countries' approaches to defense arrangements with the United States.

Philippines. The Philippines and Thailand are both treaty allies and part of the network of bilateral defense agreements that constitute the U.S. security architecture in Asia.   Throughout the Aquino and Ramos presidencies, the operation of the Philippines' defense relationship was hampered by residual acrimony over the removal of the U.S. bases and the absence of a status-of-forces agreement. Although the United States has made it clear that it takes no sides on the dispute over the Spratlys, the U.S. withdrawal from Subic Bay and Clark Air Force Base in 1992 brought about a change in the strategic environment in the South China Sea and, in the view of Philippine decisionmakers, was undoubtedly a factor in the Chinese decision to occupy Mischief Reef.[19]   Continued Chinese pressure on the Spratlys has led to renewed Philippine interest in lending substance to the bilateral defense relationship.

In any event, the episode drove home to Philippine decisionmakers the need to revitalize the security relationship with the United States, which had been damaged by the failed effort to conclude a new base agreement. In line with the new thinking in Philippine defense, the Ramos government negotiated and signed the functional equivalent

---

[18]Stein Tønnesson, "Vietnam's Objective in the South China Sea," *Contemporary Southeast Asia*, Vol. 22, No. 1, April 2000, pp. 204 and 217.

[19]The U.S.-Philippine Mutual Defense Treaty applies only to the metropolitan territory of the Philippines but calls for bilateral consultations in the event of an attack on the Philippine armed forces.

of a status-of-forces agreement—a visiting forces agreement (VFA) that would permit the resumption of cooperative military activities with the United States. The VFA was endorsed by the new government of President Joseph Estrada (a former base opponent) and was ratified by the Philippine Senate at the end of May 1999.

For the Philippines, closer military relations with the United States is a way to prevent a security vacuum from developing and reestablish deterrence in the region. The overriding Philippine concern in the defense and security area is military modernization. The Philippines simply does not have the capabilities to project power on the South China Sea. The Philippine Air Force has only five airworthy F-5s, and the Navy has World War II–era vessels in poor state of repair. A modernization plan proposed by then–Vice President Ramos during the Aquino administration called for the acquisition of a squadron of modern multirole aircraft, reconnaissance aircraft, and fast patrol boats. Although the priorities have not changed, no progress has been made in funding the modernization program.

In light of Manila's financial difficulties, the Philippines has looked to the United States for assistance with military modernization. Philippine government officials understand that there is no linkage between approval of the VFA and U.S. security assistance, but they hope for some level of U.S. assistance to bridge the gap until the Philippines can begin its military modernization program. On the matter of U.S. access to military facilities in the Philippines, the general view of Philippine security experts is that for domestic political reasons it would be difficult to give the appearance that the United States is reestablishing its bases in the Philippines. Opposition to a U.S. military presence is not as intense as it was in the immediate post-Marcos era, but it remains strong among certain groups, especially in universities, leftist political parties, and religious organizations. On the other hand, opposition to the U.S. presence is more of an elite than a broad-based sentiment. Thus, a decision by the Philippine government to allow the United States operational use of Philippine facilities in a regional security emergency is not out of the question if there is a clear Philippine national security rationale for the decision.

Thailand. The treaty-based defense relationship with the United States remains the mainstay of Thailand's security. Thailand hosts

Cobra Gold, the largest combined exercise in Asia outside Korea, which is important to the Thais as reassurance of the U.S. defense commitment. Thailand has been seeking to strengthen bilateral ties and allows the United States the use of Utapao Naval Air Station for exercises and real-life operations. Some Thai defense analysts, however, believe that with the end of the Cold War and the disappearance of the communist threat in Southeast Asia, a new rationale must be found for the U.S.-Thai defense relationship. They fear that, in the absence of this rationale, the decades-long bilateral defense relationship could wither on the vine.

The Thais were hard hit by the Asian economic crisis, which in fact began with the attack on the baht and the Thai Central Bank's decision to abandon the baht's tie to the dollar. Thailand's ambitious military modernization plans suffered as a result. The Thai Air Force canceled plans to purchase F-18 aircraft and put other programs on hold. The resumption of economic growth in Thailand in 1999 has made possible a reinstitution of a more modest program of military modernization. The Thai Air Force has requested a letter of offer and acceptance (LOA) for one squadron of F16-A/Bs (16 aircraft), which can be funded through planned overages in the Thai account in the Federal Financing Bank (FFB).

Singapore. Singapore does not have a defense treaty with the United States, but the Singaporeans see a strong coincidence of interests with the U.S., including the maintenance of freedom of navigation, access to regional markets, and global financial stability. Singapore and the United States also cooperated closely in dealing with the consequences of the regional economic crisis and the political crisis in Indonesia. The security relationship with the United States is also important to Singapore in the context of Singapore's strategy of leveraging technology to compensate for its lack of strategic depth and manpower limitations.[20] From the Singapore Air Force's standpoint, the relationship with the USAF provides the opportunity to train with the USAF, improve their capabilities, and benchmark themselves against the best in the world.[21]

---

[20]See *Defending Singapore in the 21st Century* (2000).

[21]Discussion with Major General Raymund Ng, Republic of Singapore Air Force Commander, February 2000.

Reflecting this outlook, Singapore has sought to anchor the U.S. military firmly in the region. Singapore hosts the U.S. Navy Logistic Group West Pacific (relocated from Subic Bay) and the USAF 497th Combat Training Squadron and is constructing berthing facilities to accommodate U.S. aircraft carriers. Singapore has also contributed significantly to burden sharing in the form of the provision of no-cost facilities and air force operational support. On the political side, U.S. perceptions of the Singaporean political system as authoritarian or insufficiently sensitive to U.S. conceptions of human rights were once obstacles to the development of closer bilateral cooperation, but these issues do not appear to have been a salient factor in recent years. More intractable are the problems of sheer space and geographic constraints, which place a limit on increased USAF use of Singapore facilities.[22]

Malaysia. By contrast, Malaysia has sought to diversify both its defense relationships—for instance, through the purchase of Russian MiG-29s, U.S. F/A-18s, and European naval systems—and its diplomatic relationships (i.e., through efforts to play Japan and the East Asian Economic Caucus as an economic counterweight to the United States). Malaysian policy, in fact, appears highly idiosyncratic, largely because it reflects Prime Minister Mahathir's personal proclivities as much as traditional strategic considerations.

Before the onset of the economic crisis, Malaysia conducted a broad range of military-to-military activities with the United States, but the tempo of these activities was slowed by the Malaysian defense budget squeeze. The prospects of expanded defense cooperation with Malaysia are difficult to predict and will depend largely on the future course of the Malaysian government. Prime Minister Mahathir's prickly policies and authoritarian tendencies could prove a serious obstacle to the development of closer defense relations. That said, Malaysia is now in a process of political and even generational change. Given the community of interests between the United States and Malaysia, the post-Mahathir era could open up the prospect of expanded defense cooperation.

---

[22]The policies of neighboring countries are also an important factor in the USAF's ability to optimize the use of facilities in Singapore. For instance, access to Indonesian ranges enhances training opportunities for aircraft deployed to Singapore, while Malaysia's denial of overflights renders use of Singaporean airfields more hazardous.

Indonesia. Indonesian defense policy has been informed both by the country's status as a founder and leading member of the Non-Aligned Movement and by the experience of the failed 1965 communist-backed coup. Although formally nonaligned, Indonesia's security orientation during the Suharto era coincided to a large extent with U.S. regional strategic interests. The development of a defense relationship consistent with shared security interests, however, was hampered under Suharto's New Order regime by controversies over human rights and the question of East Timor, which resonated in the U.S. Congress and led to restrictions on the transfer of U.S. military equipment and training to Indonesia.

The fall of Suharto and the transition to the new era opened a new chapter in Indonesian political development and perhaps in U.S.-Indonesian defense cooperation. A successful democratic evolution and cooperation with the international community in stabilizing East Timor would open a window for expanded bilateral defense cooperation. On the other hand, a political reversal leading either to a return to authoritarianism or to military rule, civil conflict, or a foreign policy shift in an anti-Western direction would undermine the prospects for cooperation and generate greater demands on the United States and the USAF.

The Indonesian military is acutely aware of the importance of establishing a solid relationship with the United States and the U.S. military, but it is frustrated by continuing U.S. restrictions on military-to-military relations and on the transfer of U.S. equipment and spare parts. Some harbor the suspicion that the West is seeking to keep Indonesia weak. Relations with Australia, once one of Indonesia's closest partners in regional security cooperation, have frayed badly in the wake of mutual recriminations over East Timor.

Both Air Force and Navy officers noted, in discussions in Jakarta in March 2000, that their services—unlike those of the Army—were not involved in internal security and needed U.S. help to perform their defense functions. The Air Force in particular has been hard hit both by the economic crisis and by the U.S. embargo and is unable to provide the air links critical to connect an archipelago of 17,000 islands. Of one squadron of F-16s (10 aircraft), only one-half are operational. The same holds true of Indonesia's two squadrons of C-130s. The Air Force budget has declined 50 percent in dollar terms since the onset of the crisis, and the number of flight hours has fallen by almost one-half.

Clearly there is a strong rationale for a closer relationship between the United States and the Indonesian military. If it is to shift from a politicized territorial-based force with an internal security mission to a modern military focused on external defense, and if it is to modernize its obsolescent equipment, the Indonesian armed forces need the technical support and training that the U.S. military can provide. For its part, the United States could enhance its ability to influence the most important national institution in Indonesia at a critical point in its evolution and, beyond that, help Indonesia resume its role as an agent of stability in Southeast Asia through a policy of engagement.

The obstacles to U.S. engagement with the Indonesian military are mostly political and perceptual. On the Indonesian side, there is the residual pull of the country's tradition of nonalignment and self-reliance in military matters as well as some suspicion of U.S. motives. On the U.S. side, the Indonesian military is associated with human rights violations and excesses during the East Timor crisis. These perceptions have been reflected in congressional restrictions on U.S. arms transfers and training of Indonesian military personnel. The first requirement of a policy of engagement with Indonesia, therefore, is to reduce the volatility in the relationship. This may be accomplished through a step-by-step process. As Indonesia continues to democratize, the United States should commit to deliver needed military equipment, spare parts, and training at predictable points in this process.

Vietnam. Vietnam's strategic importance derives from its long coastline on the South China Sea and its control of the base at Cam Ranh Bay—major assets in strategic competition on the South China Sea. Hence, there is an underlying logic to cooperation between the United States and Vietnam to prevent a Chinese bid for regional hegemony.

This is not to say that the U.S. military can be expected to return to Cam Ranh Bay anytime soon—aside from the fact that the Russian Navy is still there. For one thing, the threat to U.S. and Vietnamese security interests on the South China Sea has not risen to a level that would compel military cooperation. The continued rule of an authoritarian neo-communist regime in Hanoi and the legacy of the Vietnam War also constitute barriers to military cooperation between the United States and the Socialist Republic of Vietnam. This could change, however, in the context of a serious threat to regional security in which U.S. and Vietnamese strategic interests (and possibly the interests of other ASEAN states) converged. Multinational cooperation could in fact provide the cover needed to minimize historical sensitivities and bring together the two erstwhile adversaries of the Vietnam War if regional security conditions so required.

MAJOR POSSIBLE GEOPOLITICAL EVENTS IN THE SOUTHEAST ASIA REGION

The future security environment in Southeast Asia will be shaped by the interplay of a number of political and economic factors, some endogenous and others exogenous. The key factors, in our view, are the following: Southeast Asia's economic evolution; China's economic and political development and its interaction with Southeast Asia; the success of regional states in dealing with dissident movements and maintaining their national cohesion; the course of regional integration and cooperation; and the ability of key external actors, especially the United States, Japan, and Australia, to influence the regional security environment.

These drivers could interact to produce three basic scenarios, each with different implications for the political stability and security of Southeast Asian countries and for U.S. interests in the region:

(1) **Continuation of existing trends:** This would involve recovery from the economic crisis; a steady increase in Chinese influence and capabilities; a fragile trend toward democratization; continued threats to national cohesion in Indonesia and other regional states; weakened regional institutions; and a continued U.S. military presence.

(2) **Best-case scenario:** This scenario would entail steady economic recovery; a benign Chinese role in regional security; strengthening of democratic institutions in key states; resumed regional integration and a more effective role for ASEAN; and strengthened U.S. security relations with regional actors.

(3) **Downside scenario:** This would encompass economic reversal; an aggressive, hegemonic or chaotic China; an increase in ethnic and religious conflict; political breakdown or fragmentation of Indonesia; loss of cohesion of ASEAN; interstate conflict within Southeast Asia; and a regional security environment too unstable to permit successful security cooperation between ASEAN states and the United States. This scenario would also be likely to generate more severe transnational problems, including increased refugee flows, piracy, drug trafficking and smuggling, and other criminal activities.

Impact of Economic Factors

The economic evolution of Southeast Asia will clearly have a major impact in shaping the future security environment, just as the economic crisis of 1997–1998 brought about fundamental change in political and security conditions. In the best-case scenario, the regional economies would continue their recovery from the crisis. In Thailand, Malaysia, and the Philippines, currencies and stock markets would stabilize and economic growth resume. Indonesia would begin to emerge from the crisis, but the economic recovery would be fragile and vulnerable to political and social unrest.

A less optimistic scenario postulates a more uneven regional economic performance in which there would be greater differentiation among countries depending on each country's ability to maintain political stability and appropriate economic and fiscal policies. In these circumstances, Singapore and Thailand would present the best prospects for recovery and Indonesia the most problematic, and Malaysia and the Philippines would fall in between.

The worst-case scenario could come about as the result of a regional or extraregional shock—for instance, further economic deterioration in Japan, a Chinese banking crisis or currency devaluation, or competitive devaluations by other Asian countries. All Southeast Asian countries would be affected, although the political impact would be most severe in Indonesia, the country most weakened by the crisis. Economic deterioration could also threaten the stability of democratic institutions in the Philippines and Thailand, bring about the collapse of the political order in Malaysia, and aggravate interstate

tensions as governments seek foreign scapegoats for domestic difficulties.

The interplay of the trends described above could produce a number
of major geopolitical events, which would in turn generate demands
on the United States and the U.S. military. Two of the most demanding of these events—Indonesian disintegration or political breakdown and an armed conflict involving China—will be discussed
below.

Indonesian Disintegration or Political Breakdown

Indonesia's geopolitical weight makes it the key to Southeast Asia's
security. Indonesia has 40 percent of Southeast Asia's total population and a landmass greater than the rest of Southeast Asia combined. It stretches over 3000 miles and straddles critical SLOCs and
straits connecting the Western Pacific with the Indian Ocean. Although the world's largest Muslim-majority country, Indonesia is
culturally and religiously diverse and is organized as a secular state.
This vast country is currently in a process of systemic political transition in which the strategic interaction between the government,
other political actors, and the armed forces could lead to a variety of
outcomes. Three possible outcomes suggest themselves:

1. Successful Democratic Transition. The best-case scenario pre-
sumes that the current government in Jakarta will move the political
reform process forward toward a stable democratic order. However,
the coalition that elected President Wahid—which included traditional Muslims, secular-minded supporters of Vice President
Megawati Sukarnoputri, and factions of the former pro-Suharto
Golkar party—has frayed badly. A positive outcome will thus depend
on whether Wahid or his successor can build a viable parliamentary
majority. It will also depend on whether the government is able to
get a grip on the economy, bring about some improvement in the
standard of living of ordinary Indonesians, and foster the return of
the predominantly ethnic Chinese capital that has fled the country.
If the Wahid government manages these challenges successfully, the
prospects for democratic consolidation will improve. The trend lines
are, however, unclear. According to reports from Singapore, some of
the ethnic-Chinese capital that had fled Indonesia returned after
Wahid's election, but the flow of capital has since slowed because of

a lack of confidence in the Wahid government's economic management. The key problem of the corporate debt overhang has not been
cleared, for example, and the banks have not resumed lending.[23]

In addition, a number of wild cards could derail the process, one of
which is the government's handling of insurgencies and separatist
movements, particularly in Aceh. If the government's efforts to conciliate the Acehnese fail, its options would be to concede independence to Aceh as it did to East Timor, which would be unacceptable
to many Indonesians, especially in the military, or to prosecute a difficult and costly war. As mentioned earlier, there is also an armed
insurgency in the province of Irian Jaya at the opposite end of the
Indonesian archipelago as well as what amounts to a religious civil
war on some of the islands of the Moluccas, which could spread to
other parts of the country and perhaps generate unsustainable
strains on the military and the political system.

Beyond demands for outright separation, Jakarta faces a significant
political challenge in managing the demand on the part of the
provinces, especially outside Java, for greater autonomy and control
over local resources. The government has responded by passing laws
that devolve power and revenue to the provincial and village level.
In the view of some, only Indonesia's transformation into a federated
state can in the long run save the country from disintegration. On
the other hand, dismantling the old centralized state represents an
enormous challenge. The experience of the Philippines with decentralization was not entirely happy; it fostered corruption at the local
level, the creation of local fiefdoms, and reductions in government
services.[24] If not managed carefully, decentralization in Indonesia
could reduce the central government's ability to fund essential functions and could thus create greater imbalances between resource-
rich and resource-poor provinces.

2. Aborted Transition and Political Breakdown. Given this outline
of the problems confronting the Jakarta government, it goes without
saying that there is no guarantee that it will successfully navigate the

---

[23]Discussion with analysts in Singapore, February 2000.

[24]Presentation by former Philippine National Security Adviser Jose Almonte at the
Council for Security Cooperation in the Asia Pacific international seminar on
Indonesia's future challenges and implications for the region, Jakarta, March 8, 2000.

transition to a stable democratic system. One key factor in this context is leadership. By both temper and political philosophy, Wahid is well qualified to promote national conciliation and cohesion, but he has been unable to effectively address the country's pressing problems, and his political support has eroded. Vice President Megawati's political skills are unproven.

If the Jakarta government's economic and political policies were a conspicuous failure, the democratic transition could be aborted. Violence could increase and spread to Java, possibly fostered by Islamic radicals. The armed forces, which view themselves as guardians of the country's territorial integrity and political stability, could thus see no option but to reinsert themselves into politics, and the country could revert to authoritarian or military rule.

An aborted transition could widen fissures in Indonesian society, overwhelm key institutions, and lead to a breakdown of central authority. A breakdown scenario could in turn involve a collapse of authority in Jakarta, with different factions vying for power. It could, moreover, involve the loss of central control over the periphery and, in the most extreme case, the outright secession or attempted secession of outlying provinces.

3. Disintegration. This worst-case scenario could come about as a result of a split in the military, which could conceivably fracture along some of the many divides in Indonesian society, or from the simultaneous outbreak of large-scale violence in Java and secessionist or dissident challenges in the outer islands that the thinly stretched military proved unable to control. Needless to say, this scenario, while not the most likely, would be the most demanding one for the United States and the USAF. Chaotic conditions in Indonesia could generate requirements for a variety of military operations other than war (MOOTW) and at the same time raise the bar for cooperation with the Indonesian civil authorities and military.

Failure of East Timor Settlement

Indonesia's acceptance of East Timor's separation and the Indonesian military's withdrawal from the half-island have lessened considerably the prospect that East Timor will continue to be a factor of instability in Indonesia's relations with the United States and the international community. The best-case scenario would be one in which Jakarta cooperates with the international community in stabilizing East Timor. An arrangement that saves Jakarta's face and protects the interests of all of the parties—including Indonesia and its former supporters on East Timor—is most likely to produce a viable East Timorese state, strengthen the process of political reform in Indonesia, and reduce the prospects of international conflict over East Timor. Yet, despite the goodwill manifested by both President Wahid and the East Timor leadership, prospects for a favorable outcome have been clouded by continued incursions into East Timor by pro-Indonesian militias based across the border in West Timor.

Even in the best of circumstances, however, East Timor will require the employment of considerable peacekeeping assets on the part of the international community. Despite the Indonesian withdrawal and the presence of an international force, East Timor is far from stabilized. The Indonesians are unlikely to try to reassert control over East Timor, particularly if they are preoccupied with separatists in Aceh and other parts of Indonesia. In the context of political instability and power struggles in Indonesia, however, some Indonesian political and military factions might view it as in their interests to encourage continued violence and confrontation on East Timor. In this scenario, dissatisfied pro-Indonesian militias and their supporters might carry out attacks against the proindependence population and the peacekeeping force. The Indonesian authorities on West Timor might be unwilling or unable to suppress the militias— and under some circumstances might actively encourage them. The unfinished conflict on East Timor could thus become a permanent drain on international peacekeeping assets as well as a potential source of international conflict.

Threats to Democracy and Stability in the Philippines

A deterioration of conditions in Southeast Asia could also threaten democratic institutions in countries where democracy has taken root, particularly the Philippines. The democratic tradition in the Philippines strengthened steadily from the fall of the Marcos regime in 1986 to President Estrada's election in 1998. During this period, there were three successive democratic presidential elections; democratic civilian control of the military was strengthened; and former military coup makers and guerrillas alike were incorporated into the political system.

Despite the impressive achievements of Filipino democracy, strong political and economic threats to stability remain. Estrada was driven out of office in January 2001 by an uprising backed by opposition political sectors and the military. As discussed previously, the Philippine government must contend with communist and Islamic insurgents. Inadequate implementation of the peace agreement with the former Moro rebels in Mindanao—particularly the lack of tangible economic benefits for the former rank-and-file guerrillas— could undermine the viability of the accord and lead to renewed large-scale conflict. The fragility of the situation in southern Mindanao was exposed, as noted above, by Abu Sayyaf's kidnapping of foreign tourists and Filipinos in May 2000, and the Philippine military's rescue operations on Abu Sayyaf's stronghold of Basilan Island triggered the worst outbreak of violence in years. The MILF broke off peace negotiations with the Manila government in protest and staged a series of attacks in Mindanao.

Estrada's removal from office may have unpredictable consequences. Chaotic conditions could lead to a resurgence of violence and social protests—some of the conditions that undermined Philippine democracy in the past. The worst-case scenario would be a conjunction of authoritarian or chaotic political conditions in Manila with the strengthening of Islamic separatist enclaves in the southern Philippines.

Intra-ASEAN Conflict

Thirty years of interaction within ASEAN have nurtured a strong norm against the use of force to resolve conflicts among ASEAN states. Therefore, an intra-ASEAN armed conflict should be considered a low-probability event. Nevertheless, the economic crisis has weakened the ASEAN consensus and stoked intraregional tensions. Long-standing antagonisms—never far below the surface—could flare up and fuel an international conflict.

Malaysia's relations with both Singapore and Indonesia have been strained over refugee, immigration, and other economic issues. Friction between Thailand and Burma over political and border issues is also on the rise. In discussions in Bangkok in February 2000, Thai defense analysts expressed their belief that a conflict between Thailand and Burma was the most likely international conflict in mainland Southeast Asia. Potential conflicts could also arise over any of a number of land and sea border disputes.

A possible intra-ASEAN conflict between Malaysia and Singapore could come about as a result of a political crisis is Malaysia. Both countries are in the process of generational leadership transition. The Singaporean transition is proceeding at a deliberate pace and is likely to be stable, but the Malaysian transition could generate a dangerous political dynamic. Prime Minister Mahathir appears to have overcome the immediate political crisis provoked by the dismissal and imprisonment of former Deputy Prime Minister Anwar Ibrahim, but any one of a series of events, including a serious economic downturn or a rupture in the Malaysian government's Malay power base, could threaten its hold on power. In such circumstances, ratcheting tensions with Singapore could be viewed as a way to rally Malay and army support for the government. In this scenario, Kuala Lumpur might not necessarily intend the tensions to develop into an armed conflict, but crises could quickly veer out of control.

Singapore is unlikely to provoke a military conflict with Malaysia, but if Singapore is convinced that Malaysia planned to attack, its lack of strategic depth could induce it to launch an Israeli-style preemptive strike. Singapore could not sustain a prolonged conflict and would seek an early end to the fighting, with international monitoring and, to the extent possible, demilitarization of the border area.

Although a Malaysia-Singapore armed confrontation should at this time be considered a low-probability event, the consequences for regional security were it to occur would be far-reaching. It could, for example, divide Southeast Asia into antagonistic blocs and bring about the effective end of ASEAN. It could also revive the environment of national and ethnic conflict that preceded the establishment of ASEAN, endanger ethnic minorities, and invite external interference in Southeast Asian affairs.

Conflicts Involving China

The potential threats China poses to Southeast Asia can be placed in two broad categories: conventional military threats and more ambiguous and subtle challenges, possibly in the guise of maintaining regional order. It should be recognized, however, that these categories are part of a continuum: China employs both approaches as needed, beginning with more subtle or indirect threats and escalating when that approach fails or where a "lesson" is required.[25] Nevertheless, the distinction between the two kinds of threats is analytically useful: Threats in the first category are easily identifiable and therefore more amenable to deliberate planning, including deterrence and response. Because of their lower profile and more ambiguous nature, threats in the second category may be more likely to materialize but harder to anticipate or counter effectively.

1. Conventional Military Threats. In the category of conventional military threats, there are two contingencies that would require a U.S. diplomatic or military response. One would be an incident that spins out of control—for instance, if a regional state resisted a Chinese attempt at encroachment on the South China Sea or decided to challenge a Chinese outpost within its claimed area of jurisdiction. In either case, an incident could escalate into a full-scale military confrontation.

The second would be a deliberate Chinese decision to establish and maintain physical control over all or most of the Spratlys. Such a Chinese operation could feature the threat or use of force against the territory of an ASEAN state, either to compel acceptance of Chinese demands or to defeat opposing military forces.

In the event of a conventional conflict, the Chinese would quickly overrun the garrisons on the islands, since none of the Southeast Asian states, either alone or in combination, have the capability to defeat a determined Chinese attack. However, the demands of a South China Sea conflict on the logistics and operational capabilities of China and the Southeast Asian states would be substantial, as neither side has the capability to sustain operations over a prolonged period of time. That said, the Chinese might not require prolonged

---

[25]The 1979 border war with Vietnam would fall into the latter category.

operations to achieve their political aims, which could be coercion or intimidation of regional states.

2. Ambiguous Threats. Alternatively, China could expand its "salami tactics" and more ambiguous use of force to assert control over territory. The Chinese have been adept at camouflaging their politico-military operations in ostensibly innocuous garb—from the construction of "fishermen's shelters" on Philippines-claimed Mischief Reef to the July 1999 seizure, for "smuggling," of a Taiwanese vessel carrying supplies to Matsu. The Chinese could continue their "island-hopping" tactics and steadily increase their presence on disputed areas. They could also engage in selective harassment of regional states in the guise of antipiracy or order-keeping operations or protection of Chinese fishermen or so-called civilian facilities.

Under either of these circumstances, the governments under attack could request a more visible and substantial U.S. military presence including, in the event of a conventional Chinese attack, the deployment of U.S. naval vessels and combat aircraft to deter further attacks or induce China to withdraw.

If the country involved in a conflict with China were to be the Philippines, the Manila government could seek to invoke the Mutual Defense Treaty under the provision covering an attack on Philippine armed forces. The United States would then be placed in the difficult position of either complying with requests for assistance, thereby raising the prospect of involvement in a conflict with China, or refraining from doing so, which would risk diminishing the credibility of U.S. commitment to the security of the region and increase the incentive for regional states to "bandwagon" with China.

3. Spillover of Taiwan Conflict. A third and perhaps more probable scenario for a conflict in Southeast Asia involving China would involve the spillover of a conflict over Taiwan. In this scenario, the Chinese would likely seek to interdict shipping to Taiwan, possibly extending interdiction efforts to the South China Sea. If the attack on Taiwan is viewed as unprovoked—e.g., not in response to a Taiwanese declaration of independence—the ASEAN states would likely condemn it but would not be likely to provide military assistance to Taiwan. If Chinese actions were perceived as interfering with freedom of navigation on the South China Sea, some ASEAN states might be willing to join the United States in providing escorts to civilian shipping. In these circumstances, a military clash with China could not be excluded.

The stakes would be higher if the United States were to come to the defense of Taiwan. The United States could ask for the use of bases in Southeast Asia for both logistical support and combat missions. Use of air bases in Luzon could be critical in the unlikely event that Japan were to deny the United States the use of bases in Okinawa. Whether to cooperate with the United States in actual combat operations against China would be an excruciatingly difficult decision, as the political costs would be high either way. In addition, a decision to cooperate militarily with the United States could expose the cooperating countries to military retaliation by China. Therefore, in order to secure Southeast Asian military cooperation, the United States should be prepared to offer an adequate *quid pro quo* as well as protection from Chinese military retaliation, perhaps in the form of theater missile defense.

IMPLICATIONS OF CHANGES IN THE REGIONAL SECURITY ENVIRONMENT FOR REGIONAL AIRPOWER

Given the more volatile security environment in Southeast Asia and the archipelagic character of the theater, the Southeast Asian states need to upgrade their airpower both to counter growing Chinese power projection capabilities and to deal with regional contingencies. As a result of the economic crisis and a growing preoccupation with internal security problems, however, most of the ASEAN states, with the exception of Singapore, have slashed defense expenditures, weapon procurement, and force modernization. As a result, there has been a decline in combined exercises and training. Air and naval force modernization and other programs to enhance ASEAN force projection capabilities have been delayed, cut back, or canceled. Moreover, because ASEAN states have not coordinated any of these decisions, interoperability within ASEAN—which has traditionally been weak—has been dealt a further setback.

As the region pulls itself from the crisis, military modernization will resume. The Thais have requested an LOA on F-16s, and the acquisition of a modern multirole aircraft remains one of the Philippines' highest acquisition priorities.

Nevertheless, the gap in military capabilities between the ASEAN countries and China is likely to grow over the next 10 to 15 years. Therefore, the Southeast Asian states will continue to rely on the United States to maintain the regional balance of power and deter Chinese expansionism.

IMPLICATIONS OF THE CHANGES IN THE REGIONAL SECURITY ENVIRONMENT FOR THE UNITED STATES AND THE USAF

The scenarios discussed above are not predictive but suggest different sets of demands and requirements for the United States and the USAF as well as opportunities for the United States to promote its core security interests in Southeast Asia. A conflict involving China would be the most demanding scenario. The Chinese could be expected to seek to deter U.S. involvement by raising the costs of conflict through a variety of means, including challenges to U.S. global interests. In the Southeast Asian theater, Chinese ballistic or cruise missiles and submarines could place U.S. military assets at risk.

Scenarios involving political disintegration or threats to democracy in Southeast Asian countries could generate greater demands for noncombatant evacuation operations (NEO), peacekeeping and peacemaking operations, SLOC protection, and humanitarian and disaster relief operations. These requirements would increase the burden on the USAF and affect its readiness and ability to conduct major regional contingency (MRC) combat missions in the short and long run. Indonesian disintegration or political breakdown would be particularly dangerous and burdensome, not only because of the humanitarian crises such a course of events will likely generate and the accompanying demands on U.S. and USAF resources, but also because Indonesia's disintegration could change the entire geopolitical complexion of Southeast Asia in ways we cannot even begin to anticipate.

The most promising approach for the United States and the USAF is in our view to seek to affect the "demand" side through a robust shaping and hedging strategy. In this regard, the same unstable conditions that could generate greater demands would also provide greater opportunities for closer engagement with ASEAN militaries, improved multilateral cooperation, and enhanced and expanded access to regional facilities.

AN ENGAGEMENT AND HEDGING STRATEGY

From the above considerations, it follows that the United States should think of a step-by-step approach focusing on shaping a more favorable security environment through engagement with regional governments and militaries while diversifying options for U.S. access and laying the foundation for an expanded U.S. military presence if needed.

Engagement

Over the next several years, the United States will have the opportunity to cultivate stronger military ties with many ASEAN states. The priority during this period should be to expand military-to-military contacts and training to assist ASEAN countries with the modernization of their air forces and the use of their assets to combat illicit drug trafficking, smuggling, and piracy and to conduct sea monitoring, search-and-rescue, disaster relief, and humanitarian operations. Since budgetary constraints have forced ASEAN air forces to cut back on training and exercises, rotational deployments and combined exercises should be structured to minimize the counterpart country's financial outlays. Exercise Cope Thunder (which in its last iteration included Japanese, Thai, and Singaporean air force participation) could be expanded to include other ASEAN countries. The USAF could also increase periodic deployments of AWACS aircraft for training in a maritime surveillance mode with ASEAN militaries.

A democratic Indonesia should make it possible for the United States to resume international military education and training (IMET) and to provide equipment and training under the Foreign Military Sales (FMS) program. Whenever possible, the United States could foster cooperation and interoperability among regional states—for instance, by exploring the establishment of a regional "Red Flag" training center (possibly in the Philippines), an integrated air defense system, or combined interoperability programs linked to the transfer of U.S.-origin advanced weapon systems. The United States should also intensify a strategic dialogue with partners, since the importance of a shared strategic perspective cannot be underestimated in facilitating cooperation and burden sharing.

Military-to-military cooperation may be more difficult to attain if regional militaries regress into practices inconsistent with U.S. views of democratic governance and human rights. The dilemma is that, while domestic political considerations may require that the United States distance itself from local militaries, the effect may be to reduce the U.S. ability to influence a key institution on behalf of U.S. interests, including democratization and human rights improvements. Clearly, each situation would have to be evaluated on its own merits, but it could be argued that, in problematic cases, a degree of compartmentalization would serve U.S. interests. Since air forces and navies are usually less involved in internal security than ground forces, from a political perspective they can be more viable interlocutors than other elements of a regional state's armed forces.

The U.S. engagement strategy should, of course, be adapted to the historical experience and political and technical requirements of each counterpart country. With the Philippines and Thailand, the United States could build on long-standing relationships and could help, especially in the former case, with badly needed military modernization. In Singapore, as noted above, there is extensive ongoing cooperation. While Singapore is not a treaty ally, the United States would be justified in treating it as an ally, particularly with regard to high-tech transfer and advanced training. With Malaysia, there is a need to resume a normal tempo of bilateral activities, interrupted by the financial crisis, and to insulate the military-to-military relationship from controversies emanating from the political arena.

Access and Basing Arrangements

Just as engagement is key to the shaping side of the U.S. strategy, access is at the heart of its hedging component. Since the U.S. withdrawal from bases in the Philippines, there have been no permanently stationed forces in Southeast Asia, although the United States has varying degrees of access to facilities in Thailand, the Philippines, Singapore, Malaysia, and Brunei. What shape U.S. requirements will take in the future will depend largely on the way the regional security situation develops. In circumstances where their security is threatened, however, some ASEAN states would be more likely to agree to support an expanded U.S. military presence.

From a practical standpoint, it would be advisable to maximize access options to increase flexibility—that is, to adopt a "portfolio" approach to basing and access. Political considerations argue for spreading access and basing arrangements among several countries to avoid overdependence on any single country and to hedge against the loss of access or the placing of operational restrictions on U.S. forces. This approach recognizes that there is no single solution to the problem and lays the groundwork for an expansion of the U.S. military presence if required by changes in the security environment, such as the loss of bases in Northeast Asia or a more aggressive Chinese stance.

In terms of operational requirements, the near-term priorities should be the Philippines and Singapore, but the United States should also be improving military ties and cooperation with Malaysia, Indonesia, and Thailand. In the case of Malaysia and Indonesia—both of which are committed to national and regional "self-reliance" and are sensitive to their position within the nonaligned movement—the United States and the USAF will have to be patient in building trust in the relationship and improving defense capabilities. Enhanced U.S. intelligence sharing and arms transfers—especially those that enhance interoperability with U.S. forces—as well as U.S. assistance tied to improving inter-ASEAN cooperation could pave the way for expanded military cooperation.

Specific options for improved or expanded air access could include the following:

Philippines. Use of the facilities in Luzon would permit U.S. aircraft to respond to either a Taiwan or a South China Sea contingency. Despite residual controversy over the U.S. bases, the Philippine government will probably allow U.S. operational use of facilities in country if Philippine security interests are directly at stake. The United States may be asked to provide security guarantees or assistance for military modernization programs. In some envisioned circumstances, the United States would have to redefine its position on the Philippines' contested territories in the South China Sea.

Singapore. Singapore has placed at the disposal of the United States dedicated and dual-use facilities at Paya Lebar Air Base. Facilities at Singapore are close to critical straits and can be used to access Indonesian ranges. USAF operational use of facilities in Singapore is possible in the context of U.S.-Singaporean strategic cooperation. U.S. access arrangements with Singapore could be expanded into a defense agreement that would spell out conditions under which the United States could use those facilities for out-of-area contingencies, possibly including a Taiwan contingency. Geographic and space limitations, however, could constrain air operations from Singapore. There would also be political limits imposed by Malay suspicion of Singapore's relationship with the United States.

Thailand. Thailand allows the United States broad access to Utapao for exercises and real-life operations and will probably agree to an expanded U.S. presence in a regional security emergency. Unless there is further evolution in Thai attitudes toward China, Thai facilities may not be available for a China-centered contingency.

Indonesia. Indonesia has upgraded air and naval facilities at Ranai (Natuna Besar) on the South China Sea near Kalimantan. Under some circumstances arrangements could be negotiated with Jakarta, although it would require overcoming significant political obstacles on both sides. Infrastructure improvements would probably be needed.

Malaysia. Malaysia hosts regular bilateral exercises with the USAF, but operational use of Malaysian facilities for regional contingencies is unlikely unless Malaysian security was threatened. Prospects for bilateral cooperation might be better in the post-Mahathir era.

Australia. Australia is the closest U.S. ally in the Southwestern Pacific/Indian Ocean region, with vital interests in Southeast Asia. The Australians are interested in developing Tindal Air Force Base near Darwin as a training range and in accommodating Southeast Asian combined training. This could present an opportunity to expand cooperation and interoperability with regional states but will require working to rebuild trust and cooperation between Australia and Indonesia.

THE CHANGING POLITICAL-MILITARY
ENVIRONMENT: SOUTH ASIA

Ashley J. Tellis

The security environment in South Asia has remained relatively un-settled since the Indian and Pakistani nuclear tests of May 1998. The Indian government's efforts to publicly emphasize the challenges China posed in the weeks leading up to those tests—after more than a decade of mostly *sotto voce* complaints—served to rupture the or-dinarily glacial process of normalizing Sino-Indian relations. This process always possessed a certain fragility in that the gradually de-creasing tensions along the Sino-Indian border did not automatically translate into increased trust between Beijing and New Delhi. Even as both sides sought to derive tactical advantages from the confi-dence-building measures they had negotiated since 1993—for ex-ample, the drawdown of forces along the utterly inhospitable LAC in the Himalayas—each ended up pursuing larger grand strategies that effectively undercut the other's interests. Beijing, for example, per-sisted in covertly assisting the nuclear and missile programs of India's local competitor, Pakistan, while New Delhi sought in re-sponse to develop an intermediate-range ballistic missile whose comparative utility lay primarily in targeting China.

The repeated identification of China as a threat to Indian interests by both Bharatiya Janata Party (BJP) leaders and other influential Indian elites in the first half of 1998 not only underscored the fragile nature of the Sino-Indian rapprochement but also ruptured the carefully maintained façade of improving relations between the two countries.[1]   When this public finger pointing ultimately gave way to India's resumption of nuclear testing on May 11, 1998 (an event accompanied by the Indian prime minister's explicit claim that those tests were driven by the hostile actions of India's northern neighbor over the years), security competition in South Asia—which usually appears, at least in popular perceptions, as merely a bilateral affair between India and Pakistan—finally revealed itself as the "regional strategic triangle"[2] it has always been.

This appendix analyzes Indian and Pakistani attitudes toward China in the context of the triangular security competition in South Asia. Taking the 1998 nuclear tests as its point of departure, it assesses how China figures in the grand strategies of the two principal states in the Indian subcontinent and identifies the principal regional geopolitical contingencies for which the United States should prepare over the next decade.   Finally, it briefly analyzes the kinds of opportunities the region offers to the USAF as it engages, even as it prepares to hedge against, a rising China.

NUCLEAR TESTING AND THE TRIANGULAR SECURITY COMPETITION IN SOUTH ASIA

Impact of the Nuclear Tests on Sino-Indian Relations

Although Pakistan was directly affected by the Indian nuclear tests, these tests engaged Chinese security interests as well. To begin with, India's decision to resume testing made manifest New Delhi's resentment toward Beijing for its almost two-decade-long assistance to Islamabad's nuclear and missile programs. India's official claim that its resumption of nuclear testing was precipitated at least in part by various Chinese actions (such as the transfer of nuclear weapon designs, short-range ballistic missiles, and assorted technologies intended to enable Islamabad to produce strategic systems indigenously) was meant to signal the fact that India was capable of

---

[1]These early 1998 events have been summarized in Manoj Joshi, "George in the China Shop," *India Today*, May 18, 1998, pp. 10–16.

[2]For a good discussion, see Brahma Chellaney, "The Regional Strategic Triangle," in Brahma Chellaney (ed.), *Securing India's Future in the New Millennium*, New Delhi: Orient Longman, 1999, pp. 313–336.

defending its own security interests—if necessary through unilateral solutions—and that improvement in some aspects of Sino-Indian bilateral relations could not be sustained if it came at the expense of undercutting the core objective of preserving India's safety, integrity, and primacy in South Asia.[3]

Further, the decision to test and the affirmation that India would develop a nuclear deterrent implied that New Delhi would at some point seek to target China with nuclear weapons. This effort at replacing abject vulnerability with mutual vulnerability—no matter how asymmetrical it might be—suggested that Indian policymakers were unprepared to hang their hopes solely on the peacefulness of Chinese intentions, especially over the long term, given that Beijing's power is expected to grow even further and the relative differential in its strategic capabilities vis-à-vis New Delhi is likely to become even more manifest. India's decision to develop a nuclear deterrent thus suggests that India seeks at a minimum to possess the kinds of deterrent capabilities that will immunize it against possible Chinese nuclear blackmail in the event of a crisis.[4]

Finally, India's decision to resume nuclear testing has also been complemented by an effort to modernize the Indian military—an effort that has encompassed upgrading India's conventional forces, including those elements tasked with defending the mountainous border areas facing both Pakistan and China. This modernization, which slowed down during the 1990s for financial reasons, is likely to gather momentum during the coming decade as Indian security managers increasingly recognize that, irrespective of what happens in the realm of diplomatic relations, maintaining robust conventional capabilities remains not only the best insurance against deterrence breakdown but also a vital precondition for making good on India's public pledge never to use nuclear weapons first.[5]

---

[3]This theme is emphasized in J. Mohan Malik, "India Goes Nuclear: Rationale, Benefits, Costs and Implications," *Contemporary Southeast Asia*, Vol. 20, No. 2, August 1998, pp. 191–215.

[4]The critical importance of deterring blackmail in Indian calculations is highlighted in Jasjit Singh, "Why Nuclear Weapons?" in Jasjit Singh (ed.), *Nuclear India*, New Delhi: Knowledge World, 1998, pp. 9–25.

[5]For more on this calculus, see Tellis (2001).

The Sino-Indian Balance

India's recent decision to conduct nuclear tests, to develop a nuclear deterrent, and to accelerate the oft-postponed modernization of its conventional forces has often engendered the conclusion that New Delhi now views Beijing as a "clear and present danger" to its security. In point of fact, this is not the case. To be sure, the Indian capital would appear to be heavily populated by individuals, think tanks, and associations who vociferously assert the imminence of the Chinese threat. These claims are usually based either on Western revelations about Beijing's assistance to Islamabad's nuclear and missile programs and its murky activities in Burma or, alternatively, on distant fears such as the prospect of a rapidly growing China "returning" to complete its agenda of "national reunification" at a time when it will have dramatically surpassed India in most of the relevant categories of national power.[6] These challenges, however—while acknowledged both by elected Indian officials and by the higher bureaucracy in New Delhi—have not produced the kinds of reactions Indian commentators have often expected because, put simply, India's state managers have a much better grasp of the Sino-Indian power balance than many analysts give them credit for.

For more than a decade, Indian policymakers have in general pursued a subtle policy toward Beijing. Although the forceful statements of several Indian leaders in the months surrounding the nuclear tests were exceptions to this rule, more recent Indian initiatives vis-à-vis China—including the June 1999 visit of Indian Foreign Minister Jaswant Singh to Beijing—suggest that India's China policy has slowly swung back from the extreme of polemical criticism to a much more centrist effort at realistically managing the complexity and tensions inherent in the Sino-Indian relationship.[7]

The logic of this effort can best be appreciated in the context of understanding the perceptions of senior Indian security managers with

---

[6]These concerns are summarized in Amitabh Mattoo, "Complacency About Chinese Threat Called Frightening," *India Abroad*, April 5, 1996.

[7]A good description of the complexity of Sino-Indian relations can be found in Surjit Mansingh, "Sino-Indian Relations in the Post-Cold War Era," *Asian Survey*, Vol. 34, No. 3, March 1994, pp. 285–300.

respect to China.[8] All official Indian assessments of China are grounded in the recognition that while China is certainly a great power located on India's borders, it is by no means a "hegemonic" power in the international system. This means that Chinese capabilities, while significant and often superior to India's in many areas, are still regarded as insufficient to the task of bestowing on Beijing the kind of preeminence in global decisionmaking that would force India to acquiesce to Chinese preferences and actions when they undercut India's interests.

Indian policymakers certainly recognize that China is a rapidly growing economic entity, but they still see Chinese national power—on balance—as hobbled by significant domestic and external constraints. This rather sober assessment of Chinese strength is colored first by continuing uncertainty over whether China can sustain its high growth rates of the past two decades and second by the recognition that even if these growth rates were sustained, siphoning off resources for power-political purposes is unlikely to be either easy or effortless given the vast domestic development demands Beijing will have to service before it can lay claim to a managerial role at the core of the global system.[9]

These twin considerations led New Delhi to conclude that, while China may well be superior to India in power-political terms, India is by no means an "easy mark." Rather, the relative difference in power capabilities between India and China—being much less than, say, those between China and many of the smaller states along its southern periphery—provides New Delhi with a large margin within which to maneuver, thereby enabling India to respond to the growth of Chinese power with much more equanimity than is sometimes presumed justified by observers both inside and outside the country.

In fact, it is often inadequately recognized that, as far as basic security is concerned, India is actually relatively well-off vis-à-vis

---

[8]I am deeply grateful to several senior officials in the Indian Ministries of External Affairs and Defence, the Prime Minister's Office, and the headquarters of the three Indian armed services for their insights on this issue.

[9]The premises beneath this conclusion are summarized in *India: Analyst Skeptical of PRC Becoming Superpower*, FBIS-NES-97-210, July 29, 1997.

China.[10]   The Himalayan mountain ranges that divide the two countries, for example, provide a natural defensive shield against any easy Chinese aggression, and these benefits of nature have only been reinforced by Indian artifice since the disastrous border war of 1962. Today, India's conventional forces enjoy a comfortable superiority over their Chinese counterparts in the Himalayan theater; the Indian Army has superior firepower, better-trained soldiers, carefully prepared defenses, and more reliable logistics. Similarly, the Indian Air Force has better aircraft, superior pilots, and excellent infrastructure and would most likely gain tactical superiority over the battlefield within a matter of days if not hours in the event of renewed Sino-Indian hostilities. And, while the Indian Navy is not directly relevant to any Himalayan border conflict, the fact remains that it is superior to the Chinese Navy in technology, training, and war-fighting proficiency and would have little difficulty enforcing effective surface and subsurface barrier control should any Chinese naval units seek to break out into and operate within the Andaman Sea. Only in the realm of nuclear capabilities does China currently have an overwhelming, uncontestable superiority over India. Here again, however, this superiority is attenuated by two simple realities: First, the political disputes between China and India are too small to warrant any recourse to nuclear weaponry on either side; and second, the development of India's own nuclear deterrent over time will provide New Delhi with a modest means of deterring all but the most extreme Chinese threats.

All things considered, therefore, India's relative economic weakness vis-à-vis China does not by any means place it in a hopeless strategic situation as far as its northern rival is concerned. There is, in fact, a good chance that India could do as well as China economically so long as New Delhi stays the course with respect to the economic liberalization program it began in 1991. If this program continues, India could sustain average GNP growth rates in excess of 6 percent per annum over the next two decades and, moreover, could sustain such growth through the enlargement of its internal market alone. In-

---

[10]This discussion is based on Ashley J. Tellis, Chung Min Lee, James Mulvenon, Courtney Purrington, and Michael D. Swaine, "Sources of Conflict in Asia," in Zalmay Khalilzad and Ian O. Lesser (eds.), *Sources of Conflict in the 21st Century: Regional Futures and U.S. Strategy,* Santa Monica: RAND, MR-897-AF, 1998, pp. 157–158.

deed, by many key measures—such as savings rates, population composition, the durability and effectiveness of its institutions, and investments in key technologies—India's performance already compares favorably with that of China even if it does not always surpass its rival.[11]

Indian Policy Toward China

Given these considerations, Indian policymakers view the growth of Chinese power as a phenomenon that, while necessitating careful monitoring, need not warrant any panic. Since the uninterrupted growth of Chinese capabilities is by no means assured, policymakers do not believe that drastic changes are warranted in India's own grand strategy—a strategy that has focused consciously on the steady and autonomous acquisition of great-power capabilities ever since the country's independence in 1947. This autonomous quest for great-power capabilities traditionally manifested itself in two forms: in an economic policy that focused on autarkic industrialization carried out by a huge state-managed economy, and in a foreign policy centering on "nonalignment" that sought to steer clear of all competing alliances throughout the Cold War.

The autarkic, state-managed domestic economic policy has slowly given way to a more liberal economic order, since it is now widely acknowledged that state control only impedes growth and restrains innovation. To that degree, India's traditional grand strategy has thus changed.[12] Yet the desire to pursue an autonomous course in international politics remains the bedrock of New Delhi's grand strategy, based as it is on the belief that a country of India's size, heritage, power, and overall potential cannot flourish as an appendage of any ideological or power bloc. Although the demise of the bipolar order implies that the specific circumstances which gave rise to nonalignment have long disappeared, the intrinsic logic of pursuing

---

[11]For a good comparative analysis of Indian and Chinese economic performance, see Amartya Sen, *Economic Development and Social Change: India and China in Comparative Perspectives,* London: London School of Economics, STICERD Discussion Paper Series DEP-67, 1995; and A. S. Bhalla, *Uneven Development in the Third World: A Study of China and India,* New York: St. Martin's Press, 1995.

[12]For further discussion, see Ashley J. Tellis, "South Asia," in Zalmay Khalilzad (ed.), *Strategic Appraisal 1996,* Santa Monica: RAND, MR-543-AF, 1996, pp. 283–307.

an independent foreign policy—at least to the degree that one can do so within the constraints of a capabilities-driven global power-political system—remains in place in New Delhi. Thus, even in the present unipolar order, New Delhi intends neither to ally itself permanently with the United States nor to permanently oppose it. Instead, it envisages creating the requisite political space within which its national capabilities can increase and its stature can be universally recognized. To the degree that creating this space—wherein India can flourish in the safety that enables it to develop, maintain, and prosper—requires coordination with Washington, New Delhi is prepared to countenance and, indeed, even pursue such coordination even as it continuously affirms its right to choose a course of action that may deviate from U.S. preferences, especially on issues perceived to be central to India's quest for greater security, standing, and autonomy.[13]

The implications of this grand strategic preference for autonomy are profound, especially where coping with China is concerned. Put simply, India would prefer to deal even with a powerful China independently—that is, without becoming part of any formal multinational balancing coalition that may arise as a result of the enlargement of Chinese power. Toward that end, India has sought to pursue a subtle, multidimensional strategy vis-à-vis China that has several different and sometimes competing components.

First, India has sought to avoid picking fights with China—be those fights rhetorical, political, or military—to the maximum degree possible.[14] Consistent with this goal, New Delhi has negotiated a variety of confidence-building measures with Beijing: It has persisted in negotiations relating to the Sino-Indian border dispute even in the face of sluggish progress resulting from Chinese prevarication; it has accepted, in accordance with Chinese preferences, the principle that intractable issues be put on the back burner so that they do not be-

---

[13]The critical importance of the desire for autonomy in Indian grand strategy is explored in detail in Kanti Bajpai, "India: Modified Structuralism," in Muthiah Alagappa (ed.), *Asian Security Practice, Material and Ideational Influences,* Stanford, CA: Stanford University Press, 1998, pp. 157–197.

[14]For a good survey see Sujit Dutta, "Sino-Indian Diplomatic Negotiations: A Preliminary Assessment," *Strategic Analysis,* Vol. 22, No. 12, March 1999, pp. 1821–1834.

come impediments to improving relations; and it has attempted to assuage core Chinese concerns on important sovereignty disputes over Taiwan and Tibet essentially by accepting Beijing's claims on these issues even as it has sustained a tacit dialogue with the Taiwanese and provided asylum to thousands of Tibetan refugees. Even on issues that directly threaten India's security—such as the transfer of Chinese nuclear and missile technology to Pakistan and the Chinese targeting of India with nuclear weapons—Indian policymakers have traditionally been reticent to challenge Chinese actions publicly. Instead, they have responded either by politely complaining to the United States or by obliquely articulating objections to various Chinese counterparts during bilateral meetings.

Second, India has sought to improve relations with China in those issue areas where rapid improvement is possible. The most critical area of convergence is economic relations, particularly in the realm of cross-border trade.[15] India has made concerted efforts to increase the volume and composition of its trade with Beijing and has sought to enlarge the number of border outposts through which local, cross-Himalayan trade is conducted. Outside of trade issues, however, Chinese and Indian interests also converge with respect to the fight against terrorism; the threat of Islamic fundamentalism; Western pressures for human rights; fears of American intervention in sensitive domestic political questions; and a gamut of international problems such as the environment, intellectual property rights, and restrictive technology control regimes. Although India has not gone out of its way to seek or express solidarity with Chinese positions on these issues, Indian policymakers clearly recognize that the potential exists for convergent political action on many of these questions—and hence they have been careful not to foreclose any possibilities related to coordinated action should they become necessary in the future.

Third, even as India has sought to minimize the potential for discord with China, it has attempted to protect itself against the worst possible outcomes should Sino-Indian relations truly deteriorate. India's

---

[15]"Indo-China Border Trade: Trading on Top of the World," *India Today*, Vol. 17, No. 18, September 30, 1992, p. 64; Raman A. Thothathri, "Indo-Chinese Trade: A Change for the Better," *Business India*, No. 399, June 21, 1993, p. 34; and "Hindi-Chini Buy, Buy," *Business India*, No. 490, December 16, 1996, p. 77.

decision to test its nuclear capabilities and develop a modest deterrent offers the best example of such an insurance policy. Other examples include India's determination to continue its long-postponed conventional force modernization either though domestic production or foreign acquisition and to pursue a variety of research-and-development efforts in the realm of traditional strategic technologies as well as in leading-edge areas such as information technology, biotechnology, aviation, and advanced materials and manufacturing. The pursuit of these insurance policies suggests that, while New Delhi seeks to improve relations with Beijing, it is by no means blind to the ways in which Chinese power could undercut its interests. Therefore, a continued commitment to maintaining India's defensive capabilities, primarily through domesticating the best military technologies available to India on the international market, remains at the heart of Indian security policy.[16]

Fourth, the prospect of having to cope with a powerful China in the future has stimulated India to revitalize its relations with all the peripheral Asian states. Indeed, Southeast Asia and East Asia—long neglected by Indian diplomacy—now form the core of India's extraregional economic and political outreach, leading one prominent Western analyst to conclude that India's efforts at joining regional organizations like ARF and Asia-Pacific Economic Cooperation (APEC) implicitly suggests a new "look East"[17] thrust in its overall grand strategy. This effort to reach out to other states that may one day feel threatened by Chinese actions represents an ingenious attempt on India's part to add its geopolitical weight to the evolving regional balance of power without in any way compromising its long-cherished desire to maintain its freedom of action. Even as it has reached out to the Asian rimlands in this way, however, India has managed to salvage its previously disrupted military supply relationship with Russia while forging significant new relations with second-tier suppliers such as France and Israel and continuing to make

---

[16]For a good survey of some of these issues, see Kapil Kak, "India's Conventional Defence: Problems and Prospects," *Strategic Analysis*, Vol. 22, No. 11, February 1999, pp. 1639–1665.

[17]V. Jayanth, "India's 'Look East' Policy," *The Hindu*, April 2, 1998. For a systematic analysis of this policy shift, see Sandy Gordon, *India's Rise to Power*, New York: St. Martin's Press, 1995, pp. 290–317.

gradual improvements in its relations with the most important power in the international system, the United States.

All in all, this subtle and multifaceted strategy of engaging China even as it hedges against the worst consequences of emerging Chinese power implies that New Delhi believes that *the future of Sino-Indian relations is much more open-ended than most commentators usually assert.* Predictions that Sino-Indian relations are doomed to antagonism, strife and rivalry—often derived from simple "billiard-ball" models of competitive international politics—are viewed by Indian policymakers as premature at best. This is mainly because policymakers recognize that both China and India are still subordinate states in the international system and that whether Sino-Indian relations turn out to be malignantly rivalrous hinges largely on the future intentions, capabilities, and actions of many other actors, including the United States. Thus, even as they remain conscious of growing Chinese power, Indian state managers continue to seek as best they can to avoid getting locked into a relationship with China that is destined to be contentious. They believe that the best antidote to the persistently competitive and even threatening dimensions of Chinese power lies in *the complete and permanent revitalization of the Indian economy*—an arena in which the United States is seen to play a special role.

Although economic contributions in the form of increased American investments, trade, and technology transfers are important, the value of the United States to Indian grand strategy is not merely economic but also political in that it is fundamentally related to the manner in which India seeks to promote its own future as a great power. Because this is the only solution that enables India to manage the rise of China without compromising its own desire for geopolitical independence, the thrust of its engagement efforts vis-à-vis the United States centers on efforts to persuade the latter to accept New Delhi's independent foreign policy and India's own emergence as a regional hegemon as ultimately beneficial to American global interests. Toward that end, New Delhi has attempted to persuade Washington to:

- loosen the restrictive technology control regimes the United States manages so that India can enjoy greater access to sophisticated civilian, dual-use, and military technologies;

- recognize India as a great power both regionally and globally so as to allow New Delhi to secure all the benefits in capabilities, prestige, and status that would enable it to contain Pakistan's repeated challenges and deal with Beijing on an equal footing; and

- increase Indian access to the best American military technology, weapon systems, and doctrine and training so as to enable India's military-industrial complex and armed forces to further improve both through selective technology and weapons acquisitions and through greater military-to-military cooperation.

The pursuit of these objectives implies in turn that Indian security managers believe that *the best insurance against assertive Chinese power lies not in participating in any evolving anti-China alliance but rather in emerging as a strong and independent power center on China's periphery.* To the degree that the United States can help India do so, New Delhi would be able to immunize itself against the worst Chinese threats imaginable without suffering any diminution in its own cherished desire for autonomy. In pursuit of this aim, India has also sought—albeit with varying degrees of success—to deepen the quality of its engagement with other critical regional actors, including Russia, Japan, and the smaller countries of Southeast Asia.

In any case, Indian policymakers are convinced that the challenges of guaranteeing Indian security, status, and autonomy require that the country play an active and responsible role abroad even as it continues to dismantle the burdensome vestiges of *étatisme* at home. Where dealing with China is concerned, this does not require any significant shift in India's traditional preference for nonalignment and certainly does not require moving in the direction of fostering or supporting any regional anti-Chinese coalition to contain Beijing right now. In fact, even if growing fears of Chinese assertiveness were to provoke such a coalition in the future, New Delhi's intuitive preference would be to assert its strategic independence even more forcefully. Short of the most extreme threats to its security and independence, India would prefer to deal with Beijing independently, from a position of strength.

All this implies that, while future Sino-Indian relations may be competitive, they need not necessarily be antagonistic in the way that U.S.-Soviet relations were during the Cold War or Indo-Pakistani relations have remained throughout most of the postindependence period. Indeed, most of the actions India is likely to take in its pursuit of great-power capabilities—economic and technological modernization—are guided by a logic that transcends concerns about China even though they will, if successful, affect the Sino-Indian power balance over the long term. And even in those areas where Indian actions are motivated by concerns about China—e.g., conventional force improvements and nuclear modernization—the consequences of New Delhi's choices are likely to be less burdensome to Beijing than is often imagined. Indian conventional modernization will only reinforce, not change, the existing status quo—New Delhi's conventional superiority in the theater. There is no reason Beijing would view the consolidation of this existing reality as suddenly threatening to its security interests given the fact that, even if India allocates substantial resources to upgrading its military capabilities along the Himalayan border, it will still be unable to alter the predominantly defense-dominant orientation of its current posture.

Even where New Delhi's nuclear modernization is concerned, there is good reason for optimism with respect to the arms-race stability of the Sino-Indian strategic balance. This is because China already possesses a substantial nuclear arsenal (at least in relation to India) and is already capable of inflicting unacceptable punishment on New Delhi if it so chooses without any fear for the survivability of its own nuclear forces. Indian nuclear efforts over the next few decades will thus be oriented primarily toward playing catch-up. India will acquire the capabilities to hold at risk major Chinese population centers and some military targets, but it will still be weaker than China in terms of the overall nuclear balance and will remain unable to threaten the elimination of China's nuclear forces in a way that might lead to first-strike instability. The Sino-Indian nuclear interaction is thus unlikely to be violently unstable, as India will probably develop only a relatively small and mostly land-based deterrent force that will nonetheless be immune to a disarming strike by virtue of its mobility, sheer opacity, and covertness. Because the development and deployment of these capabilities will not take place simultaneously or interactively—as seems to be the case in Indo-Pakistani interactions—and because both India and China are large land powers with less asymmetricality in their power relations (compared, once again, to the Indo-Pakistani case), the worst effects of a future Sino-Indian nuclear competition can arguably be eluded.

Impact of the Nuclear Tests on Pakistani-Indian Relations

The resumption of nuclear testing by India challenged Pakistan to demonstrate its nuclear capabilities even though such an action, as was clearly understood in both New Delhi and Islamabad, would be disproportionately harmful to Pakistan's well-being. New Delhi's nuclear tests thus appeared to be part of a "competitive strategy": Although intended primarily to validate India's own nuclear weapon designs from both a technical and a political perspective, they nonetheless served to ensnare Pakistan in a dilemma. If Pakistan declined to test its own weaponry, the credibility of its covert capabilities would always be suspect both in India's eyes and in the eyes of its own populace (not to mention its other target audiences, such as the Islamic world and the assorted insurgents in Kashmir who draw solace and support from Pakistan's ability to sustain them in their war with India). By contrast, if Pakistan followed New Delhi's example and proceeded with testing, it could demonstrate its nuclear capabilities, but only at the expense of making itself vulnerable to various international sanctions that, by virtue of Islamabad's precarious domestic circumstances, would hurt Pakistan more than they would India.[18]

If India gained relative to Pakistan in the short run, however, the same judgment would not necessarily apply to the longer-term Indo-Pakistani security competition, which could well be far more troublesome than its Sino-Indian counterpart. India's decision to test its nuclear weapons in May 1998 not only provoked a Pakistani decision to follow suit but, more problematically, appears to have accelerated Islamabad's efforts at weaponization: Pakistan's decision to declare itself a nuclear power has provided its scientific community with the latitude to pursue their developmental efforts far more vigorously than might have been the case when their weapon program was for-

---

[18]For more on the pressures that compelled Pakistan to test, see Samina Ahmed, "The (Nuclear) Testing of Pakistan," *Current History*, Vol. 97, No. 623, December 1998, pp. 407–411.

mally nonexistent and their understanding of Indian capabilities largely unclear.

After the nuclear tests of May 1998, India's repeated claims about its technical capabilities, although made primarily for domestic political reasons, have had the undesirable effect of disconcerting Pakistan's strategic managers. The Indian scientific community's assertions that India could now confidently produce simple-fission, boosted-fission, thermonuclear, and enhanced radiation weapons may not be convincing in all their details but have nonetheless had the effect of spurring Pakistan's weaponization efforts and reinforcing Islamabad's fears of its own vulnerability. The draft Indian nuclear doctrine released by the National Security Advisory Board seems only to have magnified these Pakistani fears. At the very least, therefore, the Indian subcontinent is now faced with the prospect that Islamabad, believing itself to lag behind New Delhi in terms of its strategic capabilities, could finally end up with a larger and more diversified nuclear arsenal than is really necessary for its security.

This situation also holds the potential to engender greater instability at other levels. On the one hand, for example, Islamabad could become emboldened to pursue even riskier strategies vis-à-vis New Delhi were it suddenly to discover that its nuclear capabilities are far more effective than it gave itself credit for. On the other hand, New Delhi could be provoked into a substantial acceleration of its own weaponization efforts were it suddenly to discover that Pakistan's strategic capabilities were far more sophisticated than was previously believed. The former outcome would ensure that the "ugly stability"[19] currently prevailing in South Asia would be replaced by even uglier versions of the same, whereas the latter outcome could provoke a destabilizing arms race that would undermine the interest both sides currently express in deploying relatively small and finite nuclear deterrents.

Whether a destabilizing arms race would actually materialize is, however, hard to say, because Indian state managers appear at least at the moment to be unconcerned about Pakistan's nuclear capabilities. Convinced of their own superior nuclear prowess as well as

---

[19]Both the logic and the structure of "ugly stability" are detailed in Ashley J. Tellis, *Stability in South Asia,* Santa Monica: RAND, DB-185-A, 1997, pp. 30–33.

Pakistan's stark geophysical vulnerability (which its acquisition of more sophisticated strategic capabilities will not change), Indian policymakers have shown no sign of accelerating their own strategic development efforts. To the contrary, these efforts appear to be proceeding at roughly the same pace that has characterized all past activity relating to Indian strategic development programs. Despite substantial increases in the nuclear, space, and defense research and development budgets since the May 1998 tests, it is therefore hard to uncover any evidence that India has embarked on a "crash" program to expand its nuclear capabilities in particular and its strategic development programs in general.

The Future Course of Pakistani Policy Toward India

If there is reason for optimism about avoiding a high-octane nuclear arms race in South Asia, the evidence thus far does not support any expectation that Pakistan's risk-taking propensities are likely to be reduced as a result of the new nuclear capabilities demonstrated by both subcontinental states. Pakistan's willingness to continue baiting India is rooted in structural constraints that are ultimately personified by two simple realities. First, Pakistan remains the "anti–status quo"[20] state in South Asia. This phrase is not meant to convey any normative stance but is merely a description of Pakistan's circumstances: Islamabad today is not satisfied with the existing territorial order primarily because of its long-standing claims to the former princely kingdom of Jammu and Kashmir, significant portions of which are currently governed by India. Second, Pakistan is not only weaker than India but probably growing weaker in absolute terms as well. This implies that Islamabad simply lacks the resources to secure its claims over Jammu and Kashmir by force. The military solution has in fact been tried on several occasions in the past and has in all instances been unsuccessful.

The interaction of these two realities leaves Pakistan in an unenviable situation—one in which it lacks the power to resolve the dispute it feels most passionately about. Moreover, India—the stronger entity—has not only gained all the benefits that accrue from long and

---

[20]Neil Joeck, "Pakistani Security and Nuclear Proliferation in South Asia," *Journal of Strategic Studies*, Vol. 8, No. 4, December 1985, p. 80.

established control over the area most desired by Islamabad but can sustain its political control over Jammu and Kashmir indefinitely at minimal cost to its body politic. Consequently, India does not feel compelled either to change its current stance with respect to the disputed state or to enter into any negotiations with those entities committed to altering the status quo through violence.

Confronted with such a situation, Pakistan is left with only three choices:

- to negotiate with India on what will essentially be Indian terms;

- to attempt to inveigle the international community into resolving the Kashmir issue on behalf of Islamabad; or

- to conduct a low-intensity war with India in the hope of wearing down the latter and forcing it to negotiate a settlement that offers some advantages to Pakistan.

None of these individual alternatives would appear to be satisfactory.

Islamabad has never consistently pursued the alternative of negotiating with India because it has long concluded that the latter has never exhibited a sincere commitment to resolving the Kashmir issue through negotiations.[21] Thus, while both Islamabad and New Delhi have conducted several episodic discussions over the years, all these parleys have essentially deadlocked on the issue of Kashmir because both sides have been unable to move much beyond their opening gambits. Pakistan's demand for the implementation of a plebiscite in Kashmir, for example—as mandated by the U.N. resolutions of 1948—is usually met squarely by New Delhi's claim that the accession of Jammu and Kashmir to the Indian Union is effectively nonnegotiable. While India appears to be prepared to negotiate a settlement that would more or less legitimize the current realities "on the ground," Pakistan's desire to reopen the issue of Kashmir *de novo* is dismissed as an unreal exercise that is not worth any investment of New Delhi's time, energy, and resources.

---

[21]See, for example, the remarks of Pakistani Foreign Minister Abdul Sattar in "India Not Interested in Talks: Sattar," *Dawn*, February 4, 2000.

The second alternative—inveigling the international community into pressing India to negotiate the Kashmir issue—has not worked satisfactorily either, as most of the great powers have failed to demonstrate any serious interest in enforcing the existing U.N. resolutions on Kashmir given that the issue has been far removed from their vital interests. Moreover, the great powers' abiding respect for India's greater geopolitical weight, the lack of clarity about the equities of the issue after several decades of complicated regional developments, and Pakistan's own relatively poor standing in international politics have combined to make the Kashmir problem the orphan of international causes. Pakistan's early efforts at resolving the Kashmir problem by invoking U.S. assistance through the Cold War alliance system also failed conclusively, and today even Pakistan's closest ally, China, has moved a great distance away from Islamabad's position on Kashmir.

The third alternative—distracting India and possibly wearing it down through the support of low-intensity conflict—thus remains Islamabad's best hope for leveling the scales with New Delhi and bringing the latter back to the negotiating table. In the past, this alternative of "strategic diversion" was not available to Pakistan in that, Islamabad's claims notwithstanding, the Kashmiri population did not aspire to integration with Pakistan for most of the postindependence period. The popular uprising in 1989, however, reinvigorated Pakistan's commitment to changing the status quo in Kashmir as a substantial portion of the state's Muslim population appeared willing— arguably for the first time since 1947—to pursue the same goal.[22] It is important to recognize, however, that the Kashmiris are by no means universally desirous of joining Pakistan; although some of the more fervent Islamic groups would prefer to integrate the state with Pakistan, most would opt instead for some vague and undefined version of independence (*azadi*). In any case, Pakistan's longstanding claims on the territory, once combined with new opportunities presented by Kashmiri resentment against Indian misrule after 1989, led Pakistan to attempt to make the Himalayan king-

---

[22]For details, see Sumit Ganguly, *The Crisis in Kashmir: Portents of War, Hopes of Peace*, Washington, D.C.: Woodrow Wilson Center Press, 1997.

dom the newest locale for enervating Indian strength through low-intensity war, since the other alternatives—negotiations and international intervention—had both resoundingly failed thus far.

These structural conditions thus ensure that Pakistan's formal anti–status quo orientation will episodically manifest itself in a variety of efforts aimed at weakening what it perceives to be its great threat: an asymmetrically stronger India. In the early postindependence years, these efforts focused solely on recovering disputed territories such as Kashmir. After Pakistan's humiliating defeat in 1971, however, it has often appeared as if enfeebling India has become an objective that Pakistan views as worthy of pursuit for its own sake. Irrespective of what the motivations are, these efforts tend to challenge India's grand strategic objective—maintaining a stable multiethnic state with claims to greatness—and consequently guarantee that security competition between India and Pakistan will remain a fact of life well into the future even if it is expressed only through subconventional violence.

Transforming this "ugly stability" will require, at the very least, an acceptance on Pakistan's part that the status quo in Kashmir is unlikely to change significantly no matter what means are brought into play.[23] This in turn implies that both Pakistan and India would have to commit themselves to a comprehensive dialogue that would take place despite the *ex ante* impossibility of any significant transformation in the current political and territorial configuration in Kashmir. If such a dialogue is successful, a variety of alterations in the current arrangements might occur *ex post*, but the demand for radical alterations could not become either a precondition or a presumption were New Delhi to be expected to engage in serious discussions with Islamabad on Kashmir.

---

[23]Alternatively, it would require that India recognize that its current strategy in Kashmir has reached the limits of its success and therefore requires some negotiations with Pakistan that would eventually result in significant changes to the status quo. Since this possibility is highly unlikely given India's current stand and its continued willingness (and ability) to expend resources in maintaining the status quo, the only alternative left remains a change in the current Pakistani strategy of distracting India.

There is no evidence, however, that Pakistan is willing to engage in a serious dialogue with India under such conditions.[24] In fact, Pakistan's behavior since the 1998 nuclear tests suggests that Islamabad is quite willing to exploit its newly demonstrated nuclear capabilities for the strategic cover they provide in its challenges to India. The misadventure at Kargil remains a case in point. Even if other limited wars are avoided in the future, the fact that Pakistan views itself as a legitimate party to the Kashmir dispute implies that it has no other alternative but to support the Kashmiri militancy through diplomatic, moral, and material means even if such assistance ultimately fails to change the territorial status quo in any significant way. In such circumstances, the best Islamabad can hope for is that its support will keep the hope of some Kashmiri groups for *azadi* alive—and to the degree that these dreams invite greater Indian repression, they might open the door to more international attention on Kashmir and, by implication, to some external pressure that could force India into negotiating a reasonable settlement. Unfortunately for Pakistan, however, even increased international attention is by no means certain, because New Delhi has resources other than simply repression for dealing with Kashmiri aspirations.

Yet hopes for increased international pressure on New Delhi may be all that is available to Islamabad at this juncture. If so, this is likely to be poor consolation, since it implies a perpetuation of the same situation—continued Indian rule over the most attractive parts of the Himalayan state indefinitely—that Pakistan has continuously struggled against since its founding in 1947. Indeed, this is where being a weak state hurts considerably: Pakistan's poor relative capabilities imply that it has no choice but to play the only weak cards it has even though this policy may not yield either spectacular or permanent advantages. Not surprisingly, then, Pakistan will continue to support the armed struggle in Kashmir and possibly elsewhere as a means of increasing political pressure on New Delhi and wearing down its otherwise-superior adversary—in effect exploiting the protection offered by nuclear weapons against total war to wage a subconven-

---

[24]This judgment is underscored most clearly in a recent interview given by General Pervez Musharraf. See Malini Pathasarathy, "The Core Issue of Kashmir Must Be Addressed: Musharraf," *The Hindu*, January 17, 2000.

tional war against India. The apparent strategic necessity for such action is reinforced by other considerations:

- the desire to be seen as responsive to the disenchantment of the Indian Kashmiris because of its potential for enhancing legitimacy, good public order, and national unity domestically;

- the opportunity to provide gainful employment to some of the Islamist mercenaries in Pakistan by committing them to a battleground some distance away from the mainland; and

- the need to channel the abhorrence felt by the Pakistani military and intelligence services toward India in a way that harms a despised adversary even as it confirms the autonomy of the armed forces within the political life of the state.

These factors combine in different ways to compel Pakistan to pursue a variety of revisionist strategies with respect to Kashmir and elsewhere. The tactics adopted in this regard have, however, changed over time. Indeed, even the agencies that "take the point" in overseeing these efforts have varied; sometimes key initiatives are led by the Pakistan Army, at other times by the Inter-Services Intelligence Directorate, and at still other times by civilian governments. Yet in all instances, the general objective has remained the same: *to raise the costs of maintaining the status quo in Kashmir in order to force New Delhi into negotiating an outcome more favorable to Pakistan or, failing that, to wear India down so as to prevent it from being able to apply the full quantum of its political resources externally against Pakistan.*

Since this strategy is likely to continue in many variants well into the future and may even materialize in more vicious forms if Pakistan continues to decay economically and politically, the Indian state will continue to treat the possibility of conventional conflict with Pakistan as its most serious near-term external security threat. India will thus continue to maintain the large military establishment necessary to defend a vast defensive perimeter; conduct combat operations along two widely separated fronts if necessary; undertake significant internal peace operations; and retain adequate theater reserves to enable the Indian armed forces to sustain their training, maintenance, and redeployment cycles. The size, quality, and orientation of this force will in turn continue to remain a source of concern to

Pakistan. Given the conflict-ridden relations between the two states, Islamabad must reckon with the possibility that India could respond to its efforts at strategic baiting—if it has not done so already—by engaging in various cross-border operations in a crisis. This fear further reinforces Pakistan's traditional obsession with national defense—and it is in this context that Islamabad's relations with China become critical to its grand strategy.

Sino-Pakistani Relations

Pakistan's relationship with China goes back to the Sino-Indian war of 1962.[25] The rupture in Sino-Indian diplomatic relations caused by this war opened the door to a convergence of Sino-Pakistani interests that centered principally on the containment of Indian "hegemonism" in South Asia. This convergence was by no means automatic, however, because even as Beijing and Islamabad perceived new opportunities for collaborating against India after 1962, Pakistan remained a member of the U.S.-led anti-communist alliances, which were directed against both the Soviet Union and China. Nonetheless, Sino-Pakistani relations gradually developed and, in 1966, took the form of defense collaboration when China agreed to assist Pakistan in establishing an ordnance factory for the manufacture of Chinese small arms.

The constraints that inhibited the full flowering of the Sino-Pakistani relationship in the 1960s rapidly disappeared following Pakistan's defeat in the 1971 war. Perceiving itself as having been abandoned by the United States and its Middle Eastern allies during successive conflicts with India, Islamabad gradually shifted to a "look within" strategy that focused on a reliance on its own internal resources for national survival.[26] In practical terms, this meant that Pakistan continued to sustain high defense burdens to ensure the priority of military needs and continued to preserve strong bureaucratic organs of rule even as it experimented with new efforts at participatory democracy. Because these ingredients were deemed to be necessary but not sufficient to Pakistan's survival, Islamabad also embarked

---

[25]For a good review of this relationship, see Yaacov Vertzberger, *The Enduring Entente: Sino-Pakistani Relations, 1960-1980,* New York: Praeger, 1983.

[26]This strategy is described in greater detail in Tellis (1997).

clandestinely on the development of a nuclear weapon program in efforts to procure the ultimate trump in its quest for enduring security. Simultaneously, however, it accelerated the process of deepening its relationship with China, a state that had by now become a confirmed adversary of India.

By the mid-1970s, China had become a critical source of conventional military technology for Pakistan.[27] Even more important, however, it was seen to be a font of political and diplomatic support, since both countries continued to view India and its ally, the Soviet Union, as potential threats to their common security. As the U.S. security relationship with Pakistan gradually atrophied after the 1971 war, Pakistan's link with China came to be seen more and more in Islamabad as the single best external guarantee against Indian aggression. This by no means implied that China had become a formal guarantor of Pakistan's security, however; consistent with its insular foreign policy, Beijing had never expressed any interest in playing such a role and carefully avoided making any commitments to Islamabad that would have entailed such obligations.

Indeed, this posture had already become clear during the 1971 war, when China vociferously criticized Indian actions but astutely chose not to intervene militarily on Islamabad's behalf despite desperate Pakistani entreaties to that effect. This restraint clearly signaled the sharp limits of Beijing's support for Islamabad and identified the leitmotif of Sino-Pakistani security relations. In short, China would extend Pakistan every form of diplomatic and moral support that it believed to be justified in any given circumstances and would even be willing to provide Islamabad with the military instruments necessary to preserve its security and autonomy—but it would neither provide Pakistan with any formal guarantees of security nor make any efforts at extending deterrence or preparing joint defenses that implied coordinated military action vis-à-vis India. These factors suggest that China has pursued a subtle partnership with Pakistan: It appears willing to do the minimum necessary to preserve Pakistani

---

[27]For details, see Mushahid Hussain, "Pakistan-China Defense Cooperation," *International Defense Review*, 2/1993, pp. 108–111.

security from a distance but has sought to avoid all overt entanglements in Islamabad's challenges to Indian primacy in South Asia.[28]

The assistance China has extended Pakistan over the past two decades—including the transfer of nuclear and missile technologies—has in fact been entirely consistent with this premise. From Beijing's point of view, this assistance was a low-cost investment that had the potential to increase Islamabad's capability to defend itself independently but involved no public obligations or open-ended commitments on China's part to transfer technology, to make no mention of any commitment to come to Islamabad's defense.

Even as the fruits of this assistance have been exploited by Pakistan over the years, China has moved explicitly to distance itself from those Pakistani actions which could undermine stability in South Asia. Thus, for example, China has moved away from its previously unqualified support of Pakistan's position on Kashmir and has become increasingly and even visibly uncomfortable with Islamabad's support of the Taliban in Afghanistan. Beijing's unique, low-cost, low-key commitment to Pakistani security has therefore failed to translate into support for Pakistani revisionism.[29]

Beijing has deliberately imposed these subtle limits on its relationship with Islamabad because China does not view India today as its principal long-term threat. Because India could turn out to be a power that is troublesome to China over the long haul, it is seen as meriting prudent scrutiny and limited efforts at local containment.[30] The strategic assistance offered by China to Pakistan serves this purpose admirably: It keeps New Delhi focused on Islamabad, limits India's freedom of action in South Asia, and helps minimize the possibility that India will emerge as a rival to China on the larger Asian theater. While these considerations no doubt cause concern in

---

[28]This critical point is correctly emphasized in Leo E. Rose, *India and China: Forging a New Relationship*, in Shalendra D. Sharma (ed.), *The Asia-Pacific in the New Millennium: Geopolitics, Security, and Foreign Policy*, Berkeley, CA: Institute of East Asian Studies, University of California, Berkeley, 2000.

[29]Swaran Singh, "Sino–South Asian Ties: Problems and Prospects," *Strategic Analysis*, Vol. 24, No. 1, April 2000, pp. 31–49.

[30]Gary Klintworth, "Chinese Perspectives on India as a Great Power," in Ross Babbage and Sandy Gordon (eds.), *India's Strategic Future*, New York: St Martin's Press, 1992, p. 96.

New Delhi, Beijing views its assistance to Pakistan (as well as to the smaller South Asian states) as relatively small prudential investments that are justified mainly by continuing uncertainty about India's long-term capabilities and intentions.

Pakistan, in contrast, would prefer a good deal more from its relations with China. As the weaker partner in that relationship, it desires more than China has either offered to or can give. In the areas of strategic technology, Pakistan would prefer a Chinese commitment to ongoing assistance in its nuclear and missile programs. This assistance is required mainly to help Pakistani technologists overcome specific problems that currently obstruct their progress in these areas. The intention here is not to have Beijing play the role of a supplier of the completed systems; Pakistan's sorry experience with past dependence on foreign technologies has led it to be wary of all supplier relationships. Instead, Pakistan would prefer assistance in resolving certain technical problems so as to become more or less self-sufficient in the production of key strategic technologies— technologies that, in the end, remain the country's only hope for ensuring the success of its "look within" strategy.

In the area of conventional arms, Pakistan already has access to the best Chinese military technologies available. Pakistan recognizes that in most instances Chinese conventional weapons lag considerably behind their Western counterparts, but their easy availability, relatively low cost, and simpler maintenance requirements continue to make them valuable for Pakistan's defense needs. These weapons have therefore been acquired in relatively significant numbers in order to beef up the "low" end of the "high-low" mix of capabilities Pakistan has maintained in its order of battle vis-à-vis India. Given the value of these capabilities for producing "bulk" firepower, Islamabad will continue to remain an important customer for Chinese weaponry, and the Chinese military-industrial complex will likely become Pakistan's most important collaborator with respect to future product improvements, joint production ventures, and exports of low-end conventional weapons.

Aside from assistance with strategic technologies, however, what Pakistan would like most from its relationship with China is emphatic and perhaps public support for Pakistani objectives on key political issues. These include confronting Indian hegemony in

South Asia, recovering the disputed state of Jammu and Kashmir, and pacifying Afghanistan by means of complete Taliban control. China's commitment to supporting Islamabad's objectives in these areas would boost Pakistan's strategic fortunes considerably and imply a thorough endorsement of Islamabad's current grand strategy in all its details. Thus far, however, China has refused to provide either support or endorsement on any of these points. The evidence of Chinese behavior toward Pakistan and the smaller South Asian states suggests, to the contrary, that Beijing has already recognized the reality of Indian hegemony *within* South Asia, and while it has attempted to assist India's smaller neighbors in preserving their security, it has shown no interest whatsoever in leading any anti-Indian coalition of the sort that hard-liners in Islamabad would prefer. Similarly, Beijing has publicly advocated—much to Islamabad's chagrin—that the resolution of the Kashmir conflict be deferred indefinitely, and it has continued to support, albeit reluctantly, international efforts at penalizing the Taliban's brand of Islamist rule currently manifested in Afghanistan. Even as China has distanced itself from Pakistani interests in these areas, however, it has been careful to do so quietly and indirectly whenever possible. This sensitivity to Pakistani sentiments has always been appreciated by policymakers in Islamabad, who often contrast the "respect" accorded them by the Chinese—even when they disagree—with the hectoring attitude often adopted by the United States.

Islamabad's desire to preserve a close relationship with Beijing, no matter what the disagreements of the hour may be, is ultimately rooted in a simple fact of geopolitics: China, a neighboring great power, remains the only state likely to make common cause with Pakistan on the most important issue affecting its security: India. Given the asymmetry in resources between China and Pakistan, Islamabad's steadfast loyalty to Beijing—despite their divergence on many issues—should not be surprising in that even modest Chinese assistance appears indispensable from Islamabad's perspective. This gratitude is particularly justified thanks to China's past assistance in the realm of strategic technologies; not only do these instruments guarantee Pakistan's defense and allow it to whittle down India's advantages, but the mode of their transfer also enables Islamabad to claim credit for those very achievements.

In light of these realities, Pakistan is likely to remain loyal to China over the long term. The prospect of a rising China pleases Pakistan because it presages the availability of an even more powerful ally than Beijing currently represents. Given all the potential benefits that would accrue from such a possibility, Pakistan is unlikely to support any attempts at constraining China irrespective of where these may emerge. If any U.S.-led efforts materialize in this regard, they would certainly place Pakistan in a difficult position because Islamabad still seeks as best it can to retain America's friendship, support, and assistance even as it maintains its critical strategic links with China. Therefore, Pakistan will not support any hedging strategies directed against Beijing. Unlike India, which may be sympathetic to such efforts even if it does not formally participate in them, Pakistan will simply be opposed to all such solutions both in principle and in execution. If anything, Islamabad will seek to play the role of a peacemaker—i.e., a state that uses its good offices with both countries, as it did once before in 1971, to minimize differences and improve relations rather than support any efforts at coalition building vis-à-vis China. If despite its best preferences Pakistan is forced to take sides, however, Islamabad would settle for remaining loyal to Beijing. When all is said and done, this political choice would be driven primarily by Pakistan's conviction that whatever the differences between Beijing and Islamabad may be, China has always been a fair, reliable, and committed friend—in contrast to the United States, which for all its power has invariably turned out, in Pakistan's view, to be unfaithful, unreliable, and ungrateful.

MAJOR GEOPOLITICAL CONTINGENCIES

Given the broad trends described in the last section, five major geopolitical contingencies should concern the United States during the next decade.

Major Subcontinental War

A major conflict between India and Pakistan occasioned by miscalculations over Kashmir remains the most important geopolitical contingency that could emerge in South Asia today. Such a war would not, however, arise because of premeditated actions on either side. Despite what Islamabad may believe, New

Delhi today simply has no interest in pursuing any military solutions aimed at destroying, occupying, or fractionating Pakistan. And whatever Pakistan's desires may be, it simply does not possess the capabilities to pursue any of these three courses of action vis-à-vis India. Consequently, a major subcontinental war, were one to emerge, would be the unintended result of limited actions undertaken by various parties.

The key choices here remain the future of Pakistani support for the Kashmiri insurgency *and* Indian decisions about continuing its past policies of dealing with domestic militancy through purely internal counterinsurgency operations (as opposed to cross-border penetrations, which could include joint operations of limited aims). Thus far, both sides have been careful to avoid provoking the other to the point where escalation to conventional war became inevitable even though cross-border artillery exchanges, infiltration across the line of control, and terrorist acts of various sorts have been the staple of polemical accusations by both sides over the years. The recent actions at Kargil, where the Pakistan Army attempted to seize disputed territory by force, represent a new detour in the traditional pattern of Indo-Pakistani security competition. If actions such as these come to represent the norm, the likelihood of a major conflict in South Asia—which could include the brandishing of nuclear weapons—will greatly increase.

In such a situation, the kinds of demands leveled on USAF assets would depend largely on the diplomatic position the U.S. government adopts toward the conflict. At the very least, however, it is reasonable to conclude that the contingency of a regional war represents the highest levels of demand on USAF resources that could be imagined in the South Asian theater. In the run-up to a conflict as well as both during and after it, space-based assets for nuclear and conventional force monitoring and command, control, and communication (C^3), as well as CONUS-based air-breathing assets for sampling, telemetry, and electronic intelligence (ELINT) operations would be in greatest demand.

Should the U.S. government mandate the evacuation of American and foreign visitors in the region, USAF lift capabilities will be the instrument of choice. The demand for these assets both for non-combatant evacuations and for humanitarian and disaster relief will essentially come on a short-notice or no-notice basis, since traditionally the South Asian region has not been a priority area for American foreign policy. Responding to such needs would not impose structural burdens on the USAF because the lack of basing in close proximity to the region—the chief constraint on any operations involving the use of short-legged tactical assets, especially in a nonpermissive environment—would not hamper the use of strategic intelligence, national communications, and intertheater transport assets. The ready availability of these resources, however, could be constrained by competing demands that may enjoy greater priority depending on the geopolitical situation. Consequently, adjusting planning and availability factors to accommodate such circumstances may be a prudent response as far as planning for such contingencies is concerned.

Stagnation and State Failure in Pakistan

The possibility of a gradually deteriorating Pakistan that culminates in some form of state failure represents the second most serious, albeit long-term, geopolitical contingency the United States might confront in South Asia. Since the beginning of its creation in 1947, Pakistan has constantly been racked by the interaction of political, economic, social, and ideological failures. While the country has been lucky enough to muddle through a succession of crises in the past, the possibility of failure today appears more real than has ever been the case, even as the price of failure itself has become exorbitant. This threat of failure is driven primarily by decreasing state capacity in Pakistan. Islamabad's continued competition with India, which requires an overly burdensome defense economy, has become increasingly difficult to sustain because successive Pakistani regimes have been unable to increase the quantum of state revenues required to support this strategy. Unlike the Cold War era, when foreign economic and military aid was plentiful, Pakistan's mounting budgetary deficits cannot be compensated for in similar ways today. The net result has been growing external indebtedness, reduced national investments, and poor social indicators. Coupled with political failures such as misgovernance, troubled civil-military relations, and sharp interprovincial inequities, Pakistan's economic deterioration has led to increasing Islamist radicalization of domestic politics, which has in turn created growing fears about the long-term stability of important Pakistani institutions. The disconcerting aspect of decay in Pakistan is that, being essentially slow, multidimensional, and corrosive, its catastrophic effects could eventually become manifest in any number of troublesome ways. The outcomes that most observers currently fear include a sharp increase in sectarian violence in key provinces; an upsurge of potentially secessionist movements, perhaps aided from abroad; the cleaving of key institutions, including the military, on ideological grounds; and, in the most extreme scenario imaginable, a general breakdown of civil order caused by the intersection of economic failure, a chronic refugee problem, a growing drug and gun culture, and increasing mercenary violence.

Although most of these outcomes do not directly affect U.S. security, they could threaten U.S. interests were they to result in or be accompanied by an upsurge in regional tensions leading to conflict with India. It is in this context that state breakdown in Pakistan—in a manner reminiscent of 1971—could provoke a major conventional war conducted under the shadow of nuclear weaponry. The most valuable USAF resources here are the same as those relevant in the previous scenario: ISR assets for monitoring an unfolding situation and strategic lift capabilities for noncombatant evacuation, relief support, and peace operations.

"High Entropy" Proliferation of Strategic Technologies

The proliferation of strategic weapon technologies from South Asia to Northeast Asia, the Middle East, and nonstate actors represents a geopolitical contingency for the United States whose relative importance rivals the prospect of state breakdown in Pakistan as a threat to U.S. interests. Indeed, many observers conclude that this threat may even exceed that contingency in importance, as it remains a high cost–high probability outcome from the perspective of U.S. interests—in contrast to a political meltdown in Pakistan, which despite its high costs still embodies a relatively smaller probability of occurrence. In fact, many of the same factors that contribute to state breakdown are seen to apply with a vengeance where promoting the diffusion of strategic technologies is concerned: severe economic pressures and declining state control.

This assessment applies to Pakistan in particular because Islamabad's perilous economic situation offers more inducements for both state organizations and private entities to profit from the leakage of strategic technologies. The strategic technologies production complex in Pakistan is, moreover, composed of multiple scientific and bureaucratic baronies, many of which enjoy more autonomy than do their counterparts in India—a factor that opens the door to the pursuit of some parochial interests even when those might otherwise undercut the larger interests of the Pakistani state. While the challenges of guaranteeing tight controls are thus likely to be greater in Pakistan than in India, the latter is by no means immune to the problem of leakage. The chief obstacle here—which also holds true for Pakistan *a fortiori*—lies in reconciling principles with practice. If progressively instituted, as they will be under U.S. pressure, even good regulations must be effectively and consistently implemented without fear or favor, and both India and Pakistan must go some distance before concerns about their policy effectiveness are eradicated.

The problem of technology diffusion affects the USAF indirectly but in potentially lethal ways, since strategy technologies exported from South Asia might appear in the hands of other truly committed adversaries of the United States. The USAF assets that would be engaged as a result of this problem in the first instance are its intelligence resources, ranging from the tools and institutions tasked with technical intelligence collection and analysis; those among its human resources who are engaged in intelligence-counterintelligence overseas; and Air Force security services operating domestically in the United States. Insofar as the USAF is tasked by civilian policymakers to participate in joint contingency plans relating to stemming the transfer of strategic capabilities, other elements of the force would necessarily be involved as well.

High-Intensity Indo-Pakistani Nuclear Arms Racing

The possibility of serious Indo-Pakistani nuclear arms racing is an important but lower-order contingency from a U.S. perspective because an intense arms race in South Asia would most likely be more deleterious to the local protagonists than to any bystanders. The general prospect for a high-intensity arms race of the sort that occurred between the United States and the Soviet Union during the bomber and missile "gaps" in the 1950s and 1960s is quite remote, principally for economic reasons: Both India and Pakistan are relatively poor states, and neither country—particularly Pakistan—can afford to engage in any high-octane military buildups. Both countries also seem committed to developing some version of a finite deterrent that would, if implemented, minimize the opportunity for a competitive nuclear race.

While these factors combine to promise a certain modicum of arms-race stability, two other factors could subvert this promise. The first remains the pervasive misperception on both sides about the extent of the other's achievements with respect to nuclear weaponization. Should the received wisdom on this question suddenly be punctured either by unexpected revelations of capability or by asymmetric increases in transparency resulting from an intelligence coup, the stage could be set for a sharp acceleration in some dimensions of strategic programs that, because of the fear and uncertainty induced by such actions, could precipitate countervailing responses that set off a destabilizing action-reaction spiral between both states. The second factor is that both India and Pakistan have set out to develop their nuclear deterrents at roughly the same time, and while New Delhi's concerns in this regard certainly transcend Islamabad's, the latter's orientation will remain fixed on New Delhi for some time to come. In effect, India's attempts to develop a deterrent that is viable against Pakistan and China simultaneously will have the consequence of raising the threshold of sufficiency for Pakistan. Determining the appropriate equilibrium between both states will unfortunately be both a reflexive and an interactive process in which the distinctions between sufficiency and equality may easily be blurred.

An Indo-Pakistani nuclear arms race has minimal direct implications for the USAF today. Neither country treats the United States, its allies, and its dependencies as potential targets of nuclear attack, and consequently the USAF has no special defensive obligations for which to prepare other than what it would do as part of its routine planning process. The chief burden an Indo-Pakistani nuclear arms race would impose on the USAF would be connected with the demands of monitoring the progress of weaponization on both sides: This would involve the same resources already committed to observation, sampling, telemetry, and SIGINT/ELINT/COMINT/ MASINT (signals, electronic, communications, and measurement and signature intelligence) operations. In this context, as in most other contingencies in South Asia, the USAF's general ISR capabilities will become more important than ever before.

High-Intensity Sino-Indian Arms Racing

The possibility of a serious Sino-Indian nuclear arms race is the last and perhaps most unlikely contingency from the perspective of the United States. Concerns about this contingency arise mainly because the Indian nuclear program, when complete, promises to change the extant Sino-Indian strategic equilibrium in at least one fundamental respect: New Delhi will be able to target Chinese assets for the first time in much the same way that Beijing has been able to target Indian assets since the early 1970s. The rise of this new mutual vulnerability relationship often provides grounds for concern because it is feared that China might seek to recover its previous strategic advantages by responding to the development of the Indian deterrent through a major nuclear buildup oriented toward New Delhi. This outcome, however, is unlikely to obtain. In part, this is because historically China has never viewed India as a "peer competitor," and any strategic reactions suggesting otherwise at this point would only undercut Beijing's traditional attitude of treating New Delhi as a parvenu that seeks to punch above its own weight. Further, the gap in numbers and technological capabilities between the mature Chinese nuclear deterrent and New Delhi's evolving force-in-being is so large that Beijing does not have to respond in *any* way to India's incipient efforts at developing a minimum deterrent. To be sure, Chinese nuclear capabilities will expand in the decades ahead, but this expansion will be driven more by its own modernization efforts (which were under way for at least a decade prior to the Indian tests of May 1998), its perceptions of U.S. nuclear capabilities, and the future character of the nuclear regime in East Asia than by developments to the south of China. Chinese nuclear deterrence vis-à-vis India is in fact so robust that no capabilities India develops over the next decade will allow it to systematically interdict Beijing's nuclear forces either for purposes of ensuring damage limitation or for achieving counterforce dominance. Given this fact, there is little China needs to do in the face of an evolving Indian nuclear capability except what it might choose to do purely for symbolic reasons; both the range of Beijing's missiles and the yields of its warheads already allow it to hold at risk numerous Indian targets from far outside the

Chinese periphery, and consequently dramatic alterations in current Chinese deployment patterns or operating postures vis-à-vis India are unnecessary and likely will be avoided.

The principal demands on the USAF will therefore arise in the context of Chinese nuclear modernization vis-à-vis the United States rather than in the context of a Sino-Indian nuclear arms race. The American response here will continue to be the same it has always been: to maintain a robust nuclear deterrent to prevent any Chinese or, for that matter, any other nation's efforts at threatening U.S. interests through nuclear arms. In the specific case of nuclear developments in the Sino-Indian realm, the same capabilities identified in the previous scenario remain relevant, including all instruments associated with the demands of monitoring the progress of weaponization on both sides.

IMPLICATIONS FOR THE UNITED STATES AND THE UNITED STATES AIR FORCE

The nuclear tests of May 1998 heralded a new phase in security competition in South Asia. The sanctions levied on both India and Pakistan in the aftermath of the nuclear tests abruptly brought to a halt many initiatives that were intended to allow U.S. policy to reach a new equilibrium in South Asia: a deeper engagement with India consistent with the latter's steadily growing economic and strategic capabilities, coupled with the continued reassurance of Pakistan despite the downgrading of past strategic and military ties. After considerable soul searching, the United States has recognized that its larger strategic interests require a resumption of its previous efforts at engaging India and Pakistan. The efforts it has made in this direction include the waiving of sanctions imposed after the tests; the willingness on the part of the President to visit the region after a gap of more than 20 years; a restoration of U.S. support for multilateral economic development programs; and a willingness to discuss the resuscitation of previous initiatives relating to strategic cooperation, depending on the proliferation choices made by both India and Pakistan. Where the issue of nuclear proliferation is concerned, the United States has elected not to pursue chimerical goals such as rolling back the nuclear programs in South Asia but has chosen instead to focus on more limited and practical objectives, such as institutionalizing a nuclear restraint regime in both countries. Irrespective of how success eventually materializes in this area, the administration's decision to restore a semblance of normalcy to its relations with both India and Pakistan reopens opportunities for the USAF in its own military-to-military contacts with the region.

U.S. relations with both India and Pakistan are, however, still subject to considerable constraints because of many unresolved issues relating to proliferation. USAF engagement with both countries at the military-to-military level will therefore remain constrained, and the limits of these endeavors will continue to be guided by larger geopolitical and strategic considerations rather than merely by USAF needs. Nevertheless, the renewal of American relations with both India and Pakistan offers new, even if small, opportunities in the near term.

Understanding what these opportunities might be requires an appreciation of regional attitudes toward engagement with the USAF. Both India and Pakistan clearly seek to increase the quality of their cooperation with the USAF, but there are significant differences in the two states' attitudes. Since Pakistan had a long history of cooperation with the USAF, especially in the early decades of the Cold War, there is nothing more that Islamabad would like than to restore its early cooperation. Both Pakistani policymakers and their air force officers fondly recall the contributions the USAF made in assisting Pakistan with everything from combat aircraft through organization to logistics—capabilities that enabled the Pakistan Air Force to survive several wars with India. These contributions obviously occurred in the context of a different geopolitical environment, when the United States and Pakistan were formal allies in the struggle against the Soviet Union. Today this relationship has lapsed, and Pakistani decisionmakers do not seek to resurrect it because of their belief that formal alliances with other states did not serve Pakistan's interests well in the past. Consequently, they would settle for "merely" a normal relationship with the United States that includes an acceptance of the legitimacy of Pakistan's nuclear program given its strategic environment; a withdrawal of those restrictive legislative regimes which prevent Pakistan from being able to purchase American weapons, spare parts, and training; a commitment to increased economic and commercial ties, including U.S. support for Pakistani efforts at debt rescheduling; and evidence of American sensitivity to Pakistan's interest in issues such as Afghanistan and Kashmir.

Within the parameters of a normalized relationship, Pakistan seeks to improve its engagement with the USAF. This would include deepening the levels of military-to-military contacts in the form of exchanges and visits as well as increasing opportunities for training and exercises if possible. Pakistan clearly views the USAF with great respect. Having watched USAF operations in the Persian Gulf and Kosovo with interest and admiration, Pakistan would prefer to develop a relationship that allows it to increase its own technical capabilities and operational proficiency as far as air warfare is concerned—a competency that is critical to its survival in its struggle with India. The willingness to engage in any activities that further this goal, however, would not carry over to the support of hedging strategies vis-à-vis China. Rather, engaging in such activities is justified primarily by Pakistan's own security concerns which predominantly involve India. In addition, Pakistan might be willing—if relations with the United States improve considerably—to help the USAF in other ways, such as allowing for emergency staging and recovery of aircraft committed to humanitarian missions or even peace operations if these are either endorsed by the United Nations or conducted in support of friendly governments.

Like Pakistan, India is greatly interested in increasing its defense cooperation with the United States. Even more than Pakistan, however, India seeks a new, more normal, relationship with Washington that erases the mixed memories of the Cold War years and allows for at least some degree of tacit cooperation in combating the threats that may appear in the future. Because emerging as a true great power with both security and status remains at the heart of its grand strategy, India seeks to deepen its engagement with the United States, but not at the cost of its independent foreign policy. This implies that India seeks a relationship with the United States that has room for differences in opinion when New Delhi's preferences do not align with Washington's on a given issue; is not encumbered by restrictive control regimes that limit the kinds of civilian, dual-use, and military technologies available to India; and offers opportunities for greater political and military cooperation without making India appear to be a junior ally.

These objectives imply that, at least in the near term, India's attitude toward greater cooperation with the USAF will resemble that of Pakistan. India seeks to restore if not improve the levels of military-to-military contacts, exchanges, and visits that existed prior to the nuclear tests in May 1998. It had even begun a small program of exercises with the USAF, most of which were small-unit exercises, and the Indian Air Force leadership in particular is very interested in expanding the scope, regularity, and complexity of these exercises. Although it is clearly recognized that this is a gradual and long-term endeavor, both Indian security managers and the Indian Air Force leadership recognize that cooperating with the USAF would assist India in a variety of issue areas ranging from modernizing logistics through coping with downsizing to learning how to plan and execute a high-intensity air campaign. Developing a robust air warfare capability, which includes maintaining its current theater air supremacy over China, also remains an Indian Air Force goal. To the degree that engaging the USAF supports this objective, India's civilian security managers—the ultimate controlling authorities in the national command system—will permit the air force leadership to pursue various forms of engagement that at present are unlikely to go beyond combined training and exercises (although these could vary considerably in the scale and types of equipment and organizations involved).

The real value of continuing to engage India, however, will be manifested only over the longer term, when the growth of both Chinese and Indian power in Asia will create new opportunities for the USAF. At the very least, getting to know and appreciate Indian air capabilities, developing relationships with the current and emerging leadership in the Indian Air Force, and setting in place a foundation of cooperation that can be expanded if circumstances warrant remain a sound strategy for cooperating with an emerging great power whose interests will in many ways parallel U.S. objectives in Asia. These objectives—which ultimately revolve around preventing the rise of a hegemony that threatens U.S. presence in and access to the continent, sustaining an open economic order that permits secure trade flows of national resources and finished goods, and preserving a political environment that is free of extremism and violent threats to domestic order—all remain issues on which India and the United States could cooperate. The current goal of USAF engagement with

India (and of U.S. engagement in general) must therefore be to create the foundations for enhanced cooperation in each of these issue areas without in any way prejudging the forms in which such cooperation may eventually materialize. If this effort is successful, there may come a point where activities that are infeasible today—e.g., cooperative intelligence collection and sharing, opportunities for staging and recovery, and combined operations in the context of peace operations broadly understood—would be well within the realm of possibility.

BIBLIOGRAPHY

"Accomplishing the Great Cause of the Reunification of the Motherland Is the Common Wish of All Chinese People," Xinhua, January 30, 1996, reprinted in FBIS-CHI-96-021.

"ADD to Develop Spy Satellite," *Chosun Ilbo*, November 3, 1998.

"AFP: China Refuses to Launch Joint Anti-Piracy Patrols," FBIS-CHI-2000-0428, reprinted from Agence France-Presse, April 28, 2000.

AFP: Spokesman Says PRC Deports Indonesian Sailors, FBIS-CHI-98-300, reprinted from Agence France-Presse, October 27, 1998.

Ahmed, Samina, "The (Nuclear) Testing of Pakistan," *Current History*, Vol. 97, No. 623, December 1998.

Alagappa, Muthia (ed.), *Asian Security Practice: Material and Ideational Influences*, Stanford, CA: Stanford University Press, 1998.

Allen, Kenneth W., and Eric A. McVadon, *China's Foreign Military Relations*, Washington, D.C.: Henry L. Stimson Center, October 1999.

Anwar, Dewi Fortuna, "Indonesia: Domestic Priorities Define National Security," in Muthia Alagappa (ed.), *Asian Security Practice: Material and Ideational Influences*, Stanford, CA: Stanford University Press, 1998.

"Appropriation Sought for Refueling Aircraft," *Yomiuri Shimbun*, July 22, 1999.

Asher, David L., "A U.S.-Japan Alliance for the Next Century," *Orbis*, Vol. 41, No. 3, Summer 1997, pp. 343–374.

Association of Southeast Asian Nations, "ASEAN Declaration on South China Sea (1992)," available at http://www.aseansec.org/.

Babbage, Ross, and Sandy Gordon (eds.), *India's Strategic Future*, New York: St. Martin's Press, 1992.

Bajpai, Kanti, "India: Modified Structuralism," in Muthia Alagappa (ed.), *Asian Security Practice: Material and Ideational Influences*, Stanford, CA: Stanford University Press, 1998.

"Beijing Declaration by the People's Republic of China and the Russian Federation," PRC Ministry of Foreign Affairs, July 20, 2000, available at http://www.fmprc.gov.cn/english/dhtml/readhomepage.asp?pkey=2000071819160807/20/2000.

Bhalla, A. S., *Uneven Development in the Third World: A Study of China and India*, New York: St. Martin's Press, 1995.

Bhattacharjea, Mira Sinha, and C. V. Ranganathan, "India and China—I," *The Hindu*, May 8, 2000, reprinted as *Daily Analyzes India-China Relations*, FBIS-CHI-2000-0508.

Binnendyk, Hans, and Ronald N. Montaperto, *Strategic Trends in China*, Washington, D.C.: Institute for National Strategic Studies, National Defense University, 1998.

Bracken, Paul, *Fire in the East: The Rise of Asian Military Power and the Second Nuclear Age*, New York: HarperCollins, 1999.

Burles, Mark, *Chinese Policy Toward Russia and the Central Asian Republics*, Santa Monica: RAND, MR-1045-AF, 1999.

Burles, Mark, and Abram N. Shulsky, *Patterns in China's Use of Force: Evidence from History and Doctrinal Writings*, Santa Monica: RAND, MR-1160-AF, 2000.

Cha, Victor D., "What Drives Korea-Japan Security Relations?" *Korean Journal of Defense Analysis*, Winter 1999, pp. 69–87.

Chanda, Nayan, "After the Bomb," *Far Eastern Economic Review*, April 13, 2000, p. 20.

Chanda, Nayan, *Brother Enemy: The War After the War*, San Diego, CA: Harcourt Brace Jovanovich, 1986.

Chang, Felix K., "The Unraveling of Russia's Far Eastern Power," *Orbis*, Vol. 43, No. 2, Spring 1999, pp. 257–284.

Chellaney, Brahma, "The Regional Strategic Triangle," in Brahma Chellaney (ed.), *Securing India's Future in the New Millennium*, New Delhi: Orient Longman, 1999, pp. 313–336.

"Chief of General Staff Meets Japanese Defense Official," Xinhua, November 23, 1999.

"China Military Budget Up 12.7% for 2000," *China Online*, March 8, 2000, available at http://www.chinaonline.com.

"China Says Dalai Lama Using Escaped Karmapa for Own Purpose," Beijing, Agence France-Presse, March 9, 2000.

China Statistical Yearbook, Beijing: China Statistical Publishing House, 1998.

China's National Defense, Beijing: Information Office of the State Council, July 1998.

Christensen, Thomas J., "Chinese Realpolitik," *Foreign Affairs*, Vol. 75, No. 5, September/October 1996.

Christoffersen, Gaye, *China's Intentions for Russian and Central Asian Oil and Gas*, Seattle: National Bureau of Asian Research, Vol. 9, No. 2, March 1998.

Chu Shulong and Wang Zaibang, "Thoughts on [the] International Situation and China's Response," *Contemporary International Relations*, Vol. 9, No. 9, September 1999, pp. 1–13.

Chufrin, Gennady (ed.), *Russia and Asia: The Emerging Security Agenda*, New York: Oxford University Press, 1999.

Clad, James, "Fin de Siècle, Fin de l'ASEAN?" Center for Strategic and International Studies, Pacific Forum CSIS, *PacNet Newsletter*, March 3, 2000.

Cliff, Roger, "China's Peaceful Reunification Strategy," *American Asian Review*, Vol. 14, No. 4, Winter 1996.

Cliff, Roger, *The Military Potential of China's Commercial Technology*, Santa Monica: RAND, MR-1292-AF, 2001.

Cohen, William S., Secretary of Defense, *Report of the Quadrennial Defense Review*, Washington, D.C.: U.S. Department of Defense, May 1997.

"Commentary on U.S.-Japan Relations and the ABM Treaty," *Jiefangjun Bao (Liberation Army Daily)*, November 14, 1999, p. 5.

Correll, John T., "On Course for Global Engagement," *Air Force Magazine*, January 1999, pp. 22–27.

Cossa, Ralph A., "Security Implications of Conflict in the South China Sea: Exploring Potential Triggers of Conflict," *PacNet Newsletter*, available at http://www.csis.org/pacfor/pac1698.html.

Country Report: China and Mongolia, London: Economist Intelligence Unit, 1999.

Country Report: China and Mongolia, London: Economist Intelligence Unit, August 2000.

"Crisis Laws Needed, Obuchi Tells SDF," *Japan Times*, July 15, 1999.

Crispin, Shawn W., with Susan V. Lawrence, "In Self-Defense," *Far Eastern Economic Review*, July 1, 1999, pp. 22 and 24.

Da Cunha, Derek, "Southeast Asian Perceptions of China's Future Security Role in Its 'Backyard,'" in Jonathan D. Pollack and Richard H. Yang (eds.), *In China's Shadow*, Santa Monica: RAND, DC-137-CAPP, 1998.

Daimon, Sayuri, "New Defense Role: Next Step Is to Free Up SDF," *Japan Times*, May 25, 1999.

Defending Singapore in the 21st Century, Singapore: Republic of Singapore Ministry of Defense, 2000.

"Defense Agency to Delay Request for Airborne-Refuelling Aircraft," Kyodo, reprinted in *BBC Selected World Broadcasts—Far East*, FE/3604, August 4, 1999, p. E/1.

"Defense Minister Regrets 'Diplomatic' Remarks on U.S. Forces Korea," Yonhap, August 29, 1999, in *BBC Selected World Broadcasts*, FE/3626, August 30, 1999, p. D/3.

"Defense Minister's Remarks Cause Controversy," *Chosun Ilbo* (Internet version), August 26, 1999.

Defense of Japan—1999, Tokyo: Japan Defense Agency, 1999.

"Defense Spending Could Spiral Out of Control," *Asia Times*, March 4, 2000, available at http://www.asiatimes.com/indpak/BC04DfO2.html.

Defense White Paper, 1998, Seoul: Ministry of National Defense, Republic of Korea, 1999.

Deocadiz, Christina V., *Business World* (Internet version), August 6, 1998, reprinted as *Philippines: Siazon: U.S. to "Aid" Manila in Event of Spratlys Attack*, FBIS-EAS-98-218.

Dhume, Sadanand, "No Holds Barred," *Far Eastern Economic Review*, February 24, 2000, pp. 40–41.

Dong Guozheng, "Hegemonist Ambition Is Completely Exposed," *Jiefangjun Bao (PLA Daily)*, May 19, 1998, p. 5, reprinted in FBIS-CHI-98-140.

Donnelly, John, "U.S., Japan to Ink Missile-Defense Deal," *Defense Week*, July 26, 1999, pp. 1 and 12–13.

Dujarric, Robert, et al., *Korea: Security Pivot in Northeast Asia*, Indianapolis: Hudson Institute, 1998.

Dutta, Sujit, "Sino-Indian Diplomatic Negotiations: A Preliminary Assessment," *Strategic Analysis*, Vol. 22, No. 12, March 1999.

East Asian Strategic Review, 1998–1999, Tokyo: National Institute for Defense Studies, 1999.

Eberstadt, Nicholas, *The End of North Korea,* Washington, D.C.: AEI Press, 1999.

"Economic Indicators," *Far East Economic Review,* April 13, 2000.

Economy, Elizabeth, and Michel Oksenberg (eds.), *China Joins the World—Progress and Prospects,* New York: Council on Foreign Relations Press, 1999.

Faison, Seth, "Taiwan President Implies His Island Is Sovereign State," *New York Times,* July 13, 1999.

Finkelstein, David M., "China's New Security Concept: Reading Between the Lines," *Washington Journal of Modern China,* Vol. 5, No. 1, Spring 1999.

Finkelstein, David M., and John Unangst, *Engaging DoD: Chinese Perspectives on Military Relations with the United States,* Alexandria, VA: CNA Corporation, CRM-99-0046.90, October 1999.

French, Howard W., "Seoul Drawing Closer to Tokyo as Anger Fades," *New York Times,* September 20, 1999.

Friedberg, Aaron, "Ripe for Rivalry: Prospects for Peace in a Multipolar Asia" *International Security,* Vol. 18, No. 3, Winter 1993/1994, pp. 5–33.

Friedberg, Aaron, "Will Europe's Past Be Asia's Future?" *Survival,* Vol. 42, No. 3, Autumn 2000, pp. 147–160.

Funabashi, Yoichi, *Alliance Adrift,* New York: Council on Foreign Relations Press, 1999.

"FX Program Ready to Soar," *Korea Newsreview,* June 12, 1999, p. 8.

Ganguly, Sumit, *The Crisis in Kashmir: Portents of War, Hopes of Peace,* Washington, D.C.: Woodrow Wilson Center Press, 1997.

Garver, John W., "China-India Rivalry in Nepal: The Clash over Chinese Arms Sales," *Asian Survey,* Vol. 31, No. 10, October 1991, pp. 956–975.

Giarra, Paul, "Peacekeeping: As Good for the Alliance As It Is for Japan?" *Japan Digest*, February 9, 1999.

Gordon, Sandy, *India's Rise to Power*, New York: St. Martin's Press, 1995.

Green, Michael J., and Patrick M. Cronin (eds.), *The U.S.-Japan Alliance—Past, Present, and Future*, New York: Council on Foreign Relations Press, 1999.

Green, Michael J., and Benjamin L. Self, "Japan's Changing China Policy: From Commercial Liberalism to Reluctant Realism," *Survival*, Vol. 38, No. 2, Summer 1996, pp. 35–58.

Grossman, Elaine M., "Air Force's New 'Strategic Vision' to Include 'Global Vigilance,'" *Inside the Pentagon*, December 2, 1999, pp. 1–2.

Hamre, John, Deputy Secretary of Defense, Testimony to the Senate Appropriations Committee, April 1999.

Harada, Chitose, *Russia and North-east Asia*, London: International Institute for Strategic Studies, Adelphi Paper No. 310, July 1997.

"Hindi-Chini Buy, Buy," *Business India*, No. 490, December 16, 1996.

Holloway, Nigel, "Jolt from the Blue," *Far Eastern Economic Review*, August 3, 1995, p. 22.

Hoon Shim Jae, with Shawn W. Crispin, "Different Drummer—South Korea Prefers a Homegrown Missile Program," *Far Eastern Economic Review*, July 1, 1999, p. 26.

Hussain, Mushahid, "Pakistan-China Defense Cooperation," *International Defense Review*, 2/1993.

Huxley, Tim, *Insecurity in the ASEAN Region*, London: Royal United Services Institute for Defence Studies, 1993.

Huxley, Tim, and Susan Willett, *Arming East Asia*, London: International Institute for Strategic Studies, Adelphi Paper No. 329, July 1999.

Hwang Byong Moo et al., "Fifty Years of National Security in South Korea," *KNDU Review—Journal of National Security Affairs*, Vol. 3, 1998, pp. 5–180.

India: Analyst Skeptical of PRC Becoming Superpower, FBIS-NES-97-210, July 29, 1997.

"India at a Glance," World Bank fact sheet, March 28, 2000, available at http://www.worldbank.org/data/countrydata/aag/ind_aag.pdf.

"India Not Interested in Talks: Sattar," *Dawn*, February 4, 2000.

"India's Economy," *The Economist*, March 4–10, 2000.

"Indo-China Border Trade: Trading on Top of the World," *India Today*, Vol. 17, No. 18, September 30, 1992.

"Indonesia: Worse to Come," *Fast Eastern Economic Review*, July 29, 1999, p. 16.

ITAR-TASS: Russian-Chinese Statement, FBIS-SOV-1999-1210, December 10, 1999.

"Japanese Budget in Brief–1998," Ministry of Finance, Government of Japan, available at http://www.mof.go.jp/english/budget/bib004.PDF, 1998.

"Japan Opts for Domestically Made Spy Satellites," Nikkei, reprinted in *Nihon Keizai Shimbun*, September 28, 1999.

Jayanth, V., "India's 'Look East' Policy," *The Hindu*, April 2, 1998.

Joeck, Neil, "Pakistani Security and Nuclear Proliferation in South Asia," *Journal of Strategic Studies*, Vol. 8, No. 4, December 1985.

"Joint Statement by Chinese and U.S. Heads of State on the South Asian Issue, 27 June 1998, Beijing," Xinhua, June 27, 1998, reprinted in FBIS-CHI-98-178.

"Joint Statement by the People's Republic of China and the Russian Federation on the Multipolarization of the World and the Establishment of a New International Order," *Beijing Review*, May 12–18, 1997.

"Joint Statement of the Chinese Foreign Minister and Philippine Secretary of Foreign Affairs," Xinhua, May 16, 2000, reprinted as *China, Philippines Sign Joint Statement*, FBIS-CHI-2000-0516.

Joshi, Manoj, "George in the China Shop," *India Today*, May 18, 1998.

Kak, Kapil, "India's Conventional Defence: Problems and Prospects," *Strategic Analysis*, Vol. 22, No. 11, February 1999.

Khalilzad, Zalmay (ed.), *Strategic Appraisal 1996*, Santa Monica: RAND, MR-543-AF, 1996.

Khalilzad, Zalmay, and Ian O. Lesser (eds.), *Sources of Conflict in the 21st Century: Regional Futures and U.S. Strategy*, Santa Monica: RAND, MR-897-AF, 1998.

Khalilzad, Zalmay M., Abram N. Shulsky, Daniel L. Byman, Roger Cliff, David T. Orletsky, David Shlapak, and Ashley J. Tellis, *The United States and a Rising China: Strategic and Military Implications*, Santa Monica: RAND, MR-1082-AF, 1999.

Kirk, Don, "Seoul Melds Rivals into a Contender," *International Herald Tribune*, June 12–13, 1999.

Kirk, Don, "Seoul Seeks U.S. Backing for Missile Development," *International Herald Tribune*, July 2, 1999.

Kirk, Don, "U.S. Plans New Missile in Project with Japan," *International Herald Tribune*, August 7-8, 1999.

Kissinger, Henry, *Diplomacy*, New York: Simon & Schuster, 1994.

Klintworth, Gary, "Chinese Perspectives on India as a Great Power," in Ross Babbage and Sandy Gordon (eds.), *India's Strategic Future*, New York: St. Martin's Press, 1992.

"La Kha Phieu Meets with Tang Jiaxuan," Xinhua, December 31, 1999, reprinted in FBIS-CHI-1999-1231.

Lam, Willy Wo-Lap, "Deadline Debated as Taiwan Stakes Raised," *South China Morning Post*, February 22, 2000.

Layne, Christopher, "The Unipolar Illusion: Why New Great Powers Will Rise," *International Security*, Vol. 17, No. 4, Spring 1993, pp. 5–51.

Lee, Bernice, *The Security Implications of the New Taiwan*, London: International Institute for Strategic Studies, Adelphi Paper No. 331, October 1999.

Lee Sung Yul, "U.S., Russia, France Compete for Seoul's Missile Program," *Korea Herald*, September 21, 1999.

Levin, Norman D., *The Shape of Korea's Future: South Korean Attitudes Toward Unification and Long-Term Security Issues*, Santa Monica: RAND, MR-1092-CAPP, 1999.

Liu Jiangyong, "Clinton's China Visit and the New Trends in Sino-U.S.-Japanese Relations," *Contemporary International Relations*, Vol. 8, No. 7, July 1998, pp. 1–13.

Liu Yang and Guo Feng, "What Is the Intention of Wantonly Engaging in Military Ventures—India's Military Development Should Be Watched Out For," *Jiefangjun Bao (Liberation Army Daily)*, May 19, 1998, p. 5, reprinted in FBIS-CHI-98-141, May 21, 1998.

Lorell, Mark, *Troubled Partnership: A History of U.S.-Japan Collaboration on the FS-X Fighter*, Santa Monica: RAND, MR-612/2-AF, 1995.

Loveard, Dewi, "Cry for a Hold Way," *Asiaweek*, January 21, 2000.

Luo Jie and Ye Bian, "U.S. 'Missile Defense' Will Bring No End of Trouble for the Future—Sha Zukang on Topics Including [the] International Disarmament Situation and TMD," *Shijie Zhishi (World Knowledge)*, No. 13, July 1, 1999, pp. 8–11.

Ma Shikun and Zhang Yong, "The United States Makes Quicker Adjustment to DPRK Policy," *Renmin Ribao (People's Daily)*, June 24, 2000, p. 3, reprinted as *Analysis of U.S. Adjustment to DPRK Policy*, FBIS-CHI-2000-0624.

Maddison, Angus, *Chinese Economic Performance in the Long Run*, Washington, D.C.: Organization for Economic Cooperation and Development, 1998.

Maeda, Toshi, "Japan, South Korea Hold First Joint Naval Drill," *Japan Times*, August 5, 1999.

"Major Budget Item—Defense," Ministry of Finance, Government of Japan, available at http://www.mof.go.jp/english/genan11/sy001n3.htm, 1998.

Malik, J. Mohan, "China-India Relations in the Post-Soviet Era: The Continuing Rivalry," *China Quarterly*, No. 142, June 1995.

Malik, J. Mohan, "India Goes Nuclear: Rationale, Benefits, Costs and Implications," *Contemporary Southeast Asia*, Vol. 20, No. 2, August 1998.

Mann, Paul, "Asia's Recession Holds Korean Arms Hostage," *Aviation Week & Space Technology*, November 9, 1998, pp. 35–36.

Mansingh, Surjit, "Sino-Indian Relations in the Post–Cold War Era," *Asian Survey*, Vol. 34, No. 3, March 1994.

Mattoo, Amitabh, "Complacency About Chinese Threat Called Frightening," *India Abroad*, April 5, 1996.

Maxwell, Neville, *India's China War*, New York: Random House, 1970.

McCawley, Tom, "In the Middle of the War Zone," *Asiaweek*, January 21, 2000.

The Military Balance 1998/99, London: International Institute for Strategic Studies, October 1998.

Misake, Hisani, "Japan, China Consider Upgrading Security Forum," *Japan Times*, September 14, 1999.

Moon Chung In and Chung Min Lee (eds.), *Air Power Dynamics and Korean Security*, Seoul: Yonsei University Press, 1999.

Mulvenon, James C., and Richard H. Yang (eds.), *The People's Liberation Army in the Information Age*, Santa Monica: RAND, CF-145-CAPP/AF, 1999.

Nathan, K. S., "Malaysia: Reinventing the Nation," in Muthia Alagappa (ed.), *Asian Security Practice: Material and Ideational Influences*, Stanford, CA: Stanford University Press, 1998.

Noer, John H., *Chokepoints: Maritime Economic Concerns in Southeast Asia*, Washington, D.C.: National Defense University, 1996.

Okimoto, Daniel I., *The Japan-America Security Alliance: Prospects for the Twenty-First Century*, Stanford, CA: Asia/Pacific Research Center, Stanford University, January 1998.

Pathasarathy, Malini, "The Core Issue of Kashmir Must Be Addressed: Musharraf," *The Hindu*, January 17, 2000.

Pendley, William T., *Restructuring U.S.-Korea Relations and the U.S. East Asia Strategy for the Twenty-First Century*, Honolulu: East-West Center, March 1999.

Perry, William J., *Review of United States Policy Toward North Korea: Findings and Recommendations*, Washington, D.C.: U.S. Department of State, October 12, 1999.

Pillsbury, Michael, *China Debates the Future Security Environment*, Washington, D.C.: National Defense University Press, 2000.

Piracy and Armed Robbery Against Ships: Report for the Period 1 January–30 September 1999, London: International Maritime Bureau, p. 3.

Pollack, Jonathan D., "Asian-Pacific Responses to a Rising China," in Jonathan D. Pollack and Richard H. Yang (eds.), *In China's Shadow: Regional Perspectives on Chinese Foreign Policy and Military Development*, Santa Monica: RAND, CF-137-CAPP, 1998.

Pollack, Jonathan D., *Designing a New American Security Strategy for Asia*, Santa Monica: RAND, RP-541, 1996.

Pollack, Jonathan D., et al., *Chinese and Japanese Naval Power and Korean Security*, Taejon, South Korea: ROK Navy Headquarters, 1999.

Pollack, Jonathan D., and Chung Min Lee, *Preparing for Korean Unification: Scenarios and Implications,* Santa Monica: RAND, MR-1040-A, 1999.

Pollack, Jonathan D., and Richard H. Yang (eds.), *In China's Shadow: Regional Perspectives on Chinese Foreign Policy and Military Development,* Santa Monica: RAND, CF-137-CAPP, 1998.

Pye, Lucian W., *Asian Power and Politics: The Cultural Dimensions of Authority,* Cambridge, MA: Harvard University Press, 1985.

Raman, B., "Chinese Assertion of Territorial Claims: The Mischief Reef—A Case Study," Chennai, India: South Asia Analysis Group Papers, 1999.

Reese, David, *The Prospects for North Korea's Survival,* London: International Institute for Strategic Studies, Adelphi Paper No. 323, November 1998.

Risen, James, "South Korea Seen Trying to Extend Range of Missiles," *New York Times,* November 14, 1999.

ROK, Japanese Navy Officials Agree to Hold Joint Exercise, FBIS-EAS-1999-0213, reprinted from *Korean Times* (Internet version), February 13, 1999.

ROK New Agency Carries "Unofficial Translation" of South-North Joint Declaration, FBIS-EAS-2000-0614, reprinted from Yonhap, June 14, 2000.

Rose, Leo E., *India and China: Forging a New Relationship,* in Shalendra D. Sharma (ed.), *The Asia-Pacific in the New Millennium: Geopolitics, Security, and Foreign Policy,* Berkeley, CA: University of California, Berkeley, 2000.

Royal Thai Embassy, Washington, D.C., press release, "Joint Statement of the Kingdom of Thailand and the People's Republic of China on a Plan of Action for the 21st Century," signed in Bangkok on February 5, 1999, by the Thai and Chinese Foreign Ministers, available at www.thaiembdc.org/pressctr/ pr/jtthch99.htm.

Rubinstein, Gregg A., "U.S.-Japan Armaments Cooperation," in Michael J. Green and Patrick M. Cronin (eds.), *The U.S.-Japan*

Alliance—Past, Present, and Future, New York: Council on Foreign Relations Press, 1999.

Sa Benwang, "The Impact of the Kosovo War on International Situations," *International Strategic Studies*, No. 4, Serial No. 54, October 1999, pp. 1–9.

Samuels, Richard J., *Rich Nation/Strong Army: National Security and the Technological Transformation of Japan*, Ithaca, N.Y.: Cornell University Press, 1994.

Saunders, Philip C., "A Virtual Alliance for Asian Security," *Orbis*, Vol. 43, No. 2, Spring 1999, pp. 237–256.

Segal, Gerald, "Does China Matter?" *Foreign Affairs*, Vol. 78, No. 5, September/October 1999, pp. 24–36.

Sen, Amartya, *Economic Development and Social Change: India and China in Comparative Perspectives,* London: London School of Economics, STICERD Discussion Paper Series DEP-67, 1995.

"Senior Official Says Defense Budget Remains at 'Low Levels'" FTS 1999, 03080024, reprinted from Xinhua, March 8, 1999.

Sergounin, A. A., and S. V. Subbotin, *Russian Arms Transfers to East Asia in the 1990s*, SIPRI Research Report No. 15, Oxford: Oxford University Press, 1999.

Shambaugh, David, "Chinese Hegemony over East Asia by 2015?" *Korean Journal of Defense Analysis*, Vol. 9, No. 1, Summer 1997, pp. 7–28.

Shi Yinhong, "Difficulties and Options: Thoughts on the Taiwan Matter," *Zhanlue Yu Guanli (Strategy and Management)*, October 1, 1999, pp. 1–4.

Shinn, James (ed.), *Weaving the Net—Conditional Engagement with China*, New York: Council on Foreign Relations Press, 1996.

Shlapak, D. A., J. Stillion, O. Oliker, and T. Charlick-Paley, *A Global Access Strategy for the U.S. Air Force*, Santa Monica: RAND, MR-1216-AF, forthcoming.

Shlapak, David A., David T. Orletsky, and Barry Wilson, *Dire Strait? Military Aspects of the China-Taiwan Confrontation and Implications for U.S. Policy*, Santa Monica: RAND, MR-1217-SRF, 2000.

Shlapak, David A., and Alan Vick, *"Check Six Begins on the Ground": Responding to the Evolving Ground Threat to U.S. Air Force Bases*, Santa Monica: RAND, MR-606-AF, 1995.

Sims, Calvin, "U.S. and Japan Agree to Joint Research on Missile Defense," *New York Times*, August 17, 1999.

Singh, Jasjit, "Why Nuclear Weapons?" in Jasjit Singh (ed.), *Nuclear India*, New Delhi: Knowledge World, 1998.

Singh, Swaran, "Sino–South Asian Ties: Problems and Prospects," *Strategic Analysis*, Vol. 24, No. 1, April 2000.

Slocombe, Walter B., "Statement of the Undersecretary of Defense for Policy Before the House Committee on International Relations, Subcommittee on Asia and the Pacific," May 7, 1998.

Sokolsky, Richard, Angel Rabasa, and C. R. Neu, *The Role of Southeast Asia in U.S. Strategy Toward China*, Santa Monica: RAND, MR-1170-AF, 2000.

Son Key Young, "Seoul Denies Longer-Range Missile Bid," *Korea Times*, November 15, 1999.

South Korea: IFANS Report on Presence of U.S. Forces After Unification, FBIS-EAS-99-020, reprinted from Yonhap, January 21, 1999.

"South Korea to Spend $69.3 Billion in Five Year Defense Plan," Reuters, February 12, 1999.

Spencer, Geoff, "Wahid Puts China atop Foreign Agenda," *Washington Times*, October 25, 1999.

Stillion, John, and David T. Orletsky, *Airbase Vulnerability to Conventional Cruise-Missile and Ballistic-Missile Attacks: Technology, Scenarios, and U.S. Air Force Responses*, Santa Monica: RAND, MR-1028-AF, 1999.

Stokes, Mark A., *China's Strategic Modernization: Implications for the United States*, Carlisle Barracks, PA: Strategic Studies Institute, U.S. Army War College, September 1999.

Storey, Ian James, "Creeping Assertiveness: China, the Philippines, and the South China Sea Dispute," *Contemporary Southeast Asia*, Vol. 21, No. 1, April 1999.

Storey, Ian James, "Manila Looks to USA for Help over Spratlys," *Jane's Intelligence Review*, August 1999, p. 47.

Struck, Doug, "Russia, Japan Oceans Apart on Islands," *Washington Post*, September 5, 2000, p. 16.

Struck, Doug, "South Korean Says North Wants U.S. Troops to Stay," *Washington Post*, August 30, 2000, p. A1.

"Summary of 2000 Defense White Paper," *Sanbei Shimbun*, July 28, 2000, p. 2, reprinted as *Paper Carries Gist of Japan's FY2000 Defense White Paper*, FBIS-CHI-2000-0802.

Sutter, Robert G., *East Asia: Disputed Islands and Offshore Claims—Issues for U.S. Policy*, Washington, D.C.: CRS Report for Congress 92-614S, July 28, 1992.

Swaine, Michael D., and Ashley J. Tellis, *Interpreting China's Grand Strategy*, Santa Monica: RAND, MR-1121-AF, 2000.

Taiwan Affairs Office and Information Office of the State Council of the People's Republic of China, "The One China Principle and the Taiwan Issue," February 21, 2000, available at http://www.fmprc.gov.cn/english/dhtml/readsubject.asp?pkey=200002221705 11.

Takesada, Hideshi, "Korea-Japan Defense Cooperation: Prospects and Issues," *PacNet*, November 1999.

Tan, Andrew T.H., "Singapore's Defence: Capabilities, Trends, and Implications, *Contemporary Southeast Asia*, Vol. 21, No. 3, December 1999, pp. 451–474.

Tanino, Sakaturo, Japanese Ambassador to China, "Statement to Chinese Ministry of Foreign Affairs," in *BBC Selected World Broadcasts—Far East*, FE/3241/G3, May 29, 1998.

Tellis, Ashley J., *India's Emerging Nuclear Posture: Between Recessed Deterrent and Ready Arsenal,* Santa Monica: RAND, MR-1127-AF, 2001.

Tellis, Ashley J., "South Asia" in Zalmay Khalilzad (ed.), *Strategic Appraisal 1996,* Santa Monica: RAND, MR-543-AF, 1996.

Tellis, Ashley J., *Stability in South Asia,* Santa Monica: RAND, DB-185-A, 1997.

Tellis, Ashley J., Chung Min Lee, James Mulvenon, Courtney Purrington, and Michael D. Swaine, "Sources of Conflict in Asia," in Zalmay Khalilzad and Ian O. Lesser (eds.), *Sources of Conflict in the 21st Century: Regional Futures and U.S. Strategy,* Santa Monica: RAND, MR-897-AF, 1998.

"Text" of Beijing-Paris Declaration, FBIS-CHI-97-095, reprinted from Xinhua, May 16, 1997.

Thothathri, Raman A., "Indo-Chinese Trade: A Change for the Better," *Business India,* No. 399, June 21, 1993.

Tirpak, John A., "Strategic Control," *Air Force Magazine,* February 1999, pp. 20–27.

Tønnesson, Stein, "Vietnam's Objective in the South China Sea," *Contemporary Southeast Asia,* Vol. 22, No. 1, April 2000.

Trenin, Dmitri, *Russia's China Problem,* Washington, D.C.: Carnegie Endowment for International Peace, May 1999.

Tripp, R. S., Lionel Galway, Timothy L. Ramey, Mahyar Amouzegar, and Eric Peltz, *Supporting Expeditionary Aerospace Forces: A Concept for Evolving to the Agile Combat Support/Mobility System of the Future,* Santa Monica: RAND, MR-1179-AF, 2000.

"12.1% Increase Sought for Nation's Arms Budget," *Korea Herald,* June 9, 1999.

2000 National Defense Report, ROC Ministry of National Defense, available at http://www.mnd.gov.tw/report/830/html/e-03.html.

Tyler, Patrick E., "As China Threatens Taiwan, It Makes Sure U.S. Listens," *New York Times,* January 24, 1996, p. A3.

Ueno, Teruaki, "Japan, Fearing North Korea, Seeks Bigger Defense Budget," Reuters, August 31, 1999.

Umbach, Frank, "Financial Crisis Slows but Fails to Halt East Asian Arms Race," *Jane's Intelligence Review*, August 1998, pp. 23–27 (Part One), and September 1998, pp. 34–37 (Part Two).

U.S. Department of Commerce, Bureau of Economic Analysis, *Survey of Current Business*, July 1998.

U.S. Department of Commerce, *Statistical Abstract of the United States*, No. 1323, 1998.

U.S. Department of Defense, *High and Low Altitude Europe, North Africa, and Middle East*, DoD Flight Information Publication, Vol. 5, February 27, 1997.

U.S. Department of Defense, *The United States Security Strategy for the East Asia–Pacific Region*, Washington, D.C., November 1998.

U.S. Energy Information Administration, "South China Sea Region," January 2000, available at http://www.eia.doe.gov/emeu/cabs/schinatab.html#TAB2.

U.S.-Japan Security Consultative Committee, "Joint Statement," Washington, D.C.: U.S. Department of Defense, September 23, 1997.

Valencia, Mark J., *China and the South China Sea Disputes*, Oxford: Oxford University Press for the International Institute for Strategic Studies, Adelphi Paper No. 298, 1995.

Vatikiotis, Michael, et al., "Imperial Intrigue," *Far Eastern Economic Review*, September 11, 1997, p. 15.

Vertzberger, Yaacov, *The Enduring Entente: Sino-Pakistani Relations, 1960–1980*, New York: Praeger, 1983.

Vogel, Ezra (ed.), *Living with China*, New York: American Assembly, 1997.

Wall, Robert, "Japanese Recce Program Wary of FS-X Missteps," *Aviation Week & Space Technology*, August 23, 1999, p. 44.

Wanner, Barbara, *Mounting Anxiety over North Korean Security Threat Fuels Defense Debate in Japan*, Washington, D.C.: Japan Economic Institute, Report No. 33A, August 27, 1999.

Wolf, Charles, Jr., Anil Bamezai, K. C. Yeh, and Benjamin Zycher, *Asian Economic Trends and Their Security Implications*, Santa Monica: RAND, MR-1143-OSD/A, 2000.

Wolf, Charles, Jr., K. C. Yeh, Anil Bamezai, Donald P. Henry, and Michael Kennedy, *Long-Term Economic and Military Trends 1994– 2015: The United States and Asia*, Santa Monica: RAND, MR-627-OSD, 1995.

World Trade Organization press release, April 16, 1999, available at http://www.wto.org/wto/intltrad/internat.htm.

Wu, Yu-shan, "Taiwanese Elections and Cross-Strait Relations," *Asian Survey*, Vol. 39, No. 4, July/August 1999, pp. 565–587.

WuDunn, Sheryl, "In Arms Sales, Japan Coddles Its Own," *New York Times*, June 24, 1999.

Yan Xuetong, "The International Environment and Our Foreign Policy," *Contemporary International Relations*, Vol. 9, No. 9, September 1999, pp. 14–24.

Yang Bojiang, "Closer Alliance with Washington: Tokyo's Strategic Springboard for the New Century," *Contemporary International Relations*, Vol. 9, No. 6, June 1999, pp. 9–19.

Yang Bojiang, "Why [the] U.S.-Japan Declaration on [the] Security Alliance?" *Contemporary International Relations*, Vol. 6, No. 5, May 1996, pp. 1–12.

Yi Jan, "Prospects for Sino-Russian Military Cooperation," *Ching Pao*, No. 264, July 1, 1999, pp. 90–91.

Yoo Yong Weon, "Defense Minister 'Regrets' Comments on U.S. Troops," *Chosun Ilbo*, August 28, 1999.

Yoo Yong Weon, "MND to Reduce Manpower," *Chosun Ilbo*, August 20, 1999.

Zhang Changtai, "It Would Be Hard for the Indian Government to Get Out of Its Dilemma by Conducting Nuclear Tests," *Jiefangjun Bao (PLA Daily)*,May 20, 1998, p. 5, reprinted in FBIS-CHI-98-140.